WILLIAMS-SONOMA

Savoring
Appetizers

Best Recipes from the Award-Winning International Cookbooks

GENERAL EDITOR

Chuck Williams

AUTHORS

Georgeanne Brennan • Kerri Conan • Lori de Mori • Abigail Johnson Dodge

Janet Fletcher • Joyce Goldstein • Diane Holuigue • Joyce Jue

Michael McLaughlin • Cynthia Nims • Ray Overton • Jacki Passmore

Julie Sahni • Michele Scicolone • Marilyn Tausend

CONTENTS

A cook's greatest creativity is often most evident in the small dishes that begin a meal. From the tapas of Spain and the antojitos of Mexico to the elaborate appetizer platters of China and the spicy chat of India, hors d'oeuvres, snacks, and starters are often among the favorite dishes in any culture. As simple as bread sticks and garden-fresh vegetables alongside a bowl of anchovy-scented olive oil, or as elaborate as golden pastry "top hats" filled with stir-fried shrimp and crab, these savory morsels are made to pique the appetite and whet the palate for the more substantial delights to come. Served with a light aperitif before the meal, as part of a cocktail hour, or as the first course of a formal dinner, appetizers are designed for instant gratification.

In America, an ever-expanding repertoire of attractive finger foods and easy-to-serve hors d'oeuvres reflects the diversity of the country's many cultures: tortillas baked under a blanket of green chiles and melted cheese in the Southwest, dainty golden turnovers filled with hot-pepper jelly in the South, slivers of focaccia and frittata in Mediterranean-influenced California, cured salmon from the mighty rivers of the Pacific Northwest, or a Japanese-inspired, sesame-laced raw tuna *poke* with taro-root chips from tropical Hawaii.

In Mexico, a vast array of snacks and street foods has been adapted as first courses or light meals. Easy to make and fill, tortillas are used as a base for tacos, quesadillas,

flautas, and more. Fruits and vegetables are turned into delectable nibbles such as fresh squash blossoms dipped in a light egg batter and quickly fried; chile-sprinkled sticks of crisp jicama tossed with cucumber and pineapple; and starchy plantains pressed into fat, crunchy tostadas. And of course, buttery avocados are mashed or puréed to make guacamole, a perennial favorite.

Street foods are also at the heart of Asia's appetizers. In market streets from Beijing to Mumbai, dozens of busy sidewalk stalls and carts hawk everything from soup to dumplings to freshly grilled meats. The Chinese tradition of dim sum makes a sit-down meal of these delicacies—barbecued pork wrapped in fluffy steamed buns, sheer

Top: A profusion of freshly made *panini* and *pizette* is Italy's answer to fast food. **Above:** Fresh, locally made goat cheeses, or *chèvres*, are temptingly offered for tasting at a farmers' market in Provence. **Right:** The peaceful environs of the Summer Palace in Beijing are not disturbed by these early morning practioners of tai chi.

rice crepes wrapped around bits of shrimp and mushrooms, tiny flaky pastry cups filled with rich egg custard. And, especially in the north, no banquet would be complete without a selection of beautifully arranged plates heaped with hot and cold offerings.

In India, bite-sized treats and small plates, called *chat*, are an integral part of the culinary landscape. Indians traditionally love snacking—almost as much as they love going to the cinema. Here, a moviegoing experience is often accompanied by a hot treat, such as crispy spiced cashews or lentil wafers from one of the street-corner stalls that are clustered around the movie house. In restaurants and home kitchens, mouth-watering handmade specialties star on small plates: samosas and kabobs; fritters of Bombay duck, potato, or eggplant; and yam and corn dumplings.

France is home to many appetizers and first courses with classic status: A selection of *charcuterie*, including delicacies like rabbit terrine or pâté de foie gras; fresh oysters with a shallot-laced mignonette sauce; gratinéed mussels on the half shell; stuffed artichokes; salads of tomatoes, oven-dried to richness; and the staple of Provence, *le grand aïoli*—a spread of the season's best raw vegetables, served with a freshly made garlic mayonnaise for dipping.

Italians rarely drink without eating, so even the most casual glass of wine or *aperitivo* sipped at *il bar* on the corner will be paired with a selection of small bites—crunchy bread rings flavored with fennel seed; delicious chunks of Parmesan; bread sticks wrapped in prosciutto; small slices of pizza, focaccia, or panini. In restaurants, the antipasto table pays colorful tribute to the season's harvest—asparagus and fava beans around Easter, lush melon and grilled eggplant in the summer, sweet roasted red peppers and plump porcini mushrooms in the fall; bruschetta with sautéed *cavalo nero* or "black cabbage" in winter. At home, the antipasto may be simply raw vegetables arranged around a bowl of new-pressed olive oil, sliced cured meats, or squares of golden polenta with sautéed mushrooms.

Naturally, no discussion of international appetizers can conclude without a mention of the fabulous tapas of Spain. Once merely a bit of ham or cheese served alongside a glass of wine or sherry, these snacks and small plates have become a ritual in every Spanish city and town. Strolling from bar to bar, Spaniards wind down the workday with savory little bites enjoyed over drinks. Perennial favorites are spicy *patatas bravas*, "fierce" potatoes sparked with cayenne pepper; silky marinated white anchovies; fat wedges of the omnipresent Spanish *tortilla*, a thick omelet layered with onions and potatoes; and slices of nutty *jamón serrano*. In Portugal, though the tempting offerings tend to be simpler than those found in Spain, the tapas tradition is also well loved.

Left: Olive harvesting in Tuscany is most often accomplished by hand. Both men and women climb tall wooden ladders to work among supple branches heavy with the ripening fruits. **Above, left:** A peanut seller displays her goods in an artful balancing act, ready to measure out canfuls of nuts for a hungry strollers along Tonle Sap, in central Phnom Penh. **Above, right:** Italy's bakers are artisans, as evidenced by these hand-shaped loaves of fresh bread.

NORTH AMERICA

Preceding pages: Palenque, in the foothills of the Chiapas highlands in Mexico, is the most important archaeological site in the Mayan region. Top: Golden orange squash blossoms are both beautiful to look at and delectable to eat. Above: The *molcajete*, a three-legged mortar made of volcanic rock, is the classic tool for making guacamole and salsa. Right: A California baker uses a long-handled peel to remove bread from a wood-burning oven.

Lacking centuries of shared table traditions, Americans remain open-minded about what constitutes the proper start to a meal. The occasion, the crowd, and the tastes of the host are more likely to dictate how a dinner gets under way than any set of expectations. A weekday family meal may have no starter at all. A casual dinner party among friends might begin in the host's kitchen with a platter of crudités before moving into the dining room.

Many foods that are popular as starters come from the cocktail-hour tradition and the knowledge that a mixed drink requires a complement more substantial than simply a couple of olives. Consequently, Americans have become experts at finger food, one- or two-bite nibbles that guests can eat standing up with a glass in hand, as well as convenient savory starters that can be served and eaten easily with small plates and forks, including tarts, quiches, and frittatas.

Regional favorites tend to distinguish the many kinds of get-togethers that Americans traditionally cherish. At a San Francisco garden party, one may find bowls of California-grown pistachio nuts and whole heads of soft, spreadable roasted garlic to accompany Sonoma goat cheese and crusty sourdough bread. At the other end of the state, guests at a San Diego barbecue might scoop up homemade guacamole and salsa with fresh chips from a local Mexican market. In Dallas, where football is followed with religious fervor, a bubbling pot of *chile con queso*, a sort of southwestern cheese fondue, is the classic halftime diversion. At happy hour, residents of upstate New York savor the region's famous Buffalo chicken wings, deep-fried and served with celery, hot sauce, and a refreshing blue cheese dip.

Although beer may dominate at such casual events, wine appreciation is on the rise in America. In many homes, the wine hour has replaced the cocktail hour and subtly influenced the before-dinner menu. As a result, more hosts are offering wine-friendly foods in the European tradition, such as marinated olives, focaccia, grilled bruschetta, or crostini topped with a savory spread or cured fish.

With the growing awareness of the benefits of shopping for seasonal produce, more and more Americans look to the harvest when planning a meal, celebrating vegetables as a course all their own. Dinner might start with roasted bell peppers or marinated beets, with asparagus or leeks vinaigrette, or with a whole steamed artichoke for each guest. Recently, Americans have discovered sushi bars and the pleasures of raw seafood served Japanese style. Like sashimi, Hawaiian *poke*, marinated raw tuna, appeals to those with a taste for culinary adventure.

In Mexico, the foods that start many a meal in the *fondas* and restaurants of the country are often drawn from the vast repertoire of *antojitos*, the little handheld creations beloved by the Mexican people.

Masa is the basis of most *antojitos:* dried corn is processed and then ground to make a seemingly endless list of dishes, beginning, of course, with the tortilla, both the bread of Mexico and the primary utensil. This thin, round, flexible flatbread is used to scoop beans, stews, and moles from the plate to the mouth. If fried crisp, a tortilla becomes the plate itself—a tostada. In Baja California it may be topped with ceviche, in Campeche with a black bean paste and pickled red onions. When a tortilla is folded over cheese with a pungent leaf of epazote, it becomes a quesadilla. When wrapped around myriad fillings, it changes into a soft taco. Finally, when rolled and fried, it turns into a *flauta*.

A whole other world of *antojitos* is made by fashioning *masa* into stuffed morsels of different shapes and sizes and then serving them with a variety of toppings. Every region has its own specialty, and they go by a confusing array of names. The tiny dish-shaped *sopes* from Colima, filled with shredded beef in a fiery cumin-flavored salsa, may have little resemblance to similarly named ones from Jalisco. *Panuchos* may be stuffed with succulent shark and vinegar-soused red onions in Campeche, but in nearby Yucatán they carry only black beans. There are also *chalupas*, *molotes*, *memelas*, *huaraches*, *tlacoyas*, and *polkanes*, all wonderful tastes to explore.

The *antojitos* of northern Mexico differ from those of their southern neighbors. When the Spanish *conquistadores* moved north, they brought wheat with them as well as the beginning of today's vast cattle herds. As a result, flour tortillas usually replace those made with corn. And beef, thinly sliced and dried to become *carne seca*, *cecina*, or the shredded *machaca*, is, along with cheese, the base for most regional *antojitos*.

Ceviche or seafood cocktails, small portions of meats, and fanciful vegetable dishes are among the most common Mexican *entradas*, or appetizers. And not to be overlooked are *botanas*, tidbits for leisurely hours: salted nuts and seeds, various dips with *totopos* (corn chips), and fiery pickled chiles and vegetables.

Left: Rows of graceful arches surround this seventeenth-century hacienda in Yucatán, which was once known for processing henequen, the strong fiber of a type of agave, used to make rope and fabric. **Above, left:** Cinco de Mayo celebrations become especially festive when vividly costumed participants on stilts reenact the failed French invasion of 1862. **Above, right:** In the area around Castroville, California, on Monterey Bay, some three-fourths of the world's globe artichoke crop is now grown, a huge industry started by Swiss-Italian immigrants in the 1880s.

Guacamole with Corn Chips

Guacamole con Totopos • Puebla • Mexico

This is simplicity itself: a rustic *botana* that owes its flavor to the quality of the avocados. After all, the Nahuatl word *guacamole* means "avocado mixture," and that is what it should be. Some think the garnishes unbalance the flavor, and you may prefer to omit them, but many cooks like to sprinkle on one or two. Use avocados that are firm, but soft to the touch.

1 tomato, finely chopped, 1 tablespoon reserved for garnish (optional)

2 tablespoons finely minced white onion plus 1 tablespoon for garnish (optional)

3 serrano chiles, finely chopped

½ teaspoon sea salt, or to taste

3 large avocados, preferably Hass

2 tablespoons finely minced fresh cilantro (fresh coriander), plus 1 tablespoon whole leaves for garnish (optional)

Corn chips

Makes about 2 cups (1 lb/500 g)

1 Put the tomato, onion, chiles, and ½ teaspoon salt in a *molcajete* or small bowl, and smash with a pestle or fork to a coarse paste. Cut the avocados in half, remove the pits, and scoop the flesh into the tomato mixture. Add the minced cilantro and mix and mash, leaving some lumps. Taste and add more salt, if necessary.

2 If you want, sprinkle the guacamole with any or all of the garnishes and serve at once, if possible. To keep at room temperature for up to 1 hour, cover with plastic wrap pressed directly onto the surface. To keep for up to but no longer than 3 hours, do not add the cilantro until just before serving, and cover and store in the refrigerator.

3 Pass the corn chips in a basket at the table.

AVOCADOS

En route to Michoacán's hot lands lies a breathtaking area called just that, *tierra caliente*. As you descend from the pine-cloaked highlands through the deeply folded slopes of a volcanic mountain range, the climate becomes delightfully temperate. The Cupatitzio River wanders through the region, brought to life by a long waterfall, and the hillsides are canopied by dark green avocado trees. A popular destination is Uruapan, an agricultural community whose name means "Forever Springtime" in the Purépecha language.

In this peaceful town, visitors can relax in a wondrous setting, enjoy the local foods, and seek out an introduction to resident families who number among Mexico's leading avocado growers. Wandering through a plantation, you can investigate the varieties, besides the familiar Hass, that are grown. One of the most interesting is the tiny, round *criollo*, or now-cultivated "wild" avocado. The skins are so tender that you can eat the whole avocado, spitting out the pit, and the leaves are what give an anise-flavored undercurrent to so many of the regional dishes.

Hot-Pepper Jelly Turnovers

The South • America

Hot-pepper jelly, a tasty condiment that has a long history throughout the American South, is available at most well-stocked grocery stores and specialty-food shops.

PASTRY

1¼ cup (5 oz/155 g) soft winter-wheat flour (page 221)

1 teaspoon sugar

½ teaspoon salt

¼ cup (2 oz/60 g) chilled solid vegetable shortening

¼ cup (2 oz/60 g) chilled unsalted butter, cut into ½-inch (12-mm) chunks

3–6 tablespoons (1½–3 fl oz/45–90 ml) ice water

½ cup (5 oz/155 g) hot-pepper jelly (see note)

½ cup (2 oz/60 g) shredded mild Cheddar or hoop cheese (page 222)

1 egg beaten with 1 tablespoon water

Makes about 24 turnovers

1 To make the pastry, in a bowl, stir together the flour, sugar, and salt. Using a pastry blender or fork, cut in the shortening until the mixture resembles cornmeal. Cut in the butter until pea-sized balls form. Add the ice water 1 tablespoon at a time, tossing the mixture with a fork until it is moist and holds together. Gather the dough into a ball, wrap in plastic wrap, and refrigerate for 30–60 minutes before rolling out.

2 Lightly butter a baking sheet. On a lightly floured work surface, roll out the dough into a 12-inch (30-cm) round. Using a 2-inch (5-cm) round fluted cookie cutter, cut out as many rounds as possible. Place 1 teaspoon of the hot-pepper jelly and 1 teaspoon of the cheese in the center of each round. Fold the round in half, enclosing the jelly and cheese completely, and seal the edge with the tines of a fork that have been dipped in water.

3 Place the turnovers on the prepared baking sheet and refrigerate. Gather together the dough scraps, reroll, and cut out as many additional rounds as possible. Repeat the filling and folding, place on the baking sheet, and refrigerate all the turnovers for 1 hour.

4 Preheat the oven to 425°F (220°C). Brush each turnover with some of the egg-water mixture. Bake the turnovers until golden brown, 22–25 minutes.

5 Transfer the turnovers to a rack to cool. Serve warm or at room temperature.

Chorizo-Stuffed Ancho Chiles

Chiles Tolucos • Mexico, D.F. • Mexico

Stuffed dried chiles, such as large, red wine–colored anchos, are typical of the high valleys in central Mexico. Substitute whole pinto or black beans for the refried, if you like.

6 ancho chiles

1 cup (8 fl oz/250 ml) cider vinegar

1 cup (8 fl oz/250 ml) fresh orange juice

½ lb (250 g) *piloncillo* cone (page 224), chopped, or 1 cup (7 oz/220 g) firmly packed dark brown sugar

5 cloves garlic

1 bay leaf

1 teaspoon dried oregano, preferably Mexican

1 teaspoon dried thyme

2 tablespoons safflower or canola oil

¼ lb (125 g) good-quality chorizo (page 220), crumbled

1 cup (7 oz/220 g) refried beans, homemade or good-quality purchased (see note)

Sea salt to taste

½ lb (250 g) Monterey jack or other good melting cheese, cut into strips 2 inches (5 cm) long by ½ inch (12 mm) wide by ½ inch (12 mm) thick, plus ⅓ lb (5 oz/155 g), shredded

1 cup (8 fl oz/250 ml) *crema* (page 220)

1 firm but ripe avocado, preferably Hass, pitted, peeled, and sliced

10 radishes, thinly sliced

Serves 4–6

1 Leaving the stem and top intact, make a lengthwise slit in each chile and remove the seeds and veins, taking care not to break the walls.

2 In a saucepan over medium heat, combine the vinegar and orange juice and bring to a simmer. Add the *piloncillo*, garlic, bay leaf, oregano, and thyme and cook, stirring, until the sugar has dissolved. Remove from the heat. Add the chiles and soak until they feel fleshy, 15–20 minutes.

3 In a frying pan over medium heat, warm the oil. Add the chorizo and fry until cooked thoroughly, 6–8 minutes. Pour off the excess fat and stir in the beans. Season with salt. Let cool. Preheat the oven to 350°F (180°C).

4 Using tongs or a slotted spoon, transfer the chiles to paper towels to drain. Strain the soaking liquid and set aside to use as a sauce.

5 Carefully stuff the chiles with the chorizo-bean mixture and strips of cheese; the chiles should be plump. (At this point the chiles can be refrigerated for up to 1 day.) Arrange the filled chiles, seam side down, in a baking dish, and spoon the *crema* over the top. Sprinkle the top with the shredded cheese.

6 Bake the chiles until the cheese on top is melted and the chiles are heated through, about 15 minutes. Meanwhile, reheat the sauce.

7 Put 1 or 2 chiles on each individual plate, spoon the sauce around the sides, and garnish with the avocado and radish slices. Serve at once.

Wild Mushroom Tart

The Pacific Northwest • America

One of the prime fall foods of the Pacific Northwest, wild mushrooms show up in an endless variety of dishes in the region's restaurant and home kitchens. Simple quichelike tarts such as this recipe are one option. The cream cheese in the filling gives the tart a slightly firmer texture than most quiches, and the addition of hazelnuts adds a welcome nuttiness to this tasty starter. Serve the tart with a simple salad of mixed greens tossed with a classic vinaigrette in which hazelnut oil replaces some of the olive oil.

PASTRY

½ cup (2½ oz/75 g) hazelnuts (filberts), toasted and skinned (page 223)

1½ cups (7½ oz/235 g) all-purpose (plain) flour

½ teaspoon salt

6 tablespoons (3 oz/90 g) chilled unsalted butter, cut into ½-inch (12-mm) pieces

1 egg yolk

3–4 tablespoons (1½ –2 fl oz/45–60 ml) ice water

FILLING

1 tablespoon unsalted butter

½ cup (2½ oz/75 g) minced shallot or yellow onion

1½ lb (750 g) fresh wild mushrooms such as chanterelle, hedgehog, oyster, or lobster, brushed clean and coarsely chopped

Salt and freshly ground pepper to taste

¼ lb (125 g) cream cheese, at room temperature

2 eggs

1 cup (8 fl oz/250 ml) half-and-half (half cream)

2 tablespoons minced fresh flat-leaf (Italian) parsley

Serves 8

1 To make the pastry, in a food processor, combine the hazelnuts and 2 tablespoons of the flour and pulse until the nuts are very finely ground. Add the rest of the flour with the salt and pulse a few times to blend evenly. Add the butter pieces and pulse until the butter is finely chopped and the flour mixture has a coarse, sandy texture. Add the egg yolk and pulse once. Add the ice water 1 tablespoon at a time, pulsing once or twice after each addition and using only as much as needed for the dough to hold its shape when pinched between your fingers. It should be soft but not sticky. Do not overmix the dough, or it will be tough rather than flaky. Turn the dough out onto a work surface and form it into a ball. Enclose in plastic wrap and refrigerate for at least 30 minutes or for up to 1 day.

2 Preheat the oven to 375°F (190°C).

3 Remove the dough from the refrigerator and let sit for a few minutes. On a lightly floured work surface, roll out the dough into a 12-inch (30-cm) round. Drape around the rolling pin and carefully ease into a 10-inch (25-cm) tart pan with a removable bottom. Lay the overhang over the edge of the pan, and roll the pin over the dough to trim it. Following the fluted edge of the pan, gently crimp the dough rim. Line the tart shell with a piece of aluminum foil, fill with pie weights or a combination of uncooked rice and dried beans, and bake until set to the touch, 8–10 minutes. Remove the weights and foil and bake the shell until golden, about 5 minutes. Transfer to a rack and let cool. Reduce the oven temperature to 350°F (180°C).

4 To make the filling, in a large frying pan over medium-high heat, melt the butter. Add the shallot and sauté until tender and aromatic, 1–2 minutes. Add the mushrooms and sauté until they are tender and the liquid that they give off has evaporated, 5–7 minutes. Remove from the heat, season lightly with salt and pepper, and let cool completely.

5 Put the cream cheese in a bowl. Using a wooden spoon, lightly beat the cheese until smooth. Add the eggs and beat to combine. Pour in the half-and-half and continue to beat until smooth. Season with salt and pepper.

6 Pour the cream cheese mixture into the pastry shell, then evenly scatter with the cooled mushrooms, gently pressing them into the mixture. Sprinkle the parsley on top.

7 Bake the tart until the pastry edges are browned and the filling is set, about 30 minutes. Transfer to a rack and let cool completely. Remove the pan sides and place the tart on a serving plate. Serve at room temperature, cut into wedges.

DAIRY LAND

The lush pasturelands in the midwestern American states of Illinois, Indiana, Ohio, Iowa, Michigan, Wisconsin, and Minnesota attracted early European immigrants who saw their old-world landscapes in their newly adopted country. Hills of sweet alfalfa tumbled into verdant valleys of grass, ideal for grazing Brown Swiss and Holstein cows. They quickly settled in and began to re-create the dairy tradition they left behind, producing rich milk and cream, which they preserved in the form of fresh and aged cheeses, and velvety butter.

Mrs. Anne Pickett, a farm wife who bought milk from her neighbors, opened Wisconsin's first commercial "cheeserie" in 1841, in Lake Mills. Twenty years later, along came another Wisconsin innovator, Chester Hazen. He founded the first true cheese factory in 1864, and is credited with the groundbreaking idea to load railroad cars with cheese for out-of-state customers. Perhaps the most famous of these early Midwest cheeses is Colby, a cousin to Cheddar, first developed in the town of Colby, Wisconsin, in 1885. Soon Midwest dairy lands were supplying the growing nation with Cheddar, brick, Swiss, and other cheeses. Although California has since passed Wisconsin as the country's biggest milk-producing state, the Midwest as a whole does continue to dominate America's dairy industry, producing nearly half of the nation's butter and cheese. More than 350 varieties, types, and styles of cheese come from Wisconsin alone.

The growing market for artisanal cheeses has helped many new and existing midwestern cheese makers find successful niche markets with specialty cheeses, such as Mexican *queso blanco*, Italian Gorgonzola, and Greek-style feta. Small-scale producers are turning out more and more handcrafted cheeses, several of which rely on organic milk and are available only within a narrow radius of where they are made. Farmstead cheeses from Wisconsin's "Green Country," south of Madison, are winning fans and critical accolades with fine Limburger, aged Cheddar, Muenster, and Havarti. From Minnesota come creamy fromage blanc and piquant smoked sheep's milk cheese. Regional chefs can find tart and smooth goat's milk cheeses close to home, turned out in limited batches by craftspeople in Missouri and Indiana.

Summer Crudités with Ranch Dip

The Midwest · America

Ranch dressing is America's most popular. Some midwesterners like it so much that they put it on french fries and baked potatoes, as well as crisp vegetables fresh from the garden.

1 cup (8 oz/250 g) sour cream

1 cup (8 fl oz/250 ml) buttermilk

½ cup (4 fl oz/125 ml) mayonnaise

6 tablespoons (¾ oz/20 g) buttermilk powder

½ teaspoon white wine vinegar

Kosher salt and freshly ground pepper to taste

½ teaspoon sugar

4 tablespoons (⅓ oz/10 g) minced fresh flat-leaf (Italian) parsley

12–16 green (spring) onions, trimmed

2 fennel bulbs, trimmed and cut into narrow wedges

4 or 5 small red or orange beets, peeled and sliced paper-thin, or halved if small

½ lb (250 g) sugar snap or snow peas (mangetouts)

12–16 young carrots, tops trimmed

1 small head red cabbage, cut into narrow wedges

2 celery hearts, trimmed with leaves intact

2 yellow or orange bell peppers (capsicums), seeded and cut crosswise into rings

1 small zucchini (courgette) or summer squash, thinly sliced

24 cherry tomatoes

24 small radishes

Serves 12

1 In a bowl, combine the sour cream, buttermilk, mayonnaise, buttermilk powder, vinegar, salt, pepper, and sugar. Whisk until smooth. Stir in 3 tablespoons of the parsley. Taste and adjust the seasoning. Cover and refrigerate for 2 hours. Prepare all the vegetables and have them ready in the refrigerator.

2 Arrange the vegetables on a large platter. Transfer the dip to a serving bowl and sprinkle with the remaining 1 tablespoon parsley. Serve at once.

Cheese-Stuffed Shrimp Wrapped in Bacon

Camarones Rellenos Envueltos con Tocino · Veracruz · Mexico

The recipe for these bacon-wrapped shrimp, served with a fiery chipotle mayonnaise, comes from a longtime favorite seafood restaurant in Veracruz called El Lugar.

1½ cups (12 fl oz/375 ml) mayonnaise

3 *chiles chipotles en adobo*, finely chopped, with 1 teaspoon *adobo* sauce

1 clove garlic, minced

1 tablespoon minced lime zest

1 tablespoon fresh lime juice

12 medium-thick slices lean bacon, cut in half crosswise

24 large shrimp (prawns), peeled, deveined, and butterflied, with tails attached

Freshly ground pepper to taste

1½ cups (6 oz/185 g) shredded Manchego, Monterey jack, or other good melting cheese

About 4 tablespoons (2 fl oz/60 ml) olive oil

Serves 6–8

1 In a bowl or a food processor, combine the mayonnaise, chiles and *adobo* sauce, garlic, lime zest, and lime juice and stir or process to mix well. Cover and refrigerate until ready to serve.

2 Lay as many bacon slices as will fit in a single layer in a large, heavy frying pan and cook over medium-low heat until opaque but still soft, about 5 minutes. Press down with a spatula to keep the bacon flat. Transfer to paper towels to drain. Wipe out the pan and repeat to cook the remaining bacon.

3 Dry the shrimp with paper towels. Sprinkle with pepper and stuff with the cheese. Push the sides together and wrap with a cooked bacon slice, covering all of the cheese so that it will not melt out. If necessary, secure with a toothpick. In the same frying pan over medium heat, warm 2 tablespoons of the oil. Add a few of the bacon-wrapped shrimp and fry, turning frequently and adding more oil as needed to prevent sticking, until the bacon is browned and the shrimp are pink, about 10 minutes. Transfer to paper towels to drain. Repeat until all the shrimp are fried.

4 Serve the shrimp on plates and accompany with the chipotle mayonnaise.

Avocado and Cream Cheese Roll

Rollo de Queso y Aguacate · Puebla · Mexico

The salt white color, soft texture, and ripe-sour taste of fresh cream cheese make this party dish from Puebla memorable. Look for cottage-made cream cheese in specialty shops.

½ lb (250 g) cream cheese (see note), at room temperature

1 avocado, preferably Hass

2 tablespoons chopped fresh cilantro (fresh coriander)

1 tablespoon finely chopped white onion

1 serrano chile, finely chopped

¼ teaspoon fresh lime juice

Sea salt to taste

2 cups (2 oz/60 g) crumbled *chicharrones* (page 220) or 2 cups (6 oz/185 g) sesame seeds, toasted (page 225)

Corn chips or small crackers

Serves 6–8

1 Place the cream cheese between 2 sheets of parchment (baking) paper. Using a rolling pin, roll to form a rectangle about 6 inches (15 cm) by 8 inches (20 cm) and ½ inch (12 mm) thick. Remove the top sheet.

2 Cut the avocado in half, remove the pit, and scoop the flesh into a bowl. Mash until it is rather smooth, leaving some small chunks to add texture. Stir in the cilantro, onion, chile, lime juice, and salt. Spread the avocado mixture evenly over the cream cheese. Using the bottom sheet of paper, roll up the cream cheese to form a log.

3 Coat the roll completely with the crumbled *chicharrones* or sesame seeds. Cover lightly with plastic wrap and chill in the refrigerator for 15 minutes before serving. The roll can be made in advance and refrigerated for 6–8 hours, then set out at room temperature for 30 minutes before serving.

4 Unwrap the roll and place on a serving platter or tray. Serve with corn chips or crackers.

Ahi Tuna Poke

Hawaii • America

Once you try cubed raw tuna tossed with sesame-soy dressing, you'll never think of "tuna salad" the same way. Use sashimi-grade tuna, found in fish markets or the fish section of supermarkets. Other fresh tunas such as albacore can be used. *Poke* is best within a few hours of being made, although it will keep, refrigerated and tightly covered, for up to a day.

1 lb (500 g) sashimi-grade ahi tuna steaks, skin and bones removed

½ cup (2½ oz/75 g) finely chopped Maui or other sweet onion

3 tablespoons soy sauce

2 tablespoons minced fresh cilantro (fresh coriander), plus sprigs for garnish

2 teaspoons sesame seeds, toasted (page 225)

Few dashes of Asian sesame oil

Large pinch *each* of coarse sea salt and red pepper flakes

Serves 4–6

1 Using a sharp knife, cut the tuna into ¾-inch (2-cm) cubes. Place the tuna in a bowl and add the onion, soy sauce, minced cilantro, sesame seeds, sesame oil, salt, and red pepper flakes. Toss the mixture gently to blend evenly. Cover the bowl and refrigerate the *poke* until well chilled, about 1 hour.

2 Spoon the *poke* into individual small bowls. Garnish with cilantro sprigs and serve cold.

Fava Bean Bruschetta

California • America

Sweet fava beans grow particularly well in the cool coastal terrain of California. Seek out the best-quality extra-virgin olive oil for drizzling on the bruschetta before serving.

1½ lb (750 g) fresh fava (broad) beans, shelled

4 tablespoons (2 fl oz/60 ml) extra-virgin olive oil, plus oil for brushing and drizzling

1 large clove garlic, minced

Salt and freshly ground pepper to taste

6 large fresh basil leaves, torn into small pieces

12 slices coarse country bread, each about 4 inches (10 cm) long, 2 inches (5 cm) wide, and ¼ inch (6 mm) thick

4-oz (125-g) piece ricotta salata cheese

Serves 6

1 Bring a saucepan of water to a boil. Add the fava beans and blanch for 1 minute, then drain and immerse in a bowl of ice water. When the beans are cool, drain again. Using a small knife or your fingertips, slit the skin of each bean and gently squeeze to remove the bright green bean inside.

2 In a small frying pan over medium heat, warm 2 tablespoons of the olive oil. Add the garlic and sauté to release its fragrance. Add the peeled fava beans and season with salt and pepper. Add 2 tablespoons water, cover partially, reduce the heat to low, and simmer until the beans are tender, 8–10 minutes. Transfer the contents of the pan to a food processor. Add the basil and the remaining 2 tablespoons olive oil and purée until smooth. Taste and adjust the seasoning.

3 Preheat the broiler (grill). Arrange the bread slices on a baking sheet and brush both sides with olive oil. Place in the broiler and toast, turning once, until lightly browned. Divide the fava bean purée among the warm toasts, spreading it evenly. Shave ricotta salata over the purée; you may not need the entire piece. Drizzle with olive oil and serve.

Cheese-Stuffed Squash Blossoms

Buñuelos de Flor de Calabaza • Puebla • Mexico

In Mexico, cooking with goat cheese is rare. This unusual recipe from the countryside near Puebla uses it for a complementary tang inside delightfully light squash blossom fritters .

20 good-sized squash blossoms

1½ lb (750 g) fresh goat cheese

20 fresh epazote or cilantro (fresh coriander) leaves

5 eggs, separated

Sea salt and freshly ground pepper to taste

Safflower or canola oil for frying

3 tablespoons all-purpose (plain) flour

Guacamole for serving (page 17; optional)

Serves 4–6

1 Remove the pistils from the squash blossoms. Rinse the blossoms carefully by dunking them in a bowl of water. Dry on paper towels, stem end up.

2 Cut the goat cheese into 20 pieces, each about ¾ inch (2 cm) square and 1 inch (2.5 cm) long. Place a piece of goat cheese and an epazote or cilantro leaf in each blossom and lightly twist the tops of the petals together.

3 In a bowl, beat the egg whites with a whisk until soft peaks form. Add the yolks one at a time, whisking after each addition. Add a pinch of salt and a liberal grinding of pepper.

4 Pour oil to a depth of at least 1 inch (2.5 cm) into a deep, heavy frying pan or a wok and place over medium heat until the oil starts to smoke.

5 While the oil is heating, spread the flour in a shallow dish. Lightly coat the stuffed flowers with the flour. Working in batches, dip each blossom into the egg batter and place in the hot oil. Fry, turning occasionally, until golden, about 3 minutes. Using a slotted spatula, transfer to paper towels to drain.

6 Arrange on a platter and serve at once, accompanied by the guacamole, if desired.

Chiles with Melted Cheese

Chile con Queso • Chihuahua • Mexico

Northern Mexico is ranch country, and dishes made with rich dairy products, like this one, typify the cooking of the region. Serve with chips or wrap in warmed flour tortillas.

4 jalapeño chiles, seeded (page 220)

15 Anaheim chiles, roasted, peeled, seeded, and deveined (page 220)

2 tablespoons unsalted butter or safflower oil

2 small white onions, finely chopped

2 ripe tomatoes, chopped

1 cup (8 fl oz/250 ml) heavy (double) cream

¼ cup (2 fl oz/60 ml) warm water

Sea salt to taste

1 lb (500 g) *queso asadero* or other melting cheese, shredded

Serves 10–12 as a dip, 6 as a filling for tortillas

1 Cut the jalapeño and roasted Anaheim chiles into narrow strips. In a large frying pan over medium heat, melt the butter or warm the oil. Add the onions and jalapeño chiles and sauté until the onions are limp and golden, about 5 minutes. Stir in the Anaheim chiles and tomatoes and cook until all the chiles are soft, about 5 minutes longer. Pour in the cream and warm water, season with salt, and simmer for several minutes.

2 Stir the cheese into the chiles, cover, and remove from the heat. When the cheese has melted, pour the chiles into a heated serving bowl. Serve while it is still bubbling hot, as the cheese will separate and become tough and stringy if allowed to cool.

Artichokes with Aioli

California • America

Artichokes thrive in California's Monterey County. The area is also famous for garlic, so it's natural that aioli, or garlic mayonnaise, often accompanies steamed artichokes as a dip.

4 large artichokes

½ lemon

1 tablespoon mixed pickling spice

AIOLI

1 egg yolk, at room temperature (see page 221)

½ teaspoon warm water

¾ cup (6 fl oz/180 ml) extra-virgin olive oil

1 large clove garlic, or more to taste

Pinch of salt

Fresh lemon juice to taste (optional)

Serves 4

1 To trim each artichoke, cut the stem flush with the bottom. Using a serrated knife, cut about 1½ inches (4 cm) off the top of the artichoke. Using scissors, snip off the pointed tips of each leaf. Rub the artichoke all over with the lemon half.

2 Pour water to a depth of 1 inch (2.5 cm) into a large pot and add the pickling spice. Bring to a boil over high heat. Place a steamer rack in the pot, making sure that the water does not touch the rack, and add the artichokes, stem end up. Cover and adjust the heat to maintain a gentle simmer. Steam until a knife pierces the bottoms easily, 40–45 minutes. Remove the artichokes and let stand, stem ends up, on several thicknesses of paper towels for a few minutes.

3 Meanwhile, make the aioli: In a small bowl, whisk the egg yolk with the warm water, then whisk in the olive oil drop by drop. Once an emulsion has formed, gradually add the oil a little faster until all of it has been incorporated and a mayonnaise-like sauce has formed. In a mortar, combine 1 garlic clove and the salt and pound to a paste. Whisk the paste into the egg-oil mixture. Whisk in a few drops of lemon juice, if desired. Add more pounded garlic, if desired.

4 Using your fingers, gently spread apart the center artichoke leaves. Pull out the prickly innermost leaves. With a spoon, scrape out the hairy choke. Serve the artichokes hot, warm, or chilled. Spoon the aioli into the center of each artichoke or alongside it.

ARTICHOKES

Prickly on the outside but tender within, artichokes are one of nature's more peculiar vegetables. They are actually the flower bud of a large-leaved perennial in the sunflower family, and if left on the plant, the buds would gradually open to reveal glorious purple blossoms. Instead, harvesters cut them when they are tightly closed.

Many Californians consider artichokes a symbol of the Golden State. In fact, almost 100 percent of the nation's crop comes from California, with three-quarters of it grown in cool, foggy Monterey County, south of San Francisco. The tiny town of Castroville, surrounded by silvery artichoke fields and boasting the nation's only artichoke processing plant, proudly proclaims itself the Artichoke Center of the World. At harvesttime in spring, pickers move swiftly through the fields, wielding a short, sharp knife. Probing among the prickly plants, they cut the mature artichokes, leaving some of the stem attached.

Some markets carry egg-sized "baby" artichokes, which are perfect additions to pizzas, pastas, and salads. These are not immature; they are fully grown, but because they grow quite low on the plant, mostly hidden from the sun, they stay small. After paring, they are completely edible, with no fibrous choke.

Green Onion Focaccia

California • America

San Francisco's Liguria Bakery, in the heart of North Beach, is justly famous for its focaccia. The proprietors make it in large trays, slathering some with tomato sauce, garnishing others with sliced green onion. Homemade focaccia makes an impressive informal hors d'oeuvre to accompany marinated olives and the evening's first glass of wine.

1 Make the sponge 1 day before you plan to bake the bread: Put the warm water in a bowl and sprinkle the yeast over the water. Let stand for 2 minutes. Whisk with a fork to dissolve the yeast, then add the flour. Stir with a wooden spoon until smooth, then scrape down the spoon and the sides of the bowl. Cover the bowl tightly with plastic wrap and let stand in a cool place for 24 hours.

2 To make the dough, put the sponge in a heavy-duty mixer fitted with the paddle attachment. Add the water, wine, the ⅓ cup olive oil, sea salt, and 1 cup (5 oz/155 g) of the flour. Mix on low speed, slowly adding the remaining 1¾ cups (9 oz/280 g) plus 2 tablespoons flour to make a soft, sticky dough. Knead in the mixer for 5 minutes with the paddle attachment. Scrape down the paddle and the sides of the bowl, cover the bowl tightly with plastic wrap, and let rise in a cool place until doubled, about 1½ hours.

3 Grease a 12-by-17-inch (30-by-43-cm) rimmed baking sheet with the 2 teaspoons olive oil. Transfer the dough to the baking sheet and, with well-oiled fingers, pat it to cover the bottom completely. It will be very elastic and will want to bounce back. Let the dough rest for 5 minutes, then pat and prod again. If the dough still refuses to cover the sheet completely, let rest for another 5–10 minutes and try again.

4 Cover the dough loosely with oiled plastic wrap to prevent it from drying out. Let rise in a cool place until puffy, about 1½ hours. While the dough rises, line the center rack of the oven with baking tiles or a baking stone and preheat the oven to 550°F (290°C), or the highest setting, for at least 45 minutes.

5 Meanwhile, make the topping: Unless the green onions are very slender, cut them in half lengthwise. Then cut crosswise into pieces ½ inch (12 mm) thick, using all the white and pale green parts and one-third of the dark green tops. You should have about 2 cups (6 oz/185 g). In a frying pan over medium-high heat, warm 1½ tablespoons of the olive oil. Add the green onions and sauté briskly until slightly softened, about 1 minute. Let cool.

6 Carefully lift the plastic wrap off the dough. Drizzle the surface with the remaining 2 tablespoons olive oil. Scatter evenly with the green onions, then sprinkle with the coarse salt. Dimple the dough vigorously all over with oiled fingertips. Bake until lightly browned and firm to the touch, 12–14 minutes. Remove from the oven and slide out of the baking sheet onto a rack. Let cool. Use a serrated knife to cut the focaccia into pieces of the desired size.

SPONGE

1 cup (8 fl oz/250 ml) warm water

1 package (2½ teaspoons) active dry yeast

1 cup (5 oz/155 g) unbleached all-purpose (plain) flour

DOUGH

½ cup (4 fl oz/125 ml) water

⅓ cup (3 fl oz/80 ml) dry white wine

⅓ cup (3 fl oz/80 ml) extra-virgin olive oil, plus 2 teaspoons

1 tablespoon sea salt

2¾ cups (14 oz/440 g) plus 2 tablespoons unbleached all-purpose (plain) flour

TOPPING

18–20 green (spring) onions

3½ tablespoons extra-virgin olive oil

Scant 1 teaspoon coarse sea salt, lightly crushed

Serves 8

Mushroom Empanadas

Empanadas de Maíz con Hongos • Oaxaca • Mexico

These scrumptious empanadas are like chubby quesadillas. The filling is piled onto homemade tortillas, and then the tortillas are folded and browned.

FILLING

2 tablespoons unsalted butter or safflower oil

1 white onion, finely chopped

1 serrano chile, finely chopped

6 cloves garlic, minced

¾ lb (375 g) fresh mushrooms, preferably portobello, porcini, or other flavorful variety, brushed clean and coarsely chopped

2 tablespoons finely chopped fresh epazote (optional)

½ teaspoon sea salt

½ teaspoon freshly ground pepper

8–10 corn tortillas, 5 inches (13 cm) in diameter (homemade or good-quality purchased)

1½ cups (6 oz/185 g) shredded *quesillo de Oaxaca*, Muenster, mozzarella cheese, or other good melting cheese (optional)

1 cup (8 fl oz/250 ml) tomatillo salsa (homemade or good-quality purchased)

Serves 4–6

1 To make the filling, in a frying pan, melt the butter or warm the oil over high heat. Add the onion and chile and sauté until the onion is translucent, about 30 seconds. Add the garlic and continue to sauté for just a few seconds. Add the mushrooms and cook for about 4 minutes, tossing every minute or so. They will give off a heady, earthy aroma. When the mushrooms just begin to give off a liquid, stir in the epazote (if using), salt, and pepper and immediately remove from the heat. Let the filling cool.

2 Place a tortilla in the center of a sheet of plastic wrap and place 1 tablespoon of the shredded cheese, if using, in the center of the lower half of the tortilla, keeping the edges free. Spoon on some mushrooms. Fold the other half of the tortilla over the filling and press the edges together. Lift up the bottom piece of plastic wrap and turn the empanada over to remove it and set aside. Repeat with the remaining tortillas

3 Heat a griddle or large, heavy frying pan over medium-high heat. When hot, gently lay the empanada on the hot surface and cook until it starts to brown, 1 minute. Turn the empanada and move it to the side to continue cooking, while starting the next one. Repeat the process, and when the empanadas are well cooked and brown on each side, carefully remove to a low oven to keep warm.

4 Serve the empanadas at once, if possible, with the salsa on the side.

Pickled Mixed Vegetables

Verduras en Escabeche • Oaxaca • Mexico

Bowls of these brightly colored, chunky vegetables—a perfect condiment to serve with *antojitos*—are set out on the counters of market *fondas* all over Mexico.

4 garlic heads

6 carrots, peeled

6 jalapeño chiles

1 white onion, peeled

20 green beans, ends trimmed

½ cup (4 fl oz/125 ml) canola oil

4 cups (32 fl oz/1 l) mild white vinegar

2 cups (16 fl oz/500 ml) water

2 tablespoons dried oregano,
preferably Mexican

2 teaspoons *each* peppercorns and salt

3 bay leaves *and* 3 whole cloves

2 cups (6 oz/185 g) small
cauliflower florets

6–8 very small potatoes, unpeeled,
boiled until barely tender

Makes about 2 qt (2 l)

1 Remove the papery skin on the outside of the garlic heads and slice off their tops. Cut the carrots into slices ¼ inch (6 mm) thick. Cut the chiles and onion into slices ½ inch (12 mm) thick. Cut the green beans into 1½-inch (4-cm) lengths. In a large, deep frying pan over medium heat, warm the oil. Add the garlic heads and sauté, stirring often, until the skins begin to crisp, about 5 minutes. Add the carrots and cook for 2 minutes longer, then stir in the chiles and onion. Continue to cook and stir for another 2 minutes. The vegetables should still be crisp.

2 Add the vinegar, water, oregano, peppercorns, salt, bay leaves, and cloves and bring to a boil. Drop in the cauliflower and green beans and simmer until just tender, no more than 3–5 minutes. Add the potatoes and heat through.

3 Ladle the vegetables and liquid into 2 clean, sterilized jars and let cool. Seal tightly and store in the refrigerator overnight. Bring to room temperature before serving.

Tangy Jicama, Cucumber, and Pineapple Sticks with Peanuts

Jícama, Pepinos, y Piña con Cacahuates • Jalisco • Mexico

In Jalisco and other parts of Mexico, this combination, an irresistible *botana* any time of the day or night, is commonly known as *pico de gallo,* or "rooster's beak."

2 cucumbers, peeled, halved, and seeded

1 small pineapple, peeled, halved,
and cored

1 jicama, peeled

Juice of 6 limes

1 teaspoon sea salt

1 cup (5 oz/155 g) raw peanuts,
skins removed

4 árbol chiles, toasted (page 220)

Serves 6–8

1 Cut the cucumbers, pineapple, and jicama into sticks measuring about 3 inches (7.5 cm) long and ⅓ inch (9 mm) thick. Arrange the sticks in a single layer in a shallow glass dish. Sprinkle the sticks with the lime juice and salt. Cover and refrigerate, turning the pieces occasionally.

2 In a dry frying pan over medium heat, toast the peanuts, stirring often, until they are toasty gold, about 15 minutes. Remove from the heat and pour into a small bowl. Crumble the chiles over the nuts. Working in small batches, coarsely grind the peanut mixture in a spice grinder.

3 Sprinkle the ground nut mixture over the upper two-thirds of the sticks. To serve, slip the ends into a widemouthed container so that the sticks stand upright, peanut-coated side down, or lay the sticks flat on a platter.

Gravlax

The Pacific Northwest • America

A Scandinavian specialty, dill-cured salmon is perfectly at home in the Pacific Northwest, where salmon are abundant and Scandinavian heritage dates back to some of the area's earliest settlers. Traditionally, two whole fillets are cured at once, but this results in more cured salmon than most cooks are prepared to serve. This recipe calls for two smaller fillets. Plan ahead, as the gravlax should cure for a minimum of two days before serving. Lightly pickled red onions make a great finish to this elegant appetizer.

2 center-cut salmon fillet pieces of equal size, about 2½ lb (1.25 kg) total weight, with skin intact

¼ cup (2 oz/60 g) kosher salt, plus a pinch

¼ cup (2 oz/60 g) plus 1 tablespoon sugar

1 tablespoon crushed or coarsely ground white peppercorns, plus a pinch of freshly ground white pepper

1 large bunch fresh dill, coarsely chopped

2 tablespoons lemon vodka

1 small red onion

Boiling water as needed

½ cup (4 fl oz/125 ml) red wine vinegar

Thinly sliced pumpernickel cocktail bread or toasted baguette slices

Serves 20–24

1 Rub your fingers along the surfaces of the salmon fillets, and then use needle-nose pliers or tweezers to remove any fine pin bones. Lay a long piece of plastic wrap in a shallow dish, such as a baking dish, and set one of the fillet pieces, skin side down, on the plastic.

2 In a small bowl, combine the ¼ cup salt, ¼ cup of the sugar, and the 1 tablespoon crushed peppercorns and stir to mix. Scatter half of the salt mixture evenly over the salmon in the dish. Scatter the dill over the salt mixture and then drizzle with the vodka. Sprinkle the remaining salt mixture over the dill. Set the second piece of salmon, flesh side down, over the first, and draw up the plastic wrap to enclose the pieces fully. Lay a piece of aluminum foil on top, followed by another baking dish or small pan. Add a few cans of food to weight the salmon and refrigerate for 2–3 days. Every 12 hours or so, remove the weights and turn over the wrapped package of curing salmon.

3 An hour or so before you plan to serve the salmon, thinly slice the red onion and put it in a heatproof bowl. Add boiling water just to cover the onion and let stand for 5 minutes, then drain well. While the onion is still warm, return it to the bowl and add the vinegar and the remaining 1 tablespoon sugar with the remaining pinches of kosher salt and white pepper. Toss to mix until the sugar has dissolved. Let cool, then drain off the vinegar. Cover and refrigerate the onion until ready to serve.

4 When the salmon is ready, discard the plastic wrap and scrape away the dill and other seasonings. Very briefly pass the salmon under running cold water and pat dry thoroughly with paper towels. Using a sharp, narrow-bladed knife, and working at a sharp angle, cut the salmon into paper-thin slices.

5 Arrange the salmon on bread slices (halving the fish pieces first if quite large). Garnish the salmon with the pickled red onion slices and serve.

Frittata with Spring Herbs and Leeks

California • America

Because of California's large Italian American population, frittatas are almost as common as omelets in the state's home cooking. Italian delicatessens in many neighborhoods sell thick frittatas by the slice for picnics or take-home suppers. Made with the fresh, tender herbs and young leeks that flood local farmers' markets in the spring, this frittata has a distinctly California accent. Leftover frittata makes a delicious sandwich on toasted bread.

2 tablespoons unsalted butter

4 cups (12 oz/375 g) thinly sliced leeks, including tender green tops

Salt to taste, plus a pinch

Freshly ground pepper to taste

6 eggs

½ cup (¾ oz/20 g) *mixed* minced fresh flat-leaf (Italian) parsley, basil, and mint

¼ cup (1 oz/30 g) grated Parmesan cheese

Serves 4

1 In a flameproof, 10-inch (25-cm) nonstick frying pan over medium heat, melt the butter. Add the leeks, season with salt and pepper, and sauté until softened, about 15 minutes. Reduce the heat if needed to keep the leeks from browning.

2 In a large bowl, whisk the eggs to break them up. Whisk in the herbs, cheese, and pinch of salt. Add the eggs to the frying pan, stirring for just a few seconds to distribute the leeks evenly. Reduce the heat to low and cook very slowly until the eggs are set around the sides but still a little moist in the center, about 15 minutes.

3 Meanwhile, preheat the broiler (grill). When the eggs are ready, slip the frying pan under the broiler several inches from the heat source and broil (grill) until the top is lightly colored and the center is firm to the touch, 1 minute or less. Slide the frittata onto a cutting board. Serve warm, cut into wedges.

Tortilla Fritters Stuffed with Chorizo and Potatoes

Molotes • Oaxaca • Mexico

On the days before Christmas, the side streets radiating off Oaxaca's central plaza are crammed with food stalls selling spindle-shaped *molotes* filled with potatoes and chorizo, topped with a sauce of black beans and lots of condiments, and served on a lettuce leaf.

SAUCE

¾ cup (6 oz/185 g) Pot Beans (page 39) made with black beans, with some liquid, or canned black beans

½ árbol chile, toasted (page 220) and crumbled

1 small avocado leaf, toasted (page 219) and crumbled (optional)

2 teaspoons safflower or canola oil

1 tablespoon finely chopped white onion

Sea salt to taste

MOLOTES

1 guajillo chile, toasted (page 220)

½ cup (4 fl oz/125 ml) boiling water

1 teaspoon safflower or canola oil

2 oz (60 g) good-quality chorizo (page 220), crumbled

2 tablespoons finely chopped white onion

2 cloves garlic, finely chopped

2 small new potatoes, cubed, boiled, and coarsely mashed

Sea salt and freshly ground pepper to taste

8–10 corn tortillas, 5 inches (13-cm) in diameter, homemade or good-quality purchased

Peanut or safflower oil for frying

GARNISHES

12 inner leaves of romaine (cos) lettuce, plus 1 cup (2 oz/60 g) shredded

Salsa of choice, homemade (page 45) or good-quality purchased

⅓ cup (2 oz/60 g) crumbled *queso fresco* or *queso ranchero*

Serves 4–6

1 To make the sauce, put the beans and most of their broth, the árbol chile, and the avocado leaf, if using, in a blender and process until a smooth, thin purée forms. In a frying pan over medium heat, warm the oil. Add the onion and sauté until golden, about 4 minutes. Pour in the bean purée and simmer, stirring occasionally, for 5 minutes. Season with salt and keep warm.

2 Meanwhile, prepare the *molotes*: In a bowl, combine the guajillo chile and boiling water and let stand until the chile is soft, about 10 minutes. In a small frying pan over low heat, warm the oil. Add the chorizo and fry until it just starts to become crisp and brown, 3–5 minutes. Drain the chile and grind or mash it into a paste. Pour off any excess oil from the chorizo, add the onion, and cook, stirring in the chile and garlic after several minutes, until the onion is translucent, about 8 minutes. Spoon the potatoes into the chorizo mixture, stirring and mashing to combine. Season with salt and pepper. Raise the heat to medium, cook for 1 more minute, remove from the heat, and set aside.

3 Spread a small spoonful of the chorizo-potato filling in the center of a tortilla and fold the tortilla over the filling. Transfer the *molote* to a flat surface. Lightly oil your hands and form the tortilla into a tapered oblong shape with pointed ends and a bulging middle. Place under a damp kitchen towel or plastic wrap. Repeat until all the *molotes* are formed.

4 In a heavy frying pan over medium-high heat, pour in oil to a depth of 1 inch (2.5 cm) and heat until it is rippling hot. Add the *molotes* a few at a time and fry until they turn a deep golden brown, about 5 minutes. Using a slotted spoon or spatula, transfer to paper towels to drain. Keep warm in a low oven until all of the *molotes* are cooked.

5 Place a *molote* on top of each lettuce leaf. Spread with a spoonful of the bean sauce, sprinkle with shredded lettuce, and drizzle with salsa. Top with cheese and serve at once.

POT BEANS

This recipe makes about 8 cups (3½ lb/1.75 kg) of pot beans, which can be used in many recipes or served as a side dish. Store the leftovers, tightly covered, in the refrigerator for up to 4 days.

2½ cups (18 oz/560 g) dried black or pinto beans

2 tablespoons safflower or canola oil

1 white onion, finely chopped

1 clove garlic, minced

2 fresh epazote sprigs (optional)

1 teaspoon sea salt, or to taste

½ cup (2½ oz/75 g) crumbled queso fresco (optional)

Pick over the beans and discard any debris or misshapen beans. Rinse well, place in a large pot, and add water to cover by several inches. Bring to a boil, reduce the heat, and simmer.

Meanwhile, in a small frying pan over medium heat, warm the oil. Add the onion and sauté until golden, about 4 minutes. Stir in the garlic and cook for 1 minute longer. Add the onion and garlic to the beans and continue to cook, partially covered, until the beans are just tender, about 2 hours. Stir the beans occasionally and, if needed, pour in hot water to keep the water level at 1 inch (2.5 cm) above the beans. Add the epazote, if using, and salt and continue to cook until the beans are soft, about 40 minutes longer. (If time allows, let the beans cool in the broth. The earthy flavor will intensify if the beans are stored, covered, in the refrigerator for at least overnight, then slowly reheated.)

Serve the beans ladled with the broth into warmed bowls and garnished with cheese or use as directed in individual recipes.

Zucchini Quiche

Quiche de Calabacitas • Puebla • Mexico

The French may not have occupied Mexico for long—indeed, no longer than three years—but their culinary influence remains evident, especially in the central part of the country. This highly flavorful quiche, with its rich sauce of poblano chiles, pairs well with grilled meats or can easily stand on its own as a light main course. Well-cured Spanish Manchego cheese, made from sheep's milk, adds an especially distinctive flavor to the filling.

1 To make the pastry, in a bowl, mix together the cream cheese and butter until well blended, using a spoon or an electric mixer. Add the flour and salt and mix well. Turn the dough out onto a lightly floured work surface and gently knead for about 1 minute, then form into a ball, wrap with plastic wrap, and refrigerate for at least 15 minutes.

2 Preheat the oven to 350°F (180°C). Butter a 9-inch (23-cm) quiche dish or a tart pan with a removable bottom. Position a rack in the lower third of the oven.

3 To make the filling, in a frying pan over medium heat, melt the butter. Add the chile strips and onion and sauté until softened, about 3 minutes. Remove them with a slotted spoon and set aside. Put the zucchini slices in the still-hot pan along with ½ cup (4 fl oz/ 125 ml) water and 1½ teaspoons of the bouillon granules and cook until the zucchini is just tender, about 5 minutes. Drain and let cool.

4 In a blender or food processor, combine half of the onions and chile strips, the remaining 1½ teaspoons bouillon granules, and the cream cheese, eggs, cream, nutmeg, salt, and pepper. Process until puréed.

5 On a lightly floured work surface, roll out the dough into an 11-inch (28-cm) round about ⅛ inch (3 mm) thick. Drape the round over the rolling pin, transfer it to the prepared pan, and ease it into the pan. Trim off the edges even with the rim. Arrange the zucchini and the remaining onions and chile strips in the lined pan, then top with half of the shredded cheese and all of the cream cheese mixture. Top with the remaining shredded cheese.

6 Bake until a knife inserted into the center comes out clean and the top is brown, 45–60 minutes. Remove from the oven and let firm up for several minutes. If using a tart pan, remove the sides and slide the quiche onto a plate. Serve hot or at room temperature.

PASTRY

6 oz (185 g) low-fat cream cheese, at room temperature

1 cup (8 oz/250 g) unsalted butter, at room temperature

2 cups (10 oz/315 g) unbleached all-purpose (plain) flour

½ teaspoon sea salt

FILLING

⅓ cup (3 oz/90 g) unsalted butter

3 poblano chiles, roasted, seeded, and deveined (page 220), then cut lengthwise into narrow strips

1 white onion, finely chopped

2¼ lb (1.1 kg) small zucchini (courgettes), sliced ¼ inch (6 mm) thick

3 teaspoons chicken bouillon granules

¼ lb (125 g) regular or low-fat cream cheese, at room temperature

3 eggs

½ cup (4 fl oz/125 ml) heavy (double) cream

½ teaspoon freshly grated nutmeg

¼ teaspoon sea salt

Freshly ground pepper to taste

½ lb (250 g) Manchego, white Cheddar, or Monterey jack cheese, shredded

Serves 6–8

Black Bean Gorditas

Gorditas de Frijol • Veracruz • Mexico

In the bustling port of Veracruz, Sr. Atenogenes Machorro operates a small restaurant where his busy staff prepares these puffy fried tortillas with savory black beans.

1 clove garlic, unpeeled

1 cup (7 oz/220 g) Pot Beans (page 39) made with black beans, with some liquid if needed

1 avocado leaf, toasted (page 219) and crumbled (optional)

1 lb (500 g) freshly prepared tortilla *masa* or 1¾ cups (9 oz/280 g) *masa harina* (page 223)

1 teaspoon sea salt, plus more to taste

½ cup (4 fl oz/125 ml) *crema* (page 220)

2 tablespoons all-purpose (plain) flour, if needed

Peanut or safflower oil for frying

Fresh salsa (page 45 or good-quality purchased) for serving

Serves 10

1 Place a heavy frying pan over medium heat. Add the garlic clove and roast, turning it frequently, until it softens and the skin blackens, about 10 minutes. Remove from the heat. In a food processor, combine the beans and avocado leaf, if using. Peel the garlic and add it. Process to form a smooth, thick paste, adding the bean liquid as needed.

2 If using *masa*, put it in a bowl and knead with the 1 teaspoon salt, adding 1 teaspoon warm water if needed to make a soft dough. If using *masa harina*, put in a bowl, add 1 cup (8 fl oz/250 ml) warm water, and mix. Let the *masa harina* rest 5 minutes, then add the 1 teaspoon salt and knead for 1 minute. Mix together the beans, *masa*, *crema*, and salt until the dough is smooth; if too damp, knead in the flour. Form 20 balls and cover with plastic wrap. Pour oil to a depth of ½ inch (12 mm) into a heavy frying pan over medium-high heat, adjusting to maintain a temperature of 375°F (190°C) on a deep-frying thermometer.

3 Press each ball between sheets of heavy plastic in a tortilla press into a round about 4 inches (10 cm) in diameter and ¼ inch (6 mm) thick. Remove the plastic and slide the uncooked *gordita* into the hot oil. When it rises to the surface, spoon on some of the bubbling oil to help it puff. Fry until the bottom is golden and the *gordita* is puffy, about 1 minute. Turn and fry for 15 seconds, then remove the *gordita* and drain on paper towels. Keep warm in a low oven until all of the *gorditas* are cooked. Serve at once, with the salsa on the side.

Plantain Tostadas

Plátanos Machucos • Tabasco • Mexico

The hot and humid Mexican state Tabasco, Spanish for "flooded land" is home to the greatest variety of ways to prepare plantains. This recipe is a typical of the region.

Safflower or canola oil for frying

2 plantains, just beginning to ripen

1 tablespoon sea salt dissolved in 2 tablespoons water

Fresh salsa (page 45 or good-quality purchased), for serving

Makes 10–12 tostadas; serves 6

1 Pour oil to a depth of 1½ inches (4 cm) in a deep, heavy frying pan or a wok and place over medium-high heat. While the oil is heating, peel the plantains and cut them into 2-inch (5-cm) pieces. Working in batches, add the plantain pieces to the hot oil and fry, turning frequently, until just lightly golden, 1–2 minutes. Using a slotted spoon, transfer to paper towels to drain. Reduce the heat to low.

2 While the plantain pieces are still hot, press each one lightly with a paper towel to remove excess oil, then flatten it with the palm of your hand. Line a tortilla press with 2 sheets of heavy plastic cut from a plastic storage bag. Place a flattened piece of plantain on the tortilla press and press lightly. The plantain may have to be turned several times so that it is flattened evenly and is quite thin. Remove from the press and sprinkle lightly with the salt water. Repeat until all of the plantain pieces are flattened.

3 Raise the heat under the oil to medium-high. When hot, one at a time carefully lay the plantain "tortillas" in the oil and fry until crisp and brown, 1–2 minutes. Using a slotted spatula, transfer to paper towels to drain. Keep warm in a low oven while you cook the remaining tostadas.

4 Arrange the tostadas in a basket or on a plate. Serve at once with the salsa.

Tiny Tostadas with Cheese, Crab, and Shrimp

Tostaditas con Queso y Mariscos • Quintana Roo • Mexico

This casual snack, almost like the nachos of the north, is easy to make and even easier to eat. Top them with slices of pickled jalapeños, if you like.

½ lb (250 g) shrimp (prawns)

½ lb (250 g) good-quality crabmeat

10 purchased thin corn tortillas, 6 inches (15 cm) in diameter

Corn oil for frying, plus 1 tablespoon

1 tablespoon unsalted butter

1 cup (8 fl oz/250 ml) sour cream

½ teaspoon cumin seeds, toasted

Sea salt to taste

3 cups (12 oz/375 g) shredded Manchego or Monterey jack cheese

Fresh salsa (page 45 or good-quality purchased), for serving

Serves 4–6

1 Peel, devein, and coarsely chop the shrimp. Pick over the crab for shell fragments and flake the meat.

2 Stack the tortillas in 2 equal piles and cut into 4 triangular wedges. Pour oil to a depth of 1 inch (2.5 cm) into a heavy frying pan and heat to 375°F (190°C) on a deep-frying thermometer. Add the wedges a few at a time, tossing them, until light gold. Lift out with a slotted spoon and set aside on paper towels to drain. Preheat the oven to 500°F (260°C).

3 In a frying pan over medium heat, melt the butter with the 1 tablespoon oil. Add the shrimp and sauté until pink, about 3 minutes. Lift out with a slotted spoon and put into a bowl. Stir in the crabmeat and sour cream. Put the cumin seeds between 2 sheets of waxed paper and crush with a rolling pin. Mix with the shrimp and crab and season with salt.

4 Place about 1 tablespoon of the seafood mixture on each tortilla piece and sprinkle with the shredded cheese. Arrange in a large, shallow baking pan. Bake until the cheese melts, about 30 seconds.

5 Arrange the *tostaditas* on a platter and serve at once with bowls of salsa for dipping.

Broiled Oysters

The Mid-Atlantic • America

The relatively moderate ocean temperatures off the East Coast of America from Long Island to Virginia yield more subtly flavored oysters than New England's chillier waters. To savor every drop of the bivalves' liquor, cooks anchor oysters on the half shell in a bed of rock salt.

2–4 cups (1–2 lb/500 g–1 kg) rock salt

20 medium oysters such as Long Island or Chincoteague

⅔ cup (5 oz/155 g) crème fraîche

1 large shallot, minced

4 tablespoons (⅓ oz/10 g) minced mixed fresh chives, chervil, tarragon, and basil

1 teaspoon finely grated lemon zest

1 or 2 dashes Tabasco sauce or other hot-pepper sauce

Freshly ground pepper to taste

Serves 4

1 On a rimmed baking sheet, spread a ½-inch (12-mm) layer of rock salt. Rinse the oysters, then shuck them: Using a folded, thick cloth to protect your hand, hold an oyster with the flat top shell facing up. Insert the tip of an oyster knife into the dark, rounded spot at the hinge of the oyster, and then twist the knife to sever the hinge. Run the knife along the inside of the top shell, severing the muscle that attaches the oyster to the shell. Discard the top shell. Run the knife along the bottom shell to loosen the oyster, being careful to keep the oyster and its liquor in the shell. Nestle the shells in the salt.

2 Preheat the broiler (grill). In a bowl, combine the crème fraîche, the shallot, 2 tablespoons of the herbs, and the lemon zest. Season with hot-pepper sauce and ground pepper. Spoon a scant 2 teaspoons of the crème fraîche mixture on top of each oyster.

3 Place the baking sheet under the broiler 4 inches (10 cm) from the heat source and broil (grill) the oysters until the tops are just beginning to brown, 3–5 minutes. Transfer the oysters to individual plates each sprinkled with a layer of rock salt. Garnish with the remaining 2 tablespoons herbs and serve.

Fresh Tomato and Chile Salsa

Salsa Mexicana • Jalisco • Mexico

Salsa mexicana, also known as *salsa fresca*, is the reigning condiment of Mexico. It can be found on the tables of both fancy restaurants and neighborhood *taquerías*. Attain superior flavor and texture by using only freshly prepared vegetables for this recipe.

1 lb (500 g) ripe tomatoes

⅓ cup (2 oz/60 g) finely chopped white onion

¼ cup (⅓ oz/10 g) chopped fresh cilantro (fresh coriander)

2 serrano chiles, finely chopped

2 teaspoons fresh lime juice

Sea salt to taste

Makes 2 cups (16 fl oz/500 ml)

1 Cut the tomatoes into ¼-inch (6-mm) pieces, discarding the cores.

2 In a bowl, toss together the tomatoes, onion, cilantro, chiles, and lime juice. Sprinkle with salt and toss again. If the salsa is too dry, add a splash of cold water.

3 Cover and let stand for 10–15 minutes to allow the flavors to mingle, then serve.

Tostadas of Cold Vegetables in Chile-Garlic Sauce

Tostadas de Chileajo con Verduras • Oaxaca • Mexico

In Oaxaca, you might be served *chileajo*—a riotous mixture of spicy cooked vegetables named for its pungent chile and garlic sauce—piled on half a crusty bread roll or on a crispy tostada. The latter style, followed here, can be found at *fondas* in Oaxaca's Abastos market. The variety of vegetables used will often change with the season, so feel free to create your own mixture according to your preference and the ingredients available. Only the potato is a constant addition to every version of this tasty snack.

1 To make the sauce, place a heavy frying pan over medium heat. Add the garlic cloves and roast, turning them frequently, until they soften and their skins blacken, about 10 minutes. Remove from the heat and peel, discarding the skin. In a bowl, combine the toasted chiles with boiling water to cover and let soak for 15 minutes. The chiles should be quite soft. Drain the chiles, reserving the soaking water, and place in a blender with the vinegar, garlic, clove, allspice berry, and about 1 cup (8 fl oz/250 ml) of the soaking water. Process until a smooth purée forms, adding more water if necessary to facilitate blending. Pass the purée through a fine-mesh sieve placed over a bowl, pressing down with the back of a spoon. Stir in the oregano and salt and set aside.

2 To prepare the vegetables, peel and dice the potatoes. Trim the ends of the green beans and cut into ½-inch (12-mm) lengths. Peel the carrots, halve lengthwise, and cut into ½-inch (12-mm) lengths. Coarsely chop the cauliflower florets. Dice the zucchini.

3 In a saucepan, bring 4 cups (32 fl oz/1 l) water to a boil and add the 1 teaspoon salt. Add the potatoes and cook until tender, about 5 minutes. Using a slotted spoon, transfer the potatoes to a bowl filled with very cold water to stop the cooking. Repeat the process with each of the vegetables. The beans and carrots should take about 4 minutes, and the cauliflower and zucchini about 3 minutes. The vegetables should be soft but still have some bite.

4 When all of the vegetables are cooked and cooled, remove them from the water and drain on a kitchen towel. Gently stir the vegetables into the chile sauce. Taste and adjust the seasoning with salt, if needed. Cover and refrigerate for several hours.

5 Spread a thin layer of black beans over a tostada and spoon on the vegetables and sauce. Crumble the cheese and place it on top with the onion rings. Serve at once.

SAUCE

6 cloves garlic, unpeeled

6 guajillo chiles, seeded and toasted (page 220)

6 tablespoons (3 fl oz/90 ml) mild white vinegar

1 whole clove

1 allspice berry

1 tablespoon dried oregano, preferably Mexican

1 teaspoon sea salt

VEGETABLES

½ lb (250 g) new potatoes

¼ lb (125 g) green beans

¼ lb (125 g) carrots

2 cups (6 oz/185 g) cauliflower florets

¼ lb (125 g) zucchini (courgettes)

1 rounded teaspoon sea salt, plus salt to taste

TOSTADAS

1 cup (7 oz/220 g) refried black beans, homemade or good-quality purchased

12 small good-quality corn tostadas

½ lb (250 g) *queso fresco*

1 cup (3½ oz/105 g) thinly sliced small white onion, separated into rings

Serves 6

Chiles Rellenos with Green Chile Sauce

The Southwest • America

GREEN CHILE SAUCE

3 tablespoons olive oil

1 yellow onion, finely chopped

6 cloves garlic, finely chopped

1 teaspoon dried oregano,
preferably Mexican

3 tablespoons all-purpose (plain) flour

4 cups (32 fl oz/1 l) chicken stock

1 can (14½ oz/455 g) plum (Roma)
tomatoes, drained and chopped

12 large Anaheim chiles, roasted and
peeled (page 220), then chopped

1 teaspoon salt

CHILES RELLENOS

½ lb (250 g) Monterey jack cheese

8 large Anaheim chiles, roasted and
peeled (page 220)

6 eggs, at room temperature

7 tablespoons all-purpose (plain) flour

½ teaspoon salt

Corn oil for frying

Serves 4

1 To make the sauce, in a nonreactive saucepan over medium-low heat, warm the olive oil. Add the onion, garlic, and oregano, cover, and cook, stirring once or twice, until the onions soften, about 10 minutes. Add the flour and cook, stirring frequently and without browning, for 2 minutes. Gradually whisk in the stock and the tomatoes, then stir in the chiles and salt. Raise the heat to medium, bring to a simmer, and cook uncovered, stirring, until the sauce has thickened and is reduced, about 45 minutes. Taste and adjust the seasoning. Let cool to room temperature, cover, and refrigerate for up to 3 days.

2 To make the *rellenos*, cut the cheese into 8 strips, each about ½ inch (12 mm) wide, ¼ inch (6 mm) thick, and 4 inches (10 cm) long. Make a slit 2 inches (5 cm) long in each chile. With the tip of a finger, and without enlarging the slit, scrape the seeds and ribs out of each chile. Tuck a cheese strip into each of the chiles. Lay the stuffed chiles on a baking sheet, cover with plastic wrap, and refrigerate for 4 hours.

3 Line a baking sheet with paper towels. Separate the eggs, putting the yolks in a wide, shallow dish, and the whites in a bowl. Whisk 2 tablespoons of water into the yolks, then whisk in the flour and salt. Using an electric mixer or a whisk, whip the whites until soft peaks form. Stir one-third of the whites into the yolk mixture, then fold in the remaining whites just until combined. Do not overmix.

4 Pour 2 inches (5 cm) of corn oil into a wide, deep frying pan and heat to 380°F (195°C) on a deep-frying thermometer. Dip a chilled stuffed chile into the batter. Use a spatula to carefully transfer the chile to the hot oil, seam side up. Using a spoon, immediately baste the top of the chile with hot oil to seal the batter over the slit. Batter a second chile, add it to the pan, and baste it as well. Cook the chiles until browned on the bottom, then turn and continue to cook until browned on the second side, about 5 minutes total. Using the spatula, transfer the chiles to the baking sheet and keep warm in a low oven. Repeat with the remaining chiles. While the last of the chiles are frying, warm the sauce over low heat. Spoon some sauce onto 4 warmed plates. Set 2 chiles on each plate and serve at once.

Spicy Nuts and Seeds

Nueces y Pepitas Picantes • Coahuila • Mexico

Pecans are native to Mexico, as are a great variety of pumpkin seeds. Peanuts, actually a legume rather than a nut, are native to Africa, but now are plentiful in Mexico as well. All are a popular snack wherever beer and other drinks are served, especially if they have been sprinkled with chile, garlic, and lime juice. This fiery trio makes for even better nibbling.

1 tablespoon peanut oil

10 small cloves garlic, peeled

1½ cups (7½ oz/235 g) raw peanuts, skins removed

1½ cups (7½ oz/235 g) raw hulled green pumpkin seeds

1 cup (4 oz/125 g) pecan halves

About 1 teaspoon sea salt

About 1 teaspoon ground dried árbol or cayenne chile

Makes about 4 cups (1¼ lb/625 g)

1 Preheat the oven to 275°F (135°C).

2 In a frying pan over medium-low heat, warm the oil. Add the garlic cloves and sauté until they begin to turn tan, 3–4 minutes. Stir in the nuts and seeds, coating them well with the oil. Add 1 teaspoon salt and the ground chile, just a pinch at a time, until the taste just tingles the tongue.

3 Spread the nuts and seeds evenly on a baking sheet. Bake for 15–20 minutes, stirring occasionally. The air will be filled with a rich, nutty aroma. Transfer to a bowl, sprinkle with more salt, if needed, and serve warm or at room temperature.

Pumpkin Seed Dip

Zicil-P'ak • Yucatán • Mexico

The name of this dip or spread, a classic pre-Columbian dish, is a combination of the Mayan words for pumpkin seeds and tomato. That is precisely what this delightful concoction is, with only a few other ingredients thrown in for additional flavor. This version is adapted from the Restaurante El Príncipe Tutul Xio in Mani, deep in the Puuc hills south of Mérida. You can serve it either as a dip with crispy corn chips or, as the restaurant did, as a spread on top of thin slices of grilled pork wrapped in small warmed corn tortillas.

1 cup (5 oz/155 g) raw hulled green pumpkin seeds

1 large, ripe tomato or 4 plum (Roma) tomatoes

1 habanero chile, roasted (page 220)

2 tablespoons finely chopped fresh cilantro (fresh coriander)

2 tablespoons finely chopped fresh chives

1 teaspoon sea salt, or to taste

Squeeze of lime juice

Makes about 1 cup (8 fl oz/250 ml)

1 Heat a heavy frying pan over medium-low heat until quite hot. Pour in the pumpkin seeds and, as soon as they start to pop, stir constantly until they begin to puff up. Don't let them get brown. Pour onto a plate and allow to cool completely, then grind them quite fine in a spice grinder.

2 Line a cool, clean heavy-duty frying pan with heavy-duty aluminum foil, shiny side up (to prevent sticking), and place over medium heat. Add the tomato(es) and roast, turning occasionally, until the skin is blistered and begins to blacken. Trim and discard the most blackened parts of the skin and then transfer the tomato(es) to a blender or food processor. Add the chile and process briefly. Pour into a small bowl and stir in the ground pumpkin seeds, the cilantro, the chives, and the salt. Let stand for 30 minutes.

3 Just before serving, add the lime juice. Taste for salt and adjust for seasoning if desired. The dip should spread easily. If it is too thick, stir in a little water, then serve.

PEPITAS

Think twice before you discard scooped-out pumpkin seeds. Mexican cooks have used them since pre-Columbian times. Whether fat or skinny, raw or roasted, hulled or not, tasty *pepitas* are an essential ingredient in many sweets, snacks, and savory dishes.

Pipiánes, green moles thickened with ground pumpkin seeds, are, in one form or another, the regional specialties of many Mexican states. In Guerrero, cooks make a *mole verde* so thick and coarse that a fried corn chip could remain upright in it. In Puebla, a smooth, elegant pale green sauce naps chicken breasts, and in Tamaulipas, the *pipián*, mixed with cream, is spooned over fish.

Yucatán, however, boasts more different dishes using *pepitas* than any other state. A tamale with the tongue-twisting name of *dzotobichay* has a filling of chopped eggs and ground pumpkin seeds. Or, Yucatecan cooks also mix pumpkin seeds with tender white beans to stuff *polkanes*, a *masa* snack that resembles a snake head.

To make *papadzules*, tortillas are first dipped in a delicious pumpkin-seed sauce, then rolled around crumbled hard-boiled eggs, and are finally blanketed with a bright red tomato sauce beaded with rich shiny oil squeezed from the seeds. And ground pumpkin seeds, chiles, and tomatoes are combined to make one of the best dips of the region—*zicil-p'ak*.

Arizona Chile-Cheese Crisps

The Southwest · America

This appetizer, an Arizona restaurant specialty imported from Sonora, the Mexican state directly across the border, is among the most distinctive of the region's snacks, based as it is on a dramatic 18-inch (45-cm) tortilla and on service that calls for a round metal pan on a rack above a warming candle. It may be more practical to make your own 12-inch (30-cm) tortillas, unless you have a huge frying pan or a commercial range with a griddle.

TORTILLA(S)

1 cup (5 oz/155 g) unbleached all-purpose (plain) flour

½ teaspoon baking powder

½ teaspoon salt

2½ tablespoons solid vegetable shortening

⅓ cup (3 fl oz/80 ml) warm water

1 lb (375 g) mild cheese such as Colby or Monterey jack, or a combination, shredded

2 green New Mexico or Anaheim chiles, roasted and peeled (page 220), then cut lengthwise into strips ¼ inch (6 mm) wide

Fresh salsa (page 45 or good-quality purchased), for serving

Serves 4–6

1 To make the tortilla(s), in a bowl, sift together the flour, baking powder, and salt. Add the shortening to the dry ingredients and, using a pastry blender or 2 forks, cut in the fat until it forms particles the size of small peas. Add the water, stir to moisten, and then briefly knead the dough in the bowl until it begins to come together.

2 Turn the dough out onto a lightly floured work surface and knead until smooth and elastic, 10–12 times. Wrap the dough in plastic wrap and refrigerate for 1 hour.

3 For an 18-inch (45-cm) tortilla, keep the dough in 1 piece. To make two 12-inch (30-cm) tortillas, cut the dough in half. On a lightly floured work surface, roll out the dough to the desired size. Only practice will produce perfectly round tortillas, but even misshapen ones taste good. (The tortillas can be rolled out up to an hour in advance. Cover with plastic wrap and then a dampened kitchen towel.)

4 If cooking 12-inch tortillas, set a heavy, ungreased 12-inch frying pan (one with low sides will make turning the tortillas easier) over medium heat. When the pan is hot, lay a round of dough in the pan. Cook until the tortilla has puffed and the underside is dappled a golden brown, about 2 minutes. Use a spatula to release the tortilla from the pan. Flip it and cook on the other side until no longer raw, another 1–2 minutes. Repeat with the remaining dough. If cooking an 18-inch tortilla, preheat an ungreased griddle to 300°F (150°C) and cook the tortilla in the same way. The tortilla(s) can be used immediately or prepared up to 2 hours ahead. Let cool on a rack and cover with plastic wrap and a kitchen towel to prevent drying out.

5 Preheat the oven to 325°F (165°C).

6 Cover the oven rack with aluminum foil. Lay one 12-inch or the 18-inch tortilla on the rack. Scatter half of the cheese over the smaller tortilla; use all of it on the larger one. Arrange half of the green chile strips in a spoke pattern over the cheese on the smaller tortilla; use all the strips on the larger tortilla. Slide the rack into the upper third of the oven. Bake until the edges of the tortilla are lightly browned and the cheese has melted, about 10 minutes.

7 Carefully slide the tortilla onto a large serving platter. Serve at once, accompanied with the salsa. Provide diners with small plates. Diners tear off small pieces, top them with salsa, and roll them into bite-sized bundles. If making 2 crisps, bake the second tortilla while you are eating the first.

ASIA

The Chinese characters on the signs read: 黑米 红枣 豆

Preceding pages: A 100-foot (31-m) Buddha is an elaborate thirteenth-century wall carving in Sichuan, China. Top: Muslim street-stall holders sell tasty snacks wrapped in bamboo leaves in Inner Mongolia. Above: In Singapore, a stack of thin, round wrappers awaits its role in the making of *poh pia*, the Nonya version of Chinese spring rolls. Right: Plump *cha shao bao* (pork buns) originated in southern China.

T he art of the appetizer platter is unique to Chinese cuisine. It involves a specialized, skill-demanding artistic and culinary flair, and an understanding of the cultural practices. Elegantly composed on large, ornately decorated platters and accompanied by rice wine, these bite-sized selections are meant to be nibbled during toasts on formal occasions before the main courses arrive. Waiters may serve the appetizers using silver chopsticks, but at casual dinners, everyone reaches for their own choice from the plate at the center of the table.

The majority of appetizers are cold dishes, and traditional favorites include marinated mushrooms, crisp-fried dried fish, pickled cabbage, slivers of crunchy jellyfish or dry-fried duck, salty razor clams, marinated cucumbers, and cold meats. Morsels of tender, pink duck with glazed amber skin have universal appeal, as do candied walnuts. But some prefer their appetizers hot and exciting, such as Sichuan dumplings in a chile sauce, steamed or fried chicken wings, and fried spring rolls.

In the southern provinces, cold, cooked meats are enjoyed as appetizers, although the Cantonese tend not to place great importance on pre-meal nibbles, preferring to move straight on to the main course. In the north, no meal would begin without at least one dish to stimulate the appetite,

and in a restaurant, it is not unusual for a group to order as many as a dozen or more different appetizers. And, while traditionally served with tea in the morning or early afternoon, the delightful range of dim sum—roast pork buns, spring rolls, fried crab balls, steamed dumplings, and more—has been adapted as the perfect cocktail-party fare as well.

Foods that are considered appetizers in Western cuisines are more likely classified as snacks in Southeast Asia, where stopping for a quick bite at any time of the day or evening is commonplace. Thus, foods eaten between meals are ubiquitous and varied. Some are as substantial as a plate of *kway teow*, Singapore wok-fried rice noodles, while others are as simple as a *perkedel*, Indonesian corn fritters.

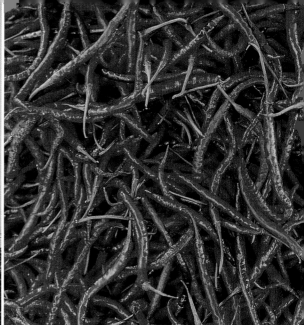

Many regional preparations, such as *satay*, *cha gio* (Vietnamese spring rolls), *sakoo sai kai* (Thai dumplings), *be ya kyaw* (Burmese split-pea fritters), and others, were once only celebratory foods, street-hawker specialties, or occasional main dishes. But with the French in Cambodia, Vietnam, and Laos; the British in Myanmar (Burma), Malaysia, and Singapore; the Dutch in Indonesia; and the Spanish in the Philippines, restaurateurs and home cooks were introduced to the Western notion of the appetizer, and they soon began making concessions to it.

The spring roll, which is time-consuming to prepare and requires practice to shape with skill, is a perfect example of a dish that has made the move from festival food to everyday snack. Traditionally, spring rolls were made for Chinese New Year, the first day of spring according to the lunar calendar, and almost every Southeast Asian country has its own version. Eventually, a year-round demand for spring rolls developed among locals, tourists, and immigrants alike, and the stuffed pastries began being served regularly at the beginning of a meal, thus trading much of their original ritual significance for widespread appreciation as a well-loved appetizer.

Similar transformations have brought what are considered informal snacks in Southeast Asia to a position of honor as favorite starters worldwide. Today, it is not uncommon to see the shrimp and sweet potato fritters of the Philippines and the sugarcane shrimps of Vietnam on menus and tables far beyond the borders of their countries of origin.

Thai *miang kum* is a delightful picturesque entry in the study of Asian snack foods turned appetizers. Trays are filled artfully with such items as dried shrimp, roasted peanuts, and toasted coconut; stacks of green herb leaves; and a syrupy sauce. Diners tuck an assortment of the ingredients into a leaf with a dab of the sauce, and the resulting packet, full of flavors and textures, is eaten in a single bite.

Many popular choices from the vast and varied repertoire of Indian *chat*, or snacks, can be made ahead of time, then reheated at a moment's notice for an elegant beginning to any meal. *Chat* originally referred to a specific spice-and-herb-laced salad, but the term now includes every conceivable Indian snack, from dumplings to fritters, fruit and noodle salads to tandoori meat tidbits and kabobs. Golden *samosas*, stuffed with a gingery potato concoction and fried in smoking hot oil; crunchy savory crackers speckled with black pepper; fritters of Bombay duck, potato, or eggplant; corn puffs; yam and corn dumplings—all are irresistible finger foods. Because these snacks are often fried, they are rich and filling. Be sure to serve them in moderation, for they are intended only to whet the palate, not to satisfy the appetite fully.

Left: In Jaipur, Rajasthan, a dancer celebrates Holi, the elephant festival. **Above, left:** According to legend, the sprawling, gold-spired Shwedagon Pagoda, the most sacred temple in Yangon (Rangoon), was built to enshrine eights hairs of the last Buddha. **Above, right:** The sixteenth-century arrival of the chile in Southeast Asia revolutionized local tables. Varying in shape, color, and degree of heat they deliver, these flavor-packed peppers are sliced and used as a garnish; set afloat in a dipping sauce; pounded into curry pastes; and added to other dishes whole or chopped.

Minced Pork and Sausage in Lettuce Cups

Shengcai Bao • Southern • China

In China, lettuce is not for salad. It is sliced as a bed for marinated bean curd, crunchy fried oysters and dumplings, or crispy-salty treats like salt-and-pepper shrimp or quail. It is also crisp-fried to serve the same purpose. It is quickly poached in oily water to serve bathed in oyster sauce as a vegetable, or dunked into the pot, along with noodles, to flavor the soup in a tabletop steamboat meal. This dish, known in Cantonese as *sang choi bao*, uses crisp iceberg lettuce to wrap a spicy filling of minced pork or squab (pigeon).

9 oz (280 g) ground (minced) pork butt

1 tablespoon light soy sauce

3 Chinese sausages

2 tablespoons canola oil

½ celery stalk, finely chopped

2 teaspoons peeled and grated fresh ginger

½ teaspoon minced garlic

½ cup (2½ oz/75 g) finely chopped bamboo shoots

½ cup (2¾ oz/80 g) finely chopped canned straw or button mushrooms

Salt and freshly ground white pepper to taste

1 tablespoon hoisin sauce, plus ½ cup (4 fl oz/125 ml)

1 tablespoon dark soy sauce

3 green (spring) onions, including tender green tops, very finely chopped

2 teaspoons cornstarch (cornflour) dissolved in ½ cup (4 fl oz/125 ml) chicken stock or water

1½ tablespoons finely chopped fresh cilantro (fresh coriander; optional)

8 firm inner leaves iceberg lettuce, edges trimmed to form cup shapes

Serves 8

1 In a bowl, combine the pork and light soy sauce, mixing well. Set aside to marinate while you prepare the sausages. Bring water to a simmer in a steamer base. Place the sausages on a heatproof plate in a steamer basket, place over the simmering water, cover, and steam until soft and plump, about 5 minutes. Remove from the steamer and let cool, then chop finely and set aside.

2 In a wok over high heat, warm the oil. Add the pork, celery, ginger, and garlic and stir-fry until the pork changes color, about 1 minute. As the pork cooks, use a spatula to break up any lumps. Add the sausage, bamboo shoots, and mushrooms and stir-fry until the meat and celery are cooked, about 40 seconds. Season with salt and pepper, the 1 table-spoon hoisin sauce, and the dark soy sauce and add the green onions and the cornstarch mixture. Cook, stirring constantly, until thickened, 20–30 seconds longer. Add the cilantro (if using), mix well, and transfer to a serving bowl.

3 To serve, divide the ½ cup (4 fl oz/125 ml) hoisin sauce among a few small sauce dishes. Place the lettuce cups on a platter. At the table, spoon an equal amount of the hot filling into each lettuce cup. Guests add their own hoisin sauce to taste, fold the lettuce around the filling, and eat out of hand.

Sesame Shrimp Toast "Coins"

Jinqian Xiabing • Northern • China

This festive and irresistible hors d'oeuvre of shrimp toast, shaped to resemble old Chinese coins, symbolizes luck and prosperity.

SWEET-AND-SOUR SAUCE

¼ cup (2 fl oz/60 ml) chicken stock or water

⅓ cup (3 fl oz/80 ml) rice vinegar

1 tablespoon light soy sauce

⅓ cup (1½ oz/45 g) superfine (caster) sugar

½ teaspoon salt

2 tablespoons peanut oil

2 teaspoons peeled and finely julienned fresh ginger

½ teaspoon crushed garlic

½ cup (2 oz/60 g) diced red bell pepper (capsicum)

½ cup (2 oz/60 g) diced, unpeeled English (hothouse) cucumber

2 green (spring) onions, including tender green tops, chopped

3 or 4 drops red food coloring (optional)

1 tablespoon cornstarch (cornflour) dissolved in 1 tablespoon water

7 oz (220 g) peeled and deveined shrimp (prawns; about 1 lb/500 g unpeeled)

1 teaspoon peeled and grated fresh ginger

1 tablespoon water

2 teaspoons light soy sauce

1 teaspoon rice wine

1 egg white

1 tablespoon cornstarch (cornflour)

½ teaspoon salt

6 large, thin slices white bread

24 small fresh cilantro (fresh coriander) leaves

2–3 tablespoons sesame seeds

Canola or peanut oil for deep-frying

Makes 24 toasts

1 To prepare the sauce, in a small bowl, combine the stock, vinegar, soy sauce, sugar, and salt and stir until the sugar dissolves. In a saucepan over medium heat, warm the oil until the surface shimmers. Add the ginger, garlic, bell pepper, cucumber, and green onions and stir-fry until slightly softened, about 1 minute. Raise the heat to medium high, pour in the vinegar mixture, bring to a boil, and simmer for 1 minute, stirring constantly. If using the food coloring, stir it into the cornstarch mixture and then stir the mixture into the sauce. Simmer over medium-high heat, stirring slowly, until the sauce is thickened and becomes clear, about 1 minute. Remove from the heat and set aside.

2 In a food processor, combine the shrimp and ginger and process to a paste. Next, add the water, soy sauce, rice wine, egg white, cornstarch, and salt and process until mixed. Spread the shrimp mixture over the bread slices. Then, using a round cookie cutter 1¾–2 inches (4.5–5 cm) in diameter, cut 4 rounds from each slice. Place a cilantro leaf in the center and evenly sprinkle the still-visible shrimp mixture with the sesame seeds, pressing them on lightly with your fingers.

3 Pour oil to a depth of 1½ inches (4 cm) in a wok, and heat until a cube of bread dropped in it turns golden, about 10 seconds. Slide in 5 of the shrimp toasts, shrimp side down, and fry until golden, about 2 minutes. Using a slotted spoon, carefully flip the toasts over and fry on the bread side until golden brown. Using the spoon, transfer to a rack over paper towels to drain. Keep warm in a low oven. Repeat with all the toasts.

4 Arrange the shrimp toasts, shrimp side up, in a single layer on a platter. Serve the toasts at once with the sauce in small dishes for dipping.

Yam Dumplings with Corn and Cinnamon

Shakkaravellikayangu Bonda • Maharashtra • India

Bondas—spicy balls of mashed vegetables, dipped in chickpea batter and deep-fried—are classic snack-time treats that are traditionally served with a beverage such as coffee or tea. The filling is left entirely up to the discretion of the cook. Although the most common are plain potato *bondas*, those made with sweet potatoes, pumpkin, cauliflower, cabbage, or any combination thereof are becoming very popular. Depending on how much you mash the filling, its texture can be varied—from smooth and creamy to coarse and chunky.

FILLING

2 sweet potatoes or yams, about 1 lb (500 g) total weight

½ teaspoon ground cinnamon

½ teaspoon salt, or to taste

2 teaspoons fresh lemon juice

1 ear of corn, husks and silk removed

1 tablespoon canola oil, plus more for deep-frying

½ teaspoon brown mustard seeds

1 yellow onion, finely chopped

¼ cup (1 oz/30 g) finely chopped pecans or cashew nuts

BATTER

1¼ cups (8½ oz/265 g) chickpea (garbanzo bean) flour

¾ teaspoon baking powder

¾ teaspoon cracked black pepper

¾ teaspoon salt, or to taste

1¼ cups (10 fl oz/310 ml) hot water

1 tablespoon canola oil

Makes 16–20 dumplings; serves 4–6

1 To make the filling, preheat the oven to 400°F (200°C). Prick the surface of the sweet potatoes several times with a fork, place them on a baking sheet, and bake until they are tender when pierced with a knife, about 45 minutes. Remove from the oven and, when cool enough to handle, peel and place in a bowl. Add the cinnamon, salt, and lemon juice and mash together with a fork or potato masher. Set aside.

2 While the potatoes are baking, use tongs to hold the ear of corn directly over the gas flame on the stove top, turning as needed to color evenly. Roast until evenly covered with several brown spots, about 5 minutes. Watch carefully, as the corn can burn and char easily. (Light charring is acceptable as it will enhance the overall flavor.) If you do not have a gas burner, place the corn on a wire rack over an electric burner and roast, turning, until it is evenly covered with brown spots, about 5 minutes.

3 Hold the roasted ear stem end down on a cutting board and, using a sharp knife, cut down the length of the ear to remove the kernels in a layer about ⅛ inch (3 mm) thick. Rotate the ear with each cut until it is fully stripped. Add the corn kernels to the potato mixture and stir to combine.

4 In a small frying pan over medium-high heat, warm the 1 tablespoon oil. When hot, add the mustard seeds and cover the pan. When the seeds stop sputtering, after about 30 seconds, uncover and add the onion. Cook, stirring occasionally, until the onion is brown and caramelized, about 6 minutes. Pour the contents of the pan over the yam mixture. Add the nuts and mix until thoroughly combined. Cover and refrigerate for 1 hour to allow the mixture to firm up and the nuts to absorb any excess moisture.

5 Divide the mixture into 16–20 portions. Lightly oil your hands and roll each portion into a ball. If making the balls ahead of time, arrange them on a baking tray in a single layer, cover, and refrigerate until you are ready to cook them. (The chilled balls hold their shape better and are easier to fry.)

6 In a *karhai* (page 72), deep-fryer, or large frying pan, pour oil to a depth of 1½ inches (4 cm) and heat to 375°F (190°C) on a deep-frying thermometer. Meanwhile, make the batter: In a bowl, combine the chickpea flour, baking powder, pepper, salt, hot water, and 1 tablespoon oil. Whisk until smooth. Dip a few of the balls into the batter, allowing the excess to drip off, and slip them into the hot oil. Do not crowd the pan. Fry, turning frequently with tongs, until the balls are nicely browned, about 4 minutes. Using a slotted spoon, transfer to paper towels to drain. Keep warm in a low oven while you fry the remaining balls the same way. Serve hot or at room temperature.

THE MARKET

Nearly every community in India, from such large, cosmopolitan cities as Bombay to the smallest rural villages that dot the coasts and deserts, boasts about its central open-air market. Indian cooks, who like to buy their groceries fresh at least every few days, if not every day, visit these traditional shopping places that are known by everyone simply as "the market."

Everything for the kitchen is available here: farm-fresh *gobhi* (cauliflower), *bhindi* (okra), *baigan* (eggplant), and other vegetables; leafy green herbs; sweetly fragrant mangoes and perfectly ripe bananas; fish such as pomfret; shellfish; meat; and live poultry. Stalls sell specialized salts, local palm sugar, freshly pressed cooking oils, pickles and chutneys typical of the area, and the spice blends, or *masalas*, that play a most important role in the cooking of each region.

Cooks can also buy clay pots (*chetti*) for cooking, iron griddles (*tava*) for baking breads, grinding stones (*sil-batta*) for making spice pastes, and cooking fuels such as haycakes, wood charcoal, and types of wood chips. A place that dazzles the senses with its vibrant colors, sounds, and heady aromas, the market reflects the strength, variety, and vitality of Indian life.

Stuffed Gold Purses

Rhoom • Thailand

Thai women use a paring knife as they shape fruits and vegetables into amazing sculptures. These delicate purses, although they don't require a knife, do need a meticulous hand and patience. They are manageable for an everyday cook, however, and the end results make the labor worthwhile. If garlic chives are unavailable, use green onion tops cut lengthwise into long, narrow strips. Pickled garlic can be found in most Asian markets.

PURSES

6 eggs, beaten

1–2 tablespoons peanut oil or corn oil

FILLING

1 teaspoon peppercorns

2 cloves garlic

1 tablespoon chopped fresh cilantro (fresh coriander) stems

1 tablespoon peanut oil or corn oil

2 shallots, minced

¾ lb (375 g) finely ground (minced) pork butt or chicken thigh meat

1 tablespoon firmly packed palm sugar or brown sugar

1½ tablespoons fish sauce

3 tablespoons unsalted dry-roasted peanuts, chopped

3 cloves pickled garlic, thinly sliced (optional)

3 red Fresno or serrano chiles, seeded and finely slivered

½ cup (½ oz/15 g) fresh cilantro (fresh coriander) leaves

18 garlic chives blanched for 5 seconds in boiling water, drained, and patted dry

Sriracha sauce for serving

Makes 18 purses; serves 6

1 To make the purses, in a pie dish or other shallow plate, beat together the eggs and 3 tablespoons water until blended. Preheat a well-seasoned 5-inch (13-cm) crepe pan or nonstick frying pan over medium-high heat until hot. To test, sprinkle with drops of water. If they dance across the surface, the pan is ready. Add a thin film of oil to the pan and wipe up any excess with a paper towel. Have the eggs near the frying pan.

2 Lay your fingers flat in the plate of eggs and then carefully position them over the frying pan. Wave your fingers back and forth in one direction, dripping long threads of egg across the width of the pan. Dip your fingers in the eggs again, and again wave them back and forth across the pan, this time dripping egg threads in the opposite direction. Repeat until you have a net, or filigree, of egg threads. Cook until the egg net sets up and is golden brown, 2–3 minutes. Carefully lift an edge and peel the net from the pan. Place on a baking sheet and cover loosely with aluminum foil. Repeat to make 18 nets in all. Set aside.

3 To make the filling, in a mortar or mini food processor, pound together or process the peppercorns, garlic, and cilantro stems to form a paste. Preheat a wok over medium-high heat and add the oil. When hot, stir in the garlic paste and shallots and stir-fry gently until fragrant, about 1 minute. Add the pork or chicken and stir-fry, breaking up any clumps of meat, until no pink remains and the mixture is crumbly and dry, 2–3 minutes. Raise the heat to high, add the palm or brown sugar and fish sauce, and cook until the sugar caramelizes and the mixture is sticky, 3–5 minutes. Stir in the chopped peanuts, transfer to a bowl, and set aside to cool.

4 To fill the purses, place 1 egg net on a flat surface. Put a heaping tablespoonful of the filling in the middle. Top with a few slices of pickled garlic, if using, a few slivers of chile, and a few cilantro leaves. Fold in the sides to form a small parcel and secure closed by tying 1 garlic chive around the middle. Repeat until all the parcels are made.

5 Arrange the purses, seam side down, on a serving plate. Top each purse with a touch of Sriracha sauce. Serve warm or at room temperature.

Crispy Spring Rolls

Cha Gio • Vietnam

This recipe comes from *The Anatomy of a Springroll*, a documentary about life in Ho Chi Minh City by Vietnamese filmmaker Paul Kwan. Look for chile-garlic sauce in Asian markets.

FILLING

10 dried Chinese black mushrooms

1 oz (30 g) dried cloud ear mushrooms

2 oz (60 g) bean thread noodles

1 small jicama, about ½ lb (250 g)

½ lb (250 g) ground (minced) pork butt

1 lb (500 g) shrimp (prawns), peeled, deveined, and coarsely chopped

1 yellow onion, minced

2 carrots, peeled and finely shredded

2 tablespoons fish sauce

1 tablespoon finely minced garlic

1 teaspoon freshly ground pepper

1 teaspoon sugar

½ teaspoon sea salt

1 egg, lightly beaten

1 package (12 oz/375 g) dried round rice papers, 8 inches (20 cm) in diameter

DIPPING SAUCE

1 cup (8 oz/250 g) sugar

½ cup (4 fl oz/125 ml) white vinegar

5 tablespoons (2½ fl oz/75 ml) fish sauce

2 tablespoons finely minced garlic

1 tablespoon fresh lime juice

1 tablespoon Vietnamese chile-garlic sauce (see note)

2 red Fresno or serrano chiles, chopped (optional)

Coarsely chopped unsalted roasted peanuts for garnish

Peanut or canola oil for deep-frying

1 head red-leaf or butter (Boston) lettuce, leaves separated

Leaves from 1 small bunch fresh mint

Makes 36 spring rolls; serves 12

1 To make the filling, place the black mushrooms, cloud ear mushrooms, and bean thread noodles in separate bowls with warm water to cover. Soak the noodles for 15 minutes, the cloud ear mushrooms for 20 minutes, and the black mushrooms for 30 minutes.

2 Drain the noodles and cut into 2-inch (5-cm) lengths. Drain the cloud ear mushrooms, squeeze out the excess water, and remove the tough knots from the undersides. Drain the black mushrooms, squeeze out the excess water, remove and discard the stems, and thinly slice the caps. Roll up the mushrooms and cut crosswise into long, thin shreds.

3 Peel the jicama and shred it finely using the small holes on a box grater-shredder. Squeeze out the excess water. Put both mushrooms and the noodles in a large bowl and add the jicama, pork, shrimp, onion, carrots, fish sauce, garlic, pepper, sugar, salt, and egg. Mix well and set aside.

4 To form the spring rolls, lay 1 rice paper round on a flat surface. Using a pastry brush, brush the rice paper with warm water and leave it for 30 seconds or longer until it is softened and feels like wet tissue. Put a heaping tablespoon of the filling in a line across the lower third of the wrapper. Mold the filling to form a log 3 inches (7.5 cm) long by 1 inch (2.5 cm) wide. Fold the bottom edge of the rice paper over the log, then fold both sides toward the middle to enclose the ends. Roll up into a taut roll and place on a tray. Cover with a damp kitchen towel. Repeat until all of the filling is used.

5 To make the dipping sauce, in a bowl, stir together the sugar and vinegar until the sugar completely dissolves. Add ½ cup (4 fl oz/125 ml) water, the fish sauce, garlic, lime juice, chile-garlic sauce, and the chiles, if using. Divide the sauce among small saucers. Garnish with the peanuts.

6 To fry the rolls, preheat a wok or deep saucepan over medium-high heat until hot. Add oil to a depth of 2½ inches (6 cm) and heat slowly to 365°F (185°C) on a deep-frying thermometer.

7 Slip a batch of the spring rolls, one at a time, into the hot oil. Do not crowd the pan. Fry until golden, about 5 minutes. Using a skimmer, transfer the spring rolls to paper towels to drain. Keep warm in a low oven and repeat until all the rolls are fried.

8 To serve, arrange the lettuce leaves and mint leaves on a platter. Arrange the spring rolls, whole or cut in half, on a separate platter. To eat, place a spring roll on a lettuce leaf with some mint and roll up the leaf. Dip the roll into the sauce and eat out of hand.

Eggplant Fritters

Katrika Bajji · Karnataka · India

Eggplant is a popular vegetable in Karnataka, especially in the form of traditional spicy, asafetida- or garlic-laced fritters, tinted orange by pungent turmeric.

1 lb (500 g) small to medium-sized eggplants (aubergines), cut into slices ⅛ inch (3 mm) thick

BATTER

1½ cups (7½ oz/235 g) chickpea (garbanzo bean) flour

¼ cup (1 oz/30 g) rice flour

2 teaspoons salt

1 teaspoon cayenne pepper

1 teaspoon ground turmeric

½ teaspoon powdered asafetida (page 219) or 2 teaspoons minced garlic

2 tablespoons canola oil

1½ cups (12 fl oz/375 ml) hot water

Canola or corn oil for deep-frying

Serves 6

1 Place the eggplant slices in a bowl with salted water to cover (using ½ teaspoon salt for each 1 cup/8 fl oz/250 ml water). This will keep the eggplants from discoloring while you make the batter.

2 To make the batter, in a bowl, combine the chickpea flour, rice flour, salt, cayenne pepper, turmeric, asafetida or garlic, and 2 tablespoons oil. Mix until combined, then gradually add the hot water, stirring, until you have a pancakelike batter. (Depending upon the humidity, you may not need all of the water.) Whisk the batter until smooth.

3 In a *karhai* (page 72), deep-fryer, or large frying pan, pour oil to a depth of 1½ inches (4 cm) and heat to 375°F (190°C) on a deep-frying thermometer. Meanwhile, drain the eggplant slices and pat them dry on paper towels. When the oil is ready, dip a few slices in the batter, letting the excess drain off, and gently slip them into the oil. Do not crowd the pan. Fry, turning frequently with tongs, until golden, about 4 minutes. Using a slotted spoon, transfer to paper towels to drain. Keep warm in a low oven while you fry the remaining fritters in the same way. Serve at once.

Deep-Fried Crab Balls

Zha Pangxie Qiu • Southern • China

Tamarind concentrate is a tart seasoning produced by scraping the flesh from dried tamarind pods. It is readily available at most well-stocked Asian markets.

DIPPING SAUCE

⅓ cup (2½ oz/75 g) firmly packed light brown sugar

½ teaspoon tamarind concentrate (see note) or 2 tablespoons fresh lime juice

1½ tablespoons thick soy sauce

CRAB BALLS

7 oz (220 g) crabmeat

2½ oz (75 g) ground (minced) pork butt

⅓ cup (2 oz/60 g) finely chopped water chestnuts

1 tablespoon chopped green (spring) onion, white part only

1 slice white bread, crusts removed and roughly chopped

1 egg white

1–2 tablespoons tapioca starch or cornstarch (cornflour)

½ teaspoon salt

½ teaspoon freshly ground white pepper

Sunflower or corn oil for deep-frying

Makes 18–20 crab balls

1 To prepare the sauce, in a small saucepan over medium heat, combine the sugar and ½ cup (4 fl oz/125 ml) water, bring to a simmer, and simmer until the sugar melts and the syrup is golden brown and reduced by half, about 10 minutes. Add the tamarind or lime juice and soy sauce and stir to mix. Pour into small dishes and set aside.

2 To prepare the crab balls, in a food processor, combine the crabmeat and pork and process to form a smooth paste. Add the water chestnuts, green onion, bread, egg white, 1 tablespoon of the tapioca starch or cornstarch, the salt, and the pepper and process until smooth. A soft, moist mixture may be difficult to roll but will result in light-textured balls. If it is too moist to form, add an extra 1 tablespoon tapioca starch or cornstarch.

3 Pour oil to a depth of 2 inches (5 cm) in a wok and heat to 375°F (190°C) on a deep-frying thermometer. Using a tablespoon, scoop up balls of the crab mixture and carefully drop them into the oil. Do not crowd the pan. Fry, turning as needed to cook evenly, until golden brown, about 1½ minutes. Using a wire skimmer or slotted spoon, transfer to a rack placed over paper towels to drain. Keep warm in a low oven and repeat until all the crab mixture is cooked.

4 Arrange the crab balls on a serving plate and serve at once with the dipping sauce.

Creamy Corn and Crab Soup

Yumi Xierou Geng • Southern • China

Cutting wonton wrappers, found in most Asian markets, into thin strips and frying them until golden adds a nice garnish to this popular sweet-and-savory soup.

1 can (14½ oz/455 g) creamed corn

4 cups (32 fl oz/1 l) chicken stock

1–2 teaspoons chicken bouillon granules

2 teaspoons light soy sauce

Salt and ground white pepper to taste

2 tablespoons cornstarch (cornflour) dissolved in ⅓ cup (3 fl oz/80 ml) water

¼ lb (125 g) crabmeat

3 egg yolks or 2 whole eggs

2 tablespoons finely chopped green (spring) onion, including tender green tops

Wonton wrapper garnish (see note; optional)

Serves 6–8

1 In a saucepan over high heat, combine the creamed corn, stock, bouillon granules, and soy sauce and bring to a boil. Season with salt and pepper. Stir in the cornstarch mixture, reduce the heat to medium, and cook, stirring, until the soup thickens, about 1½ minutes.

2 In a small bowl, combine the crabmeat and egg yolks or whole eggs, mixing well.

3 Remove the soup from the heat, add the crabmeat mixture, and let stand for 30 seconds, then slowly stir into the soup. The eggs will form short strands. Reheat gently if the egg has not set sufficiently or if the soup has cooled too much to serve. Do not allow to boil.

4 Ladle the soup into warmed individual bowls and garnish with the green onion, the fried wonton wrappers (if using), and a dusting of pepper. Serve at once.

Water Chestnut and Beef Cakes

Ma Ti Niurou Gao • Southern • China

The poetic name for this dish means "triumph and exultation." Serve it hot, with light soy sauce or sweet chile sauce for serving. The best water chestnuts are from the city of Guilin.

7 oz (220 g) ground (minced) lean beef

2 oz (60 g) ground (minced) pork butt

1 teaspoon peeled fresh ginger

1 teaspoon garlic-chile sauce

1 tablespoon light soy sauce

½ teaspoon salt

½ cup (3 oz/90 g) chopped water chestnuts

¼ cup (¾ oz/20 g) finely chopped green (spring) onion, white part only

⅓ cup (1½ oz/45 g) cornstarch (cornflour)

Canola oil for frying

½ teaspoon freshly ground white pepper

Makes about 16 cakes

1 In a food processor, combine the beef, pork, and 2 tablespoons of water and process to a paste. Add the ginger, garlic-chile and soy sauces, and salt and process until well mixed. Add the water chestnuts and green onion and pulse to mix them without crushing them.

2 Shape the mixture into about 16 small balls about 1¼ inches (3 cm) in diameter. Spread the cornstarch in a shallow bowl and coat the balls evenly, tapping off the excess. Lightly press each ball to flatten into a cake ½ inch (12 mm) thick. If time allows, cover and chill for 1 hour before frying.

3 Pour oil to a depth of ¼ inch (6 mm) in a shallow, wide pan over medium-high heat. When the oil is hot, add the cakes, in batches, and fry until golden brown on one side, about 2½ minutes. Turn and cook on the other side until golden brown, 1½–2 minutes longer. Using a slotted spoon, transfer the cakes to paper towels to drain for about 1 minute, then arrange on a warmed serving plate. Sprinkle with the pepper and serve hot.

THE KARHAI

The *karhai* is the most important and versatile cooking utensil in India. This round-bottomed metal pan is similar in shape to the better-known Chinese wok, but is much heavier. It is used for everything from deep-frying *pakoras* (fritters) and *pooris* (balloon breads) to stir-frying vegetables and other ingredients, steaming dumplings, and making sweets.

Up until the last few decades, before melamine *thali* plates and plastic *ghara* (water jugs) infiltrated the village life of India, *karhais* were also commonly used as babies' bathtubs. Or, painted with prayers, they housed the family's sacred *tulsi* (holy basil) plant.

The pans come in a wide range of sizes. Tiny 5-inch (13-cm) *karhais* are just right for roasting spices. The mammoth 40-inch (1-m) versions are used in catering. *Karhais* are made of iron, aluminum, silver, stainless steel, or tin-lined brass or copper. Perhaps the most standard and versatile is the hand-hammered iron *karhai*, 12 inches (30 cm) in diameter. After an initial scrub with soap and water, *karhais* are virtually maintenance free. Their weight makes them stable, but a wok ring can be used as a support, if desired.

Savory Crackers with Black Pepper

Mathari • Punjab • India

These rich crackers are a favorite treat in northern India. Enjoy them alone or with a hot pickle or sweet chutney. Store in an airtight container in a cool place for up to four months.

1½ cups (7½ oz/235 g) all-purpose (plain) flour, plus more for dusting

1 teaspoon salt

Pinch of baking powder

¼ cup (2 oz/60 g) *usli ghee* (page 221) or vegetable shortening, melted

1 tablespoon cracked black peppercorns, preferably Tellicherry peppercorns

¼ teaspoon *ajowan* seeds or 1 teaspoon dried thyme

⅓ cup (3 fl oz/80 ml) cold water, or as needed

Canola oil for deep-frying

Makes about 50 small or 24 large crackers

1 In a bowl, mix together the flour, salt, baking powder, *usli ghee*, pepper, and *ajowan* or thyme. Gradually add the water and mix until a stiff dough forms. (You may not need all of the water.) Turn out onto a lightly floured work surface and knead gently, dusting with extra flour as needed, until smooth, about 3 minutes. Divide the dough into 4 portions. Cover each with plastic wrap until ready to use.

2 On a lightly floured work surface, roll out 1 portion of dough at a time, dusting often with flour, until it is ⅛ inch (3 mm) thick. Cut out plain rounds using a 2-inch or 4-inch (5-cm or 10-cm) cookie cutter. With a fork, prick each circle in several places to prevent it from puffing too much during frying.

3 In a *karhai* (page 72), deep-fryer, or large saucepan, pour oil to a depth of 1½ inches (4 cm) and heat to 375°F (180°C) on a deep-frying thermometer. When the oil is ready, gently slip a few rounds of cracker dough into it. Do not crowd the pan. Fry over medium heat, turning occasionally, until both sides are golden, about 3 minutes. Using a slotted spoon, transfer to paper towels to drain. Make the remaining crackers in the same way. Serve hot or at room temperature.

Plantain Fritters

Bhajjia • Kerala • India

Popular in southern India, the plantain, a banana variety, is prized for its chewy texture. Plantains are available in most grocery stores. Firm, underripe bananas may be substituted.

1 large or 2 medium unripe green plantains

½ cup (4 oz/125 g) plain yogurt

BATTER

1 cup (5 oz/155 g) chickpea (garbanzo bean) flour

2 tablespoons rice flour

1½ teaspoons salt

1 teaspoon cayenne pepper

¾ teaspoon ground turmeric

24 fresh or 48 dried kari leaves, finely shredded (page 222)

1 tablespoon canola oil, plus oil for deep-frying

Serves 6

1 Peel the plantain and cut on the diagonal into slices ⅛ inch (3 mm) thick. In a bowl, whisk 1 cup (8 fl oz/250 ml) water and the yogurt until smooth. Add the plantain slices and mix to coat them with the yogurt. (This will keep the plantain from turning dark.)

2 To make the batter, in a bowl, combine the chickpea flour, rice flour, salt, cayenne pepper, turmeric, and kari leaves. Add the 1 tablespoon oil and mix well. Slowly add about ½ cup (4 fl oz/125 ml) hot water, stirring constantly, until you have a pancakelike batter. (Depending upon the humidity, you may not need all of the water.) Whisk the batter until it is smooth.

3 In a *karhai* (page 72), deep-fryer, or large frying pan, pour oil to a depth of 1½ inches (4 cm) and heat to 375°F (190°C) on a deep-frying thermometer. Meanwhile, drain the plantain slices and pat them dry on paper towels. When the oil is ready, dip a few slices in the batter, letting the excess drain off, and gently slip them into the oil. Do not crowd the pan. Fry, turning often, until the fritters are golden, about 4 minutes. Using a slotted spoon, transfer to paper towels to drain. Keep warm in a low oven while you make the remaining fritters in the same way. Serve at once.

Stuffed Tapioca Dumplings

Sakoo Sai Kai • Thailand

Asians are fond of soft, gelatinous, sticky foods. In Thailand, tapioca is enjoyed for this trio of features. Here, tapioca pearls are used as a coating for sweet-savory meat-filled dumplings. Just before serving, the dumplings receive a drizzle of garlic oil, a favorite Thai condiment. Unless you have tried this dumpling in its homeland, it is difficult from reading the recipe to imagine how all the textures and flavors come together in a single delicious bite. Preserved radish can be purchased from well-stocked Asian markets.

GARLIC OIL

⅓ cup (3 fl oz/80 ml) canola oil

8 garlic cloves, chopped

FILLING

½ teaspoon black peppercorns

5 cloves garlic

1 tablespoon chopped fresh cilantro (fresh coriander) stems

½ teaspoon salt

1 tablespoon peanut oil or corn oil

½ cup (2½ oz/75 g) minced shallots

½ lb (250 g) finely ground (minced) pork butt or chicken thigh meat

½ cup (2½ oz/75 g) chopped unsalted dry-roasted peanuts

¼ cup (1½ oz/45 g) preserved radish, minced (see note)

¼ cup (2 oz/60 g) firmly packed palm sugar or brown sugar

2 tablespoons fish sauce

2 tablespoons chopped fresh cilantro (fresh coriander)

TAPIOCA COATING

2 cups (12 oz/375 g) small tapioca pearls

3 tablespoons tapioca flour

1½–2 cups (12–16 fl oz/375–500 ml) boiling water

1 banana leaf

Makes about 4 dozen dumplings; serves 12

1 To make the garlic oil, preheat a small frying pan over medium heat. Add the oil and heat to 325°F (165°C) on a deep-frying thermometer or until a piece of garlic dropped into the oil sizzles without burning. Add the garlic and fry, stirring with a spoon to break up any clumps. When the garlic turns golden, after about 3 minutes, remove the pan from the heat and let the garlic continue to fry until golden brown, about 2 minutes longer. Let cool to room temperature, pour through a fine-mesh sieve into a bowl, cover, and set aside. (The garlic oil will keep, refrigerated in a tightly sealed glass jar, for up to 1 month.)

2 To make the filling, in a mortar, pound together the peppercorns, garlic, cilantro stems, and salt to form a paste. Preheat a wok over medium heat and add the oil. When hot, stir in the garlic paste and stir-fry gently until fragrant, about 1 minute. Raise the heat to high, add the shallots and pork or chicken, and stir-fry, breaking up any clumps of meat, until no pink remains and the mixture is dry and crumbled, about 3 minutes. Add the peanuts, preserved radish, palm or brown sugar, and fish sauce and continue to stir-fry over high heat until the sugar caramelizes and the mixture is sticky, 3–5 minutes. Remove from the heat, let cool, and stir in the chopped fresh cilantro.

3 To make the tapioca coating, in a large mixing bowl, combine the tapioca pearls and tapioca flour. Stirring constantly, gradually pour in enough boiling water to make a thick paste. Turn the dough out onto a flat work surface and knead for 2 minutes. It should be thick and sticky. If the dough becomes dry while you are kneading it, add a little more water. Let cool.

4 You will need two bamboo steamer baskets or 2 heat-resistant shallow pie dishes that will fit comfortably into a tiered steamer. Cut out 2 banana leaf rounds each about ½ inch (12 mm) smaller in diameter than the basket or pie dish. Put the leaf rounds into the baskets or dishes and set aside.

5 Dip your fingers into a bowl of cold water. Pinch off a 1½-inch (4-cm) piece of tapioca dough and roll it into a ball. Flatten it into a 3-inch (7.5-cm) round. Pack 1 teaspoon of filling into the center of the dough, then fold up the edges around the filling and form a ball. Place the ball on a banana-leaf round. Repeat to make 42–48 balls in all and place them, without touching, on the banana leaves. Cover the steamers with their lids.

6 Add water to a wok or other pan for steaming and bring to a rolling boil. Place the steamers, stacked, over the water and steam until the dumplings are translucent and cooked through, 10–12 minutes.

7 To serve, remove the baskets or dishes from over the water. Drizzle the dumplings with garlic oil and serve warm.

Corn Puffs

Makka Poa • Maharashtra • India

These corn fritters—studded with bell peppers, green onion, and fresh cilantro and scented with cumin and garam masala—come from the Bombay Cricket Club, where they are served with ice-cold beer.

TAMARIND CHUTNEY (OPTIONAL)

1½-inch (4-cm) ball tamarind pulp

8 pitted dates

1 teaspoon cumin seeds, roasted and ground

1 teaspoon cayenne pepper

1 teaspoon salt

MINT CHUTNEY (OPTIONAL)

2 yellow onions, finely chopped

4 fresh serrano chiles, stemmed

2 teaspoons lemon juice

1¼ teaspoons salt

1 small unripe mango

1 cup (2 oz/60 g) fresh mint leaves

½ cup (1½ oz/60 g) fresh cilantro (fresh coriander) leaves

1¼ cups (9 oz/280 g) all-purpose (plain) flour

2 teaspoons baking powder

1½ teaspoons salt

1 teaspoon cumin seeds, toasted

1 teaspoon garam masala

1 cup (8 fl oz/250 ml) milk

1 egg, beaten

1 tablespoon unsalted butter, melted

1 cup (6 oz/185 g) corn kernels

½ cup (1½ oz/45 g) sliced green (spring) onions, including tender green tops

½ cup (2½ oz/75 g) minced red bell pepper (capsicum)

½ cup (¾ oz/20 g) chopped fresh cilantro (fresh coriander)

Canola oil for deep-frying

Serves 6

1 To make the tamarind chutney, if using, in a heatproof bowl, combine the pulp with 1½ cup (12 fl oz/375 ml) boiling water and let stand until softened, about 30 minutes. Using your fingers, squeeze and press the tamarind to release as much pulp as possible into the water. Strain, discarding the fibrous residue. Pour into a blender or food processor and add the dates, cumin, cayenne pepper, and salt and process until liquefied and smooth. Cover and set aside.

2 To make the mint chutney, if using, in a blender or food processor, combine the onions, chiles, lemon juice, and salt. Process until the ingredients are finely minced. Prepare the mango as directed on page 223, add to the blender a few pieces at a time, and process until puréed. Add the mint and cilantro a little at a time and process until a smooth paste forms. Add 1–2 tablespoons water, if needed for smoothness, and set aside.

3 In a bowl, combine the flour, baking powder, salt, cumin, and garam masala. In a small bowl, whisk the milk, egg, and butter. Pour over the flour mixture. Mix quickly to form a lump-free batter. Fold in the corn, green onion, bell pepper, and cilantro.

4 In a *karhai* (page 72), deep-fryer, or large frying pan, pour oil to a depth of 1½ inches (4 cm) and heat to 375°F (190°C) on a deep-frying thermometer. Using a teaspoon or a melon baller, gently slip heaping spoonfuls of the batter, a few at a time, into the oil. Do not crowd the pan. Fry the puffs, turning occasionally, until they are golden, about 5 minutes. Using a slotted spoon, transfer to paper towels to drain. Keep warm in a low oven while you cook the remaining puffs.

5 Serve hot or at room temperature with the chutneys, if desired.

Fried Vegetarian Spring Rolls

Chun Bing • Western • China

Black "wood ear" fungus introduces an appealing crunchiness to the filling of these crisp, golden snack rolls. You can find it in Asian markets and natural-food stores.

FILLING

3 large dried black mushrooms, soaked in hot water to cover for 25 minutes and drained

1½-inch (4-cm) square dried black fungus (see note), soaked in hot water to cover for 25 minutes and drained

1 cup (2½ oz/75 g) finely julienned carrot

½ cup (1¾ oz/50 g) finely julienned celery

¼ cup (1¼ oz/40 g) finely julienned bamboo shoots

1 cup (2 oz/60 g) finely sliced napa cabbage

1 cup (1½ oz/45 g) bean sprouts

2 green (spring) onions, including tender green tops, cut into 1½-inch (4-cm) lengths and then julienned lengthwise

2 tablespoons hoisin sauce or oyster sauce

1 tablespoon tapioca starch or cornstarch (cornflour)

20 spring roll wrappers, each 5 inches (13 cm) square

Canola or peanut oil for deep-frying

Sweet-and-Sour Sauce (page 60) or light soy sauce for serving

Makes 20 rolls

1 To prepare the filling, remove and discard the stems from the mushrooms and the woody parts from the fungus if necessary. Finely slice the mushroom caps and fungus. Set aside.

2 Bring a saucepan three-fourths full of water to a boil, add the carrot and celery, and blanch for 1½ minutes. Using a wire skimmer, lift out the vegetables and drain well. Add the bamboo shoots, cabbage, bean sprouts, and green onions to the same boiling water, blanch for 1 minute, and drain well.

3 In a bowl, combine all the well-drained vegetables, mushrooms, fungus, and the hoisin sauce. Mix well, then stir in the tapioca starch or cornstarch to absorb any excess liquid.

4 To assemble each spring roll, place a wrapper on a clean work surface, with one corner pointing toward you. Place about 2 tablespoons of the filling in the center of the wrapper and fold the point nearest you over the filling, tucking the end in and nudging the filling with your fingers to form the roll shape. Fold the 2 side edges in over the filling. Moisten the tip of the remaining flap with cold water and roll up, giving the spring roll a gentle squeeze to secure the end flap. The roll should be about 2½ inches (6 cm) long and 1 inch (2.5 cm) in diameter. Repeat until all of the rolls are formed.

5 Pour oil to a depth of 2 inches (5 cm) in a wok or large, heavy saucepan and heat to 325°F (165°C) on a deep-frying thermometer, or until a small cube of bread dropped into it begins to turn golden in 5–10 seconds. Slide in half of the rolls and fry, turning several times, until golden brown, 1½–2 minutes. Using a wire skimmer or slotted spoon, transfer to a rack placed over paper towels to drain. Keep warm in a low oven while you fry the remaining rolls.

6 Arrange the hot spring rolls on a platter and serve at once with the sweet-and-sour sauce or light soy sauce in small bowls for dipping.

Potato Fritters

Aloo Bhajia • Andhra Pradesh • India

Every state in India has its own distinct version of the classic fritter recipe. This one, from Andhra Pradesh, is very spicy and quite delicious. The fritters are just as tasty when made with zucchini, pumpkin, or eggplant.

1 lb (375 g) Yukon gold or new potatoes

BATTER

1½ cups (7½ oz/235 g) chickpea (garbanzo bean) flour

2 teaspoons ground cumin

1–2 teaspoons cayenne pepper

1 teaspoon *nigella* seeds (optional)

1 teaspoon *each* salt and ground turmeric

1 cup (8 fl oz/250 ml) hot water

Canola oil for deep-frying

Serves 6

1 Scrub but do not peel the potatoes. Slice into pieces ⅛ inch (3 mm) thick and place in a bowl. Add water to cover and set aside.

2 To make the batter, in a bowl, combine the chickpea flour, cumin, cayenne pepper to taste, *nigella* (if using), salt, turmeric, and hot water. Whisk until smoothly blended.

3 In a *karhai* (page 72), deep-fryer, or large frying pan, pour oil to a depth of 1½ inches (4 cm) and heat to 375°F (190°C) on a deep-frying thermometer. Meanwhile, drain the potato slices and pat them dry on paper towels. When the oil is ready, dip a few slices in the batter, allowing the excess to drain off, then gently slip them into the oil. Do not crowd pan. Fry, turning frequently, until golden, about 4 minutes. Using a slotted spoon, transfer to paper towels to drain. Keep warm in a low oven while you fry the remaining slices in the same way. Serve at once.

Herb Leaf–Wrapped Bundles

Miang Kum • Thailand

When served, this dish looks somewhat like a relish tray, and enjoying it depends on a skillful combining of the ingredients. Diners take a small fresh herb leaf and put one or two bits of each item onto it, spoon sauce on the mixture, and fold it up into a bundle. In Thailand, *cha plu* leaves, relatives of betel leaves, are traditionally used, but spinach may be substituted. Be sure to cut each ingredient into the size indicated.

½ cup (2 oz/60 g) unsweetened grated dried coconut, toasted

½ cup (2½ oz/75 g) unsalted roasted peanuts

¼ cup (1½ oz/45 g) dried shrimp, each about ½ inch (12 mm) long

¼ cup (2 oz/60 g) peeled and diced fresh ginger (¼-inch/6-mm dice)

1 thin-skinned lime, unpeeled, cut into ¼-inch (6-mm) dice

⅓ cup (1½ oz/45 g) diced shallot (¼-inch/6-mm dice)

2 tablespoons chopped green serrano or Thai chile

½ cup (½ oz/15 g) fresh cilantro (fresh coriander) leaves

18 *cha plu* (see note), spinach, or *shiso* leaves

SAUCE

¼-inch (3-mm) ball tamarind pulp

¼ cup (2 fl oz/60 ml) boiling water

¼ cup (1 oz/30 g) unsweetened grated dried coconut, toasted

2 tablespoons dried shrimp powder

3 tablespoons ground unsalted roasted peanuts

1 slice fresh galangal, ½ inch (12 mm) thick, peeled and chopped

½ teaspoon dried shrimp paste

⅓ cup (3 oz/90 g) firmly packed palm sugar or brown sugar

1 tablespoon fish sauce, or to taste

1 teaspoon dark soy sauce

½ teaspoon salt

½ cup (4 fl oz/125 ml) water

Serves 6

1 Prepare a platter with piles of coconut, peanuts, dried shrimp, ginger, lime, shallot, chile, and cilantro leaves. Arrange the *cha plu* or other leaves on a serving plate.

2 To make the sauce, in a glass bowl, combine the tamarind pulp and boiling water. Let stand until soft, 15–20 minutes. Squeeze as much pulp as possible from the tamarind, strain, and set aside, discarding the fibrous residue. In a blender, combine the coconut, shrimp powder, peanuts, and galangal and process. Transfer the mixture to a saucepan and add the shrimp paste, palm sugar, tamarind water, fish sauce, soy sauce, salt, and water. Bring to a boil over high heat, reduce the heat to medium, and cook, stirring occasionally, it is syrupy and a caramel color, 2–3 minutes. Pour into a saucer and let cool.

3 Diners take a leaf and puts a bit of each ingredient onto it. The total ingredients should amount to no more than a small mouthful. Then he or she spoons a dab of the sauce on top, folds up the leaf, and pops it into the mouth.

Steamed Shrimp with Soy-Chile Sauce

Zheng Xiao Xia Lajiangyou · Southern · China

What great pleasure comes from a simple meal of cooked shellfish, salty fresh from the sea. The Chinese prefer the crustaceans to be served whole in the shell, making the eating a messy but enjoyable hands-on dining experience that calls for a plastic tablecloth and plenty of napkins. In many Chinese restaurants, a bowl of cold tea is brought to the table to serve as a finger bowl for rinsing sticky fingers once the last shrimp is eaten.

18 large shrimp (prawns) in their shells, about 1½ lb (750 g) total weight

SOY-CHILE SAUCE

2½ tablespoons dark soy sauce

1½ tablespoons light soy sauce

2 slices fresh ginger, each about ⅛ inch (3 mm) thick, peeled and very finely chopped

1 green (spring) onion, including tender green top, very finely chopped

1 hot red or green chile, seeded and very thinly sliced

1½ tablespoons peanut or canola oil

Serves 6–8

1 Rinse the shrimp but do not peel. Place in a bowl with ice water to cover. Leave for at least 10 minutes or for up to 1 hour to firm and crisp the flesh.

2 To prepare the sauce, in a small bowl, lightly whisk together the dark and light soy sauces, 2 tablespoons water, the ginger, green onion, chile, and oil. Pour into small serving bowls for dipping.

3 Bring water to a boil in the base of a steamer. Place the shrimp in a steamer basket and set in the steamer. Cover tightly, reduce the heat so the water continues to simmer, and steam until the shrimp are pink-red and firm, 8–10 minutes. Remove from the steamer and tip onto a platter.

4 Serve the shrimp at once with the dipping sauce.

SOY SAUCE

From humble beginnings as a cottage industry to a multimillion dollar international revenue earner, the manufacture of soy sauce has spanned three millennia in the world's most populous country. Making soy sauce (*jiangyou*) is a relatively simple process.

Yellow soybeans are cooked until tender, mashed, mixed with roasted wheat or barley flour, salted (and in some instances sugared), and packed into tubs to ferment, then brined and refermented with the *Lactobacillus spp.* bacteria. The first extraction, after about forty days, is a light amber brown, delicate in flavor, and pleasantly salty. Left to ferment longer, the flavor and color develop in intensity,

although the saltiness declines. Further processing involves the addition of sugar or caramelized sugar for dark-colored, glossy sauces in which sweet and salty flavors balance and complement, and of ingredients such as mushroom and shellfish, which contributes rich, complex flavors.

Use light soy sauce for flavor and saltiness in stir-fries and marinades and as a dip; dark soy (some types of which are called mushroom soy) for richness and color in braised dishes (called "red cooking"), spicy stir-fries, and dark sauces; and sweet thick soy where specified. Special dietary low-sodium and wheat-free soy sauces are also available.

"Top Hats" Filled with Crab and Vegetables

Kueh Pai Tee • Singapore

A great party dish, these dainty, fluted shells are filled with a braised mixture of seafood and vegetables. Each shell is made with a steel mold that is dipped into batter and plunged into hot oil. When crisp and brown, the shell slips off the mold. You can find the molds in some of the better Southeast Asian markets in the West. Or substitute wonton skins: Press a 1½-inch (4-cm) wide, stainless-steel ladle into the middle of a skin and hold it down in the hot oil. Failing that option, use small, premade Western pastry shells.

BATTER

¾ cup (4 oz/125 g) all-purpose (plain) flour

¼ cup (1 oz/30 g) rice flour

¼ teaspoon salt

1 egg, lightly beaten

Canola oil for deep-frying

FILLING

¼ lb (125 g) fresh shrimp (prawns)

2 tablespoons canola oil

3 cloves garlic, minced

2 teaspoons dried shrimp, minced

1 cup (4 oz/125 g) julienned bamboo shoots

1 large carrot, peeled and finely shredded

½ lb (250 g) daikon, peeled and finely shredded

1 tablespoon sugar

1 teaspoon salt

¼ lb (125 g) fresh-cooked crabmeat, picked over for shell fragments and flaked

¼ cup (⅓ oz/10 g) chopped fresh cilantro (fresh coriander), plus about 36 whole leaves for garnish

Sriracha sauce for serving

Makes about 3 dozen pastries; serves 12

1 To make the batter, in a bowl, stir together the all-purpose and rice flours and the salt. Add the egg. Slowly add ¾ cup (6 fl oz/180 ml) water, stirring until the mixture is smooth.

2 To fry the pastry shells, pour the oil to a depth of 3 inches (7.5 cm) in a wok or deep saucepan and heat to 365°F (185°C) on a deep-frying thermometer. When the oil is hot, season the pastry mold (see note) by holding its handle and dipping it into the hot oil for 1 minute. Remove the mold from the oil, shaking to remove any excess oil, then dip it into the batter up to, but not over, the top edge. Lift the mold out of the batter and let the excess batter drip back into the bowl. Lower the coated mold into the hot oil and deep-fry until the pastry can retain its shape, about 1 minute. With chopsticks or tongs, nudge the top edge of the mold to help release the shell into the oil. Fry the shell until it is golden brown, about 1 minute longer. Remove and transfer to paper towels to drain. Repeat until all the batter is used. Let the shells cool completely. (The shells can be stored in an airtight container at room temperature for up to 3 days.)

3 To make the filling, bring a saucepan three-fourths full of water to a boil. Add the fresh shrimp and boil until they turn bright orange-pink, 1–2 minutes. Drain, let cool, then peel, devein, and cut into ¼-inch (6-mm) dice.

4 Place a wok over medium-high heat and add the oil. When it is hot, add the garlic and dried shrimp and sauté until the garlic is golden, about 30 seconds. Raise the heat to high and add the bamboo shoots, carrot, daikon, and diced fresh shrimp, and stir and toss in the hot oil for a few seconds. Add 1 cup (8 fl oz/250 ml) water, the sugar, and salt and continue cooking, stirring gently, until the vegetables are tender and all the liquid has evaporated, 8–10 minutes. Remove from the heat and let cool.

5 Add the crabmeat and chopped cilantro to the cooled filling and mix well. Using chopsticks or a spoon, put about 2 teaspoons of the filling into each pastry shell. Garnish each filled shell with a whole cilantro leaf, top with a drop of Sriracha sauce, and serve.

Fish and Eggplant Purée in Lettuce Leaves

Tom Ponh • Laos

A popular dish in Laos, this fish purée typifies the complex herbaceous flavors present in the traditional foods of Indochina. If you prefer, you can broil the fish instead of grilling it.

1 lb (500 g) catfish or other whitefish fillets such as cod or snapper

Canola oil for brushing

1 large globe eggplant (aubergine) or 4 large Asian (slender) eggplants, 1¼ lb (625 g) total weight

6 cloves garlic, unpeeled

2 shallots, unpeeled

2 tablespoons fish sauce, or to taste

3 red Fresno or serrano chiles, seeded and finely chopped

2 green (spring) onions, including 1 inch (2.5 cm) of the green tops, minced

3 tablespoons chopped fresh mint

2 tablespoons chopped fresh Thai basil

2 tablespoons fresh cilantro (fresh coriander) leaves

2 fresh dill sprigs, chopped

1 teaspoon salt, or to taste

DIPPING SAUCE

1 fresh red chile, seeded and finely minced

3 tablespoons fish sauce

¼ cup (2 fl oz/60 ml) fresh lime juice

1 tablespoon sugar

1 head red-leaf or butter (Boston) lettuce, leaves separated

1 handful fresh Thai basil leaves

1 handful fresh cilantro (fresh coriander) leaves

1 handful fresh polygonum leaves

1 handful fresh mint leaves

1 cucumber, peeled, seeded, and cut into thin strips ⅛ inch (3 mm) wide and 2 inches (5 cm) long

Serves 4–6

1 Prepare a medium-hot fire in a charcoal grill.

2 Brush the fish fillets with oil. Place the fish on the grill rack and grill, turning once, until opaque throughout, about 5 minutes total per ½ inch (12 mm) at the thickest point of the fillets. Transfer the fish to a platter and let cool. Break up the cooled fish into chunks, and set aside.

3 Using a skewer, puncture the eggplant(s) in several places and set over the charcoal fire. Grill, turning occasionally, until the skin(s) blacken and the flesh is very tender, about 20 minutes for the globe eggplant and 10 minutes for the Asian eggplants. Remove from the grill and let cool. Cut in half lengthwise and scoop out the tender flesh; set aside.

4 Meanwhile, thread the garlic cloves and shallots on a metal skewer and set over the charcoal fire. Grill, turning occasionally, until charred and tender, 10–15 minutes. Remove from the grill and set aside to cool. Peel the garlic and shallots, reserving 2 garlic cloves to add to the dipping sauce.

5 In a food processor, combine the fish chunks, eggplant flesh, 4 of the garlic cloves, the shallots, fish sauce, chiles, green onions, mint, basil, cilantro, and dill. Process until a smooth purée forms. If it is too thick, thin the purée with a little water to the consistency of a thick dip. Add the salt and taste and adjust the seasoning. Transfer to a serving bowl.

6 To make the dipping sauce, in a mortar, combine the remaining 2 grilled garlic cloves and the chile and pound to a purée. Stir in the fish sauce, lime juice, sugar, and ¼ cup (2 fl oz/60 ml) water. Pour into a saucer.

7 Arrange the lettuce, basil, cilantro, polygonum, and mint along with the cucumber strips around the edges of a large platter around the bowl of fish-eggplant purée.

8 Each diner takes a lettuce leaf, scatters a few herb leaves and strips of cucumber in the center, adds a dollop of the purée, rolls up the lettuce leaf, dips the roll into the sauce, and eats it out of hand.

Fresh Vegetable Spring Rolls

Poh Pia • Singapore

Every country in Southeast Asia has its own version of the spring roll, and fresh ones—that is, not fried—are particularly popular in Singapore and Malaysia, where the Nonya kitchen flourishes. The filling for this recipe is inspired by the *poh pia* served at Singapore-born Chris Yeo's Straits Café in San Francisco.

FILLING

2 tablespoons canola oil

1 teaspoon chopped garlic

3 shallots, thinly sliced

¼ lb (125 g) shrimp (prawns), peeled, deveined, and cut into ¼-inch (6-mm) pieces

2 carrots, peeled and finely julienned

1 small jicama, 7–8 oz (220–250 g), peeled and finely julienned

1 cup (4 oz/125 g) julienned bamboo shoots

1 cup (3 oz/90 g) finely shredded cabbage

1 tablespoon distilled white vinegar

1 teaspoon sugar

¼ teaspoon salt

3 eggs, lightly beaten (optional)

1–3 teaspoons canola oil, if using eggs

1 package (1 lb/500 g) lumpia wrappers or fresh spring roll wrappers

3 Chinese sausages, steamed and coarsely chopped (optional)

1 small English (hothouse) cucumber, peeled, seeded, and julienned

3 green (spring) onions, white part only, finely slivered

2 red Fresno or serrano chiles, seeded and finely slivered

16 fresh cilantro (fresh coriander) sprigs

1 cup (8 fl oz/250 ml) hoisin sauce

⅓ cup (3 fl oz/80 ml) Sriracha sauce

Makes about 16 rolls; serves 16

1 To make the filling, preheat a wok over medium-high heat and add the oil. When it is hot, add the garlic and shallots and stir-fry until the shallots are translucent, 1–2 minutes. Add the shrimp and stir-fry until they turn bright orange-pink, about 2 minutes. Raise the heat to high, add the carrots, jicama, bamboo shoots, and cabbage, and stir-fry until the vegetables are tender, about 5 minutes. Add the vinegar, sugar, salt, and ¼ cup (2 fl oz/ 60 ml) water, stir well, cover, and simmer gently until the vegetables are cooked but still crisp, about 5 minutes longer. Pour the vegetables into a colander to drain and let cool.

2 While the filling cools, prepare the remaining ingredients: If you are using the eggs, preheat a 9-inch (23-cm) frying pan over medium-high heat until hot. To test, sprinkle with drops of water. If they turn to beads and dance across the surface, the pan is ready. Add 1 teaspoon oil to the pan and wipe up the excess with a paper towel. (Too much oil will not work for this recipe.) Reduce the heat to low. Pour in about one-third of the beaten egg, then swirl the pan to spread it evenly over the bottom. Let cook for 1 minute, or until the bottom is light brown and the edges start to shrink back. Carefully peel loose at the edge and turn out onto a cutting board. Roll up the omelet jelly-roll style and cut crosswise into very thin shreds. Toss and lift the pieces to fluff them and set aside. Cook the remaining egg in two batches and cut into shreds.

3 Arrange the wrappers, the omelet shreds and sausage (if using), the cucumber, green onion, chiles, cilantro sprigs, and filling on a platter. Pour the hoisin and Sriracha sauces into 2 dipping saucers.

4 Invite your guests to wrap their own *poh pia*: To make a spring roll, lay 1 wrapper on a flat surface. Scatter a tablespoon of the vegetable filling across the lower third of the wrapper, top it with a small amount of egg shreds and Chinese sausage (if using), cucumber strips, green onions, chile slivers, and cilantro sprigs. Top with some hoisin sauce and a dribble of Sriracha sauce. Roll up the bottom of the wrapper to enclose the filling and form a log. Fold in the sides to enclose the ends, then finish rolling until the log is totally enclosed. Leave the roll whole or cut in half crosswise and eat out of hand.

Indian Flat Bread Stuffed with Spicy Lamb

Murtabak • Singapore

In Singapore, *murtabak* hawkers are true artisans, spinning small lumps of dough in the air to transform them into sheets as thin as filo. The bread, called *roti*, is folded and grilled. To make this *murtabak*, wrap the uncooked dough around seasoned lamb before browning it on a griddle. Cut up *murtabak* into squares to serve as a hearty appetizer. Left whole and doused with curry sauce, it makes an excellent light lunch. In either case, serve it with milky Indian coffee. For a vegetarian version, try filling the *roti* packet with egg, onion, and peas.

1 To make the Indian layered bread dough, in a bowl, sift together the flour and salt. Stir in the 5 tablespoons (2½ fl oz/75 ml) ghee until crumbly. Slowly stir in enough of the milk to form a soft, spongy, slightly sticky dough. Turn out onto a lightly floured surface and knead, dusting with flour to prevent sticking, until a smooth ball forms, about 10 minutes. Transfer to a bowl, cover with a towel, and let rest in a warm spot for 30 minutes. Turn the dough out onto a work surface and cut into 8 equal pieces. Shape each piece into a ball, brush with some of the remaining ghee, and set the balls, not touching, on a tray. Cover with a damp kitchen towel and let the dough rest for 4 hours.

2 To make the filling, in a wok or frying pan over medium heat, warm the ghee or oil. Add the shallots, garlic, and ginger and sauté until translucent, about 1 minute. Do not allow to brown. Add the lamb, curry leaves (if using), curry powder, sugar, and salt, breaking up any large clumps of meat. Continue to cook, stirring often, until the meat is no longer pink and all the liquid has evaporated, 5–8 minutes. The mixture should be dry and crumbly. Taste and adjust the seasoning. Remove from the heat and let cool, then mix in the egg.

3 Preheat a griddle or large frying pan over medium-high heat. Add a little ghee or oil and tilt the pan to coat the bottom thinly.

4 Working quickly, take 1 ball of dough and place it on a large work surface brushed with ghee or oil. With a rolling pin or your fingers, flatten the ball of dough. Roll or spread it out into a 12-inch (30-cm) or larger round. Scatter one-eighth of the onion slices and one-eighth of the meat mixture onto the middle of the round. Fold in all 4 sides so the edges overlap in the middle, completely enclosing the filling and making a 5-inch (13-cm) square packet.

5 Place the square, folded side up, on the griddle. Fry until the bottom is nicely browned, about 3 minutes. Turn the square over and brown the second side, about 3 minutes longer. Transfer to a platter and keep warm while you fry the remaining packets.

6 Cut each griddled bread into several pieces and arrange on a platter. Serve at once.

INDIAN LAYERED BREAD DOUGH

3½ cups (17½ oz/545 g) bread (hard-wheat) flour

1 teaspoon salt

5 tablespoons (2½ oz/75 ml) ghee (page 221)

1¼–1½ cups (10–12 fl oz/310–375 ml) milk, heated to lukewarm

FILLING

2 tablespoons ghee (page 221) or canola oil

4 shallots, minced

2 cloves garlic, minced

1 slice fresh ginger, peeled and finely minced

1 lb (500 g) ground (minced) lamb

2 tablespoons curry leaves (optional)

1 tablespoon Indian-style curry powder

1 teaspoon sugar

1 teaspoon salt

1 egg, lightly beaten

Ghee (page 221) or canola oil for frying

1 white onion, thinly sliced

Makes 8 stuffed breads; serves 8

Royal Lucknow Kabobs

Kakori Kabab • Uttar Pradesh • India

Made with lamb, cashews, and fragrant spices, these *kakori kabab*, perfected in food stalls in the city of Lucknow after India achieved independence in 1947, have a complex flavor.

1 teaspoon poppy seeds

3 tablespoons chickpea (garbanzo bean) flour or roasted split peas

2 tablespoons *usli ghee* (page 221)

1 small yellow onion, finely chopped

¼ cup (1 oz/30 g) cashew nuts, ground to a coarse powder in a food processor or mortar

1 tablespoon garam masala

1 teaspoon freshly ground black pepper

½ teaspoon ground cardamom

¼ teaspoon ground nutmeg

1 lb (500 g) ground (minced) lamb or beef

¼ cup (1 oz/30 g) grated green papaya, potato, jicama, or zucchini (courgette; optional)

1 teaspoon salt

¼ teaspoon saffron threads, crushed

Mint Chutney (page 77)

Makes 16 kabobs; serves 4

1 In a small, dry frying pan over high heat, toast the poppy seeds until they are fragrant and turn darker, about 4 minutes. If you are using chickpea flour, add it now and toast for 2 minutes more. Transfer to a mortar, blender, or coffee grinder reserved solely for spices and pound or process until powdered. If you are using split peas, add them now and pound or process until finely powdered.

2 In a frying pan over medium-high heat, warm the *usli ghee*. When it is very hot, add the onion and cook, stirring often, until it is caramel brown, about 7 minutes. Stir in the cashew powder, garam masala, pepper, cardamom, and nutmeg. Transfer the mixture to a large bowl. Add the meat, papaya (if using), salt, saffron, and poppy seed mixture. Mix well and set aside for 30 minutes at room temperature to allow the flavors to blend. Divide the mixture into 16 portions. Using your hands, shape each portion into a cylinder.

3 The kabobs can be grilled or broiled. If using a charcoal grill, prepare a fire for direct-heat cooking. Position the grill rack 5 inches (13 cm) from the fire. Allow the coals to burn until white ash covers them and the heat is moderate. If using the broiler (grill), preheat it to the maximum temperature, positioning the broiler pan 5 inches (13 cm) from the heat source. Place the kabobs on the grill rack or broiler pan and cook, turning them 3 times, until cooked through and nicely browned, 8–11 minutes. Serve hot with the mint chutney alongside in a bowl.

Green Onion Pastries

You Yuan • Eastern • China

Asian sesame oil is a deep-amber oil pressed from toasted sesame seeds. The paler gold-colored variety is not a suitable flavor substitute, but it can be used for sautéeing.

2 cups (10 oz/315 g) all-purpose (plain) flour

1 cup (8 fl oz/250 ml) boiling water

3 tablespoons Asian sesame oil (see note)

Coarse or flaked salt for sprinkling

1¼ cups (3¾ oz/110 g) chopped green (spring) onion tops

Canola oil for frying

Serves 6

1 Sift the flour into a bowl and make a well in the center. Pour the boiling water into the well. Using a wooden spoon, quickly work the water into the flour to make a fairly stiff, but not dry, dough. Knead gently in the bowl until the dough forms a ball. Remove the dough from the bowl and brush it lightly with some of the sesame oil. Invert the bowl over the dough and leave to cool, about 6 minutes.

2 Knead the dough very lightly until smooth and elastic, rub with more of the sesame oil, and place in a plastic bag. Set aside for 30–60 minutes.

3 Using your palms, roll the dough out on the work surface to form a log about 10 inches (25 cm) long. Cut into 6 equal pieces. Roll each piece into a ball. Working with 1 piece at a time, roll out each ball into a very thin round about 7 inches (18 cm) in diameter. Brush generously with sesame oil. Sprinkle with salt and then cover evenly and lightly with one-sixth of the green onion. Roll up the round into a cigar shape, twist into a tight coil, and brush the top with more sesame oil. On a lightly oiled work surface, flatten the coil with a rolling pin to make a round about 5 inches (13 cm) in diameter. Try to avoid having the onions break through the pastry. Repeat until all the pastries are made.

4 When all of the pastries are ready, pour oil to a depth of 1 inch (2.5 cm) in a large, wide, shallow pan and heat over medium-high heat until hot. Working with 2 or 3 pastries at a time, place them in the hot oil and fry, turning once, until a light golden brown, about 3 minutes on each side.

5 Transfer the pastries to a serving platter, sprinkle with additional salt, and cut into quarters. Serve at once.

STREET FOOD

The best way to experience true Southeast Asian cooking is to spend time eating hawker fare, authentic dishes served up in plain stalls at bargain prices. Made according to recipes passed down through generations, these street foods are the labor of legions of entrepreneurial cooks.

Old-timers in Singapore recall the days when hawkers commuted to work each day by negotiating the busy streets at the helm of their portable restaurants, wood-and-tin structures on bicycle wheels with small stools hanging from the sides and a faded canopy covering the "kitchen." Some even wore their places of business across their shoulders, balancing bamboo poles with pots and woks, bowls and plates dangling from each end. Those itinerant hawkers are gone now, replaced by the government's efficient, sanitary, highly convenient food centers, populated with large numbers of permanent stalls—literally hundreds in Chinatown's Kreta Ayer center—and tables gathered together under a single roof. Some locals lament the loss of the traveling hawker, but others appreciate the orderliness that the city-state's regulations have delivered.

Singapore has the most organized system of food stalls in Southeast Asia, but every community boasts clusters of talented street-based cooks. In the night markets of Chiang Mai, locals fuel up on *khao soi* (curry noodles), *khanom jiin* (noodles with spicy fish), and other dishes. Near the train station in Hanoi, in alleyways off Hang Bong Street, bureaucrats and students, families and pensioners perch on stools to consume bowls of herbal chicken soup and plates of fish cakes and *cha gio* (spring rolls). And just beyond central Yangon's (Rangoon's) cavernous Bogyoke Market stands an open-air market thick with steam rising from pots of *mohingha*, the typical Burmese breakfast.

Grilled Minced Beef Rolled in La-Lot Leaves

Bo La-Lot • Vietnam

When a special occasion is at hand, and the Vietnamese have money in their pockets, they like to go out and eat the banquet known as *bo bay mon*, or beef cooked seven ways. Seven is considered a fortuitous number, so the name of this celebratory meal carries good luck. The banquet often includes *bo la-lot*, seasoned beef wrapped in *la-lot* leaves and grilled. The *la-lot* plant has shiny, heart-shaped leaves and an aniselike flavor and camphor aroma. They can be found in Asian markets. The Japanese *shiso* leaf is a good substitute.

NUOC CHAM DIPPING SAUCE

1 large clove garlic

¼ cup (2 fl oz/60 ml) fresh lime juice

5 tablespoons (2½ fl oz/75 ml) fish sauce

3 tablespoons sugar

1 fresh red chile, seeded (page 220), and thinly sliced

2 tablespoons grated carrot

1 lb (375 g) lean beef round, finely ground (minced)

1 tablespoon canola oil

2 tablespoons finely minced lemongrass (from midsection of 2 stalks; see page 222)

2 large shallots, finely minced

4 cloves garlic, finely minced

1 tablespoon fish sauce

2 teaspoons sugar

1 teaspoon five-spice powder

1 teaspoon salt

¼ teaspoon freshly ground pepper

¼ teaspoon ground turmeric

30 *la-lot*, *shiso*, or bottled grape leaves (see note)

Canola oil for brushing

ACCOMPANIMENTS

30 butter (Boston) lettuce leaves

30 fresh cilantro (fresh coriander) sprigs

2 cups (2 oz/60 g) fresh mint leaves

2 cups (2 oz/60 g) fresh Thai basil leaves

Makes 30 rolls; serves 8–10

1 To make the sauce, in a mortar, pound the garlic until puréed. Mix in the lime juice, fish sauce, sugar, and 6 tablespoons (3 fl oz/9 ml) water. Add the chile and carrot. Pour into a dipping saucer, cover, and set aside.

2 In a bowl, combine the beef, oil, lemongrass, shallots, garlic, fish sauce, sugar, five-spice powder, salt, pepper, and turmeric. Mix well, cover, and marinate for up to 2 hours at room temperature or as long as overnight in the refrigerator.

3 Place 6 bamboo skewers, each 6 inches (15 cm) long, in water to cover. Prepare a medium-hot fire in a charcoal grill or preheat the broiler (grill).

4 Rinse the *la-lot* or *shiso* leaves with cold water and pat dry with paper towels. If using grape leaves, rinse thoroughly in cold water to remove the brine, then trim off the stems. Place the leaves, shiny side down and with the stem end toward you, on a work surface. Put 1 tablespoon of the filling on the stem end of each leaf and mold it into a log 2 inches (5 cm) long. Fold over the end nearest you and roll tightly from the bottom to enclose the log but leave the ends open. (If using grape leaves, fold in the sides to enclose the roll completely.) Repeat until all the rolls are made.

5 Drain the skewers and thread 5 rolls horizontally onto each skewer, allowing the rolls to touch. Set the skewers on a tray and brush the rolls with oil.

6 Place the skewers on the grill rack about 5 inches (13 cm) above the fire or on the broiler pan positioned about 5 inches from the heat source. Grill or broil, turning once, until crisp and browned on both sides, about 3 minutes on each side.

7 To serve, arrange the lettuce leaves, cilantro sprigs, and mint and basil leaves on a platter. To eat, put a roll on a lettuce leaf with some of the fresh herbs. Roll up the lettuce to enclose everything, dip it into the sauce, and eat out of hand.

Steamed Pork Dumplings

Jiaozi • Northern • China

DOUGH

2–2½ cups (10–12½ oz/315–390 g) all-purpose (plain) flour

1 tablespoon baking powder

⅔ cup (5 fl oz/160 ml) water

FILLING

7 oz (220 g) ground (minced) lean pork

1½ teaspoons peeled and grated fresh ginger

1½ tablespoons canola oil

2 tablespoons light soy sauce

About ½ cup (4 fl oz/125 ml) water

¾ cup (2 oz/60 g) finely chopped napa cabbage, plus 2 large whole leaves

¼ cup (¾ oz/20 g) finely chopped green (spring) onion, including tender green tops

1 tablespoon sesame oil

Red vinegar or light soy sauce

Makes about 20 dumplings

1 To prepare the dough, sift together 2 cups (10 oz/ 315 g) of the flour and the baking powder into a bowl. Make a well in the center and pour the water into the well. Using a large spoon, mix quickly to form a workable dough. It should be soft enough to work easily, but not so sticky that it will adhere to the work surface. Add more flour if it is too moist. Turn it out onto a very lightly floured work surface and knead until firm and elastic, about 2 minutes. Cover with a damp kitchen towel and let rest while you make the filling.

2 To prepare the filling, in a food processor, process the pork to a smooth paste. Add the ginger, oil, and soy sauce and mix well. Gradually add up to ½ cup (4 fl oz/125 ml) water as needed, 1 tablespoon at a time, to form a soft, moist filling. Add the chopped cabbage, green onion, and sesame oil and pulse until evenly mixed, but not puréed.

3 Cut the dough into 1-inch (2.5-cm) pieces. On the floured board, lightly roll out each piece into a thin 3½-inch (9-cm) round, making it slightly thinner at the edges. Cover the rounds with a clean, dry cloth. You should have about 20 rounds. To form dumplings, place a round in the palm of your hand and put a spoonful of filling in the center of it. Using 3 fingers of the other hand, gather the edge of the dough in small pleats, bringing it together at the top to enclose the filling. Twist the top into a point. Gently tap the dumpling on the work surface so that it forms a round.

4 Boil water in the base of a steamer. Line bamboo steamer baskets or metal steamer racks with the whole cabbage leaves and top with the dumplings, leaving space between them. Set the baskets in the steamer, cover, reduce the heat so the water simmers steadily, and steam until the dumplings are puffy and feel soft-firm to the touch, 7–9 minutes. Remove the baskets from the steamer. Serve at once with vinegar or soy sauce in small dishes alongside for dipping.

Sugarcane Shrimp

Chao Tom • Vietnam

A signature Vietnamese dish, sugarcane shrimp is seasoned shrimp purée molded around the center of a sugarcane skewer, then grilled. It is eaten by easing the purée off the cane, combining it with lettuce, mint, cucumber, and cilantro, and then rolling them up in rice paper and dipping the bundle into a sauce. Fresh sugarcane is used for the skewers in this recipe. If unavailable, look for canned sticks packed in syrup, sold in Asian markets.

3 sections sugarcane, each 6 inches (15 cm) long

1 tablespoon chopped shallot

1 teaspoon chopped garlic

1-oz (30-g) piece pork fat, chopped

1 lb (500 g) shrimp (prawns), peeled, deveined, and patted dry

1 tablespoon toasted rice powder

2 teaspoons sugar

1 teaspoon cornstarch (cornflour)

½ teaspoon baking powder

¼ teaspoon freshly ground pepper

About ¼ cup (2 fl oz/60 ml) canola oil

ACCOMPANIMENTS
Nuoc Cham Dipping Sauce (page 94)

12 dried round rice papers, 8 inches (20 cm) in diameter

12 red-leaf or butter (Boston) lettuce leaves

½ cup (½ oz/15 g) fresh cilantro (fresh coriander) leaves

½ cup (½ oz/15 g) fresh mint leaves

½ English (hothouse) cucumber, peeled and finely slivered

Serves 6

1 Using a sharp knife, split each sugarcane section in half lengthwise, then split each half in half again. You should have a total of 12 skewers each 6 inches (15 cm) long. Set aside.

2 Prepare a fire in a charcoal grill. In a food processor, combine the shallot and garlic and process to mince finely. Transfer to a bowl. Add the pork fat to the processor and process to form a purée. Add the shrimp and process to form a coarse paste. Return the garlic and shallot to the processor and add the rice powder, sugar, cornstarch, baking powder, and pepper. Pulse a few times to mix.

3 Oil the lattice bottom of a bamboo steamer. Oil your hands, scoop up 2 tablespoons of the shrimp paste, and mold it evenly around the middle section of a sugarcane stick, leaving 1 inch (2.5 cm) exposed on each end. Place on the oiled steamer. Repeat with the remaining shrimp paste and sugarcane sticks, placing them, without touching, in the steamer. Add water to a wok or other steaming pan and bring to a rolling boil. Place the bamboo steamer over the boiling water, cover, and steam until the shrimp paste is almost cooked, 3–5 minutes.

4 Remove the steamer from over the water, then remove the sugarcane sticks. Pat dry. Place the sticks on the grill rack over the hot fire and grill, turning often, until they are nicely charred with grill marks, about 2 minutes. Transfer to a platter.

5 To serve, pour the dipping sauce into a saucer. Place the rice paper rounds on a plate. Arrange the lettuce, cilantro, and mint leaves and cucumber slivers on a platter. Set a wide bowl of warm water on the table.

6 To eat, take a round of rice paper, slip it briefly into the warm water, and then lay it down on a plate and leave it for 30 seconds or longer until it is softened and feels like a wet tissue. Put a lettuce leaf on top and then a few mint and cilantro leaves and slivers of cucumber. Strip away the shrimp paste from the sugarcane (it can still be hot or at room temperature) and lay it in the middle of the herbs. Fold in one end and roll the rice paper into a cylinder. Dip it into the sauce and eat. Chew on the sugarcane sticks for sweetness.

RICE PAPER

While traveling through the countryside of Southeast Asia, one will see small rice paper "factories" at individual homesteads, identifiable by rows of rice-paper rounds drying on bamboo trays in the strong afternoon sun.

To make the paper, the cook pours a thin film of rice-flour batter over a piece of muslin stretched across a vat filled with boiling water. As one round is being steamed, a second "drum steamer" is used and the process is repeated. When the first round is done, the cook slips a large, flat wooden paddle under it and lifts the enormous circle of wet rice paper onto a woven bamboo tray. It is then carried outdoors and propped at an angle facing the sun to dry. Each dried round, perhaps two hundred of which are made by a single hardworking cook in one day, carries the "watermark" of the bamboo tray.

Around a makeshift factory like this, for as far as the eye can see, thousands of white disks lie drying in the sun. Such sizable output is necessary, though, for the Vietnamese use rice-paper rounds, made by hand and by machine, in huge numbers as coverings for their ubiquitous fresh and fried spring rolls and for wrapping pieces of grilled meat or seafood, herbs, and garnishes into easy-to-eat packets at the table.

Spiced Cashews

Masala Kaju • Gujarat • India

These zesty cashew nuts are utterly irresistible. They pose a real threat as a meal spoiler if you don't pay careful attention to how many you consume.

¼ cup (2 fl oz/60 ml) canola oil

2 cups (10½ oz/330 g) raw cashew nuts, preferably large whole nuts

1½ teaspoons *chat masala* or mango powder

½ teaspoon salt

¼–½ teaspoon cayenne pepper

Serves 8

1 In a *karhai* (page 72) or large frying pan over medium-high heat, warm the oil. Add the nuts and fry, stirring and tossing, until they turn light brown, about 6 minutes. Using a slotted spoon, transfer to a baking sheet or a large plate so that the nuts are in a single layer. Before the cashews cool completely, combine the chat masala or mango powder, salt, and cayenne pepper to taste. Sprinkle over the nuts and mix lightly. (Do not overmix, or the spices will slip away from the nuts.)

2 The nuts can be served warm or at room temperature. Store in an airtight container for up to 3 weeks.

Chicken Fritters

Murghi ke Pakore • Punjab • India

These fritters have a thick, spongy chickpea-batter crust laced with mango powder, *ajowan* seeds, garam masala, and green chiles. A popular appetizer in Indian restaurants serving Moghul fare, they are just as delicious made with shrimps, scallops, fish, or paneer.

BATTER

1¾ cups (8½ oz/265 g) chickpea (garbanzo bean) flour

¼ cup (1½ oz/45 g) rice flour or all-purpose (plain) flour

1½ teaspoons garam masala

1 teaspoon mango powder or 1 tablespoon fresh lemon juice

1 teaspoon baking powder

½ teaspoon ground turmeric

½ teaspoon freshly ground black pepper

¼ teaspoon *ajowan* seeds

4 fresh hot green chiles such as serrano, coarsely chopped

1 teaspoon salt, or to taste

1⅓ cups (11 fl oz/340 ml) hot water

½ cup (¾ oz/20 g) fresh cilantro (fresh coriander), leaves and tender stems

Canola oil for deep-frying

1 skinless, boneless whole chicken breast, about 1 lb (500 g), cut into strips 3 inches (7.5 cm) long by 1 inch (2.5 cm) wide by ¼ inch (6 mm) thick

Mint Chutney (page 77) or Tamarind Chutney (page 77) for serving

Serves 8

1 To make the batter, in a food processor or blender, combine the chickpea flour, rice or all-purpose flour, garam masala, mango powder or lemon juice, baking powder, turmeric, pepper, *ajowan* seeds, chiles, salt, and water. Process until smooth. Add the cilantro and process only until it is finely chopped; a little texture in the cilantro will add to the appeal of the fritters. (If mixing the batter by hand, mince the chiles and chop the cilantro before combining them in a bowl with the other ingredients.)

2 In a *karhai* (page 72), deep-fryer, or large frying pan, pour oil to a depth of 1½ inches (4 cm) and heat to 375°F (190°C) on a deep-frying thermometer.

3 Meanwhile, pat the chicken pieces dry on paper towels. When the oil is ready, dip a few pieces of the chicken into the batter, letting the excess drain off, then gently slip them into the hot oil. Do not crowd the pan. Fry, turning frequently, until the coating is golden brown, about 6 minutes. Using a slotted spoon, transfer to paper towels to drain. Keep warm in a low oven while you fry the remaining chicken pieces in the same way. Serve the fritters at once with the chutney.

Roast Pork Buns

Cha Shao Bao • Northern • China

Bread is as much a part of a Chinese meal in the north as rice is in the south. Vast fields in the northern provinces provide the wheat for the noodles and the many varieties of baked, fried, and steamed breads. As Chinese kitchens traditionally were not equipped with ovens, steaming and dry cooking on a griddle were effective ways to cook breads. Steaming has endured as a favorite technique that renders the bread to a silky sponginess, combined in these delectable buns with the sweet saltiness of a roast pork filling.

DOUGH STARTER

1 cup (5 oz/155 g) all-purpose (plain) flour

¼ cup (2 oz/60 g) superfine (caster) sugar

1½ teaspoons active dry yeast

1 cup (6 fl oz/180 ml) lukewarm water

RED ROAST PORK

2 tablespoons light soy sauce

1½ teaspoons dark soy sauce

1½ tablespoons superfine (caster) sugar

1½ teaspoons five-spice powder

¾ teaspoon baking soda (bicarbonate of soda)

1 teaspoon crushed garlic

1½ tablespoons canola oil

3 or 4 drops red food coloring (optional)

1 or 2 pork tenderloins, about ¾–1 lb (375–500 g) total weight, trimmed, cut in half lengthwise, and then cut crosswise into 6-inch (15-cm) pieces

1 cup (8 fl oz/250 ml) water

FILLING

1½ tablespoons hoisin sauce

1 tablespoon cornstarch (cornflour) dissolved in 3 tablespoons water

DOUGH

1¼ cups (6½ oz/200 g) all-purpose (plain) flour

2 teaspoons baking powder

1½ tablespoons melted lard or canola oil (optional)

⅓ cup (3 fl oz/80 ml) lukewarm water

Makes 20 buns

1 To prepare the dough starter, in a bowl, stir together the flour, sugar, and yeast. Make a well in the center. Pour the lukewarm water into the well and stir with a fork to mix thoroughly. Cover with plastic wrap and set aside in a warm place until bubbly and doubled in size, about 3 hours.

2 To prepare the pork, in a wide, flat dish, combine the light and dark soy sauces, sugar, five-spice powder, baking soda, garlic, oil, and food coloring (if using), mixing well. One by one, dunk the pork strips into the marinade, turning to coat evenly, then arrange them in a single layer in the dish. Cover and refrigerate for 1½ hours, turning every 20 minutes. Position a rack in the second highest level in the oven. Pour the water into a drip pan and place it on a rack below. Preheat the oven to 400°F (200°C). Arrange the marinated pork on the rack, allowing space between the strips, and roast for 12 minutes. Turn and roast for 5 minutes longer. The surface should be glazed and charred at the edges, and the meat inside still pink and tender. Remove from the oven allow to rest for 6 minutes, then dice.

3 To prepare the filling, in a small saucepan over medium-low heat, combine the pork, hoisin sauce, and cornstarch mixture and heat gently, stirring, until the meat is glazed with the sauce, about 1 minute. Remove from the heat and let cool.

4 To prepare the dough, in a bowl, sift together the flour and baking powder. Make a well in the center. Add the lard or oil, if using, the dough starter, and the lukewarm water to the well and, using your fingers, work the mixture into a smooth dough.

5 Shape the dough into a ball and transfer to a lightly floured work surface. Using your palms, roll the dough into a log 20 inches (50 cm) long. Cut crosswise into 20 pieces each 1 inch (2.5 cm) long.

6 To make the buns, working with 1 piece of dough at a time, gently roll it into a ball, then, using your fingers or a rolling pin, flatten it into a 3-inch (7.5-cm) round that is thinner on the edges than in the center. Place about 2½ teaspoons of the filling in the center and pull the dough up and around the filling, pinching the edges together.

7 Cut out 20 pieces of waxed paper or parchment (baking) paper each 1½ inches (4 cm) square. Place a piece of paper beneath each bun. Place the buns in 2 steamer baskets, or on 2 racks of a metal steamer, spacing them ¾ inch (2 cm) apart to allow for expansion during steaming. If you do not have 2 baskets or a double-tiered steamer, cook the buns in 2 batches. Let rise for 10 minutes.

8 Bring water to a simmer in the steamer base. Place the steamer baskets or racks over the simmering water, cover, and steam until well expanded and dry on the surface, about 8 minutes. Serve at once.

Vegetarian Appetizer Platter

Sucai Lengpan • Western • China

Dried mushrooms to honor the guests, spicy cucumber to whet the appetite, and peanuts to absorb the wine: this is a typical appetizer for a Sichuan banquet or a full vegetarian dinner. In China, formal dinners encourage a chef's artistic flair and imagination. Ingredients are artistically shaped to depict the phoenix for good fortune, the peacock for success, and the crane for longevity. Experts can sculpt carrots into peonies, onions into chrysanthemums, or tomatoes into roses, to bloom beside the meticulously positioned tidbits.

MARINATED MUSHROOMS

6 large dried black mushrooms

1 teaspoon salt

1 tablespoon rice wine

1 tablespoon light soy sauce

1 teaspoon Asian sesame oil

1 teaspoon superfine (caster) sugar

1 teaspoon peeled and grated fresh ginger

BOILED PEANUTS

1 cup (5 oz/155 g) raw peanuts

2 teaspoons salt

SPICY CUCUMBERS

2 English (hothouse) cucumbers, about 9 oz (280 g) total weight

Salt for sprinkling

1½ tablespoons rice vinegar

1 tablespoon superfine (caster) sugar

½ teaspoon crushed garlic

1 small, hot red chile, seeded and finely julienned (optional)

Serves 4–8

1 To prepare the mushrooms, place them in a saucepan with water to cover and the salt. Bring to a boil over high heat, cover, reduce the heat to low, and simmer gently until plump and soft, about 20 minutes. Remove from the heat and allow the mushrooms to cool in the water. Drain well, trim off and discard the stems if necessary, and finely slice the caps. In a small bowl, combine the rice wine, soy sauce, sesame oil, sugar, and ginger and stir until the sugar is dissolved. Add the mushrooms, mix well, and set aside to marinate while you prepare the peanuts and cucumber. Drain the mushrooms just before serving.

2 To prepare the peanuts, place them in a small saucepan with water to cover and the salt. Bring to a boil over high heat, reduce the heat to low, and simmer, uncovered, for 10 minutes. Remove from the heat and allow the peanuts to cool in the water. Drain well and set aside.

3 To prepare the cucumbers, cut each cucumber lengthwise into slices ⅓ inch (9 mm) thick, then cut the slices into sticks 2 inches (5 cm) long and ⅓ inch (9 mm) wide. Place the cucumber sticks in a colander and sprinkle generously with salt. Let stand for about 15 minutes, then gently knead with your fingers to rub the salt into the sticks. Rinse lightly under running cold water.

4 In a bowl large enough to hold the cucumbers, stir together the vinegar, 1½ tablespoons water, and the sugar until the sugar is dissolved. Add the garlic and cucumbers, toss to mix, and marinate for 20 minutes, turning frequently. Add the chile, if using, and taste and adjust the seasoning with salt.

5 To serve, arrange the drained mushrooms, the peanuts, and the cucumbers in separate mounds on a platter. Serve at room temperature.

Dried Bombay Duck Fritters

Sookha Bomla nu Cutless • Maharashtra • India

These are delicious, and fairly easy to prepare once you have the Bombay duck. Look for it in Indian grocery stores specializing in dried fish.

4 dried Bombay ducks
(see sidebar, below)

½ cup (½ oz/15 g) fresh cilantro (fresh
coriander), leaves and tender stems

¼ cup (1 oz/30 g) unsweetened
flaked coconut

4 fresh hot green chiles, such as serrano

1 large clove garlic

½ teaspoon ground cumin

½ teaspoon ground coriander

½ teaspoon salt

1½ teaspoons white wine vinegar

Canola oil for frying

1 egg

1 cup (4 oz/125 g) dried bread crumbs

Tamarind Chutney (page 77; optional)

Serves 4

1 Soak the Bombay ducks in cold water to cover for 3 hours. Drain, squeezing out as much water as you can, and pat dry on kitchen towels. Remove the heads and tails and cut the fish in half crosswise. Using your fingers, carefully remove the center bone and discard. Place the fish in a shallow bowl.

2 In a food processor, blender, mortar, or grinding stone, combine the cilantro, coconut, chiles, garlic, cumin, ground coriander, salt, and vinegar. Process or pound until finely puréed. Rub the herb paste into the fish. Set aside to marinate for 10 minutes.

3 In a large frying pan over high heat, pour oil to a depth of ½ inch (12 mm) and heat to 350°F (180°C) on a deep-frying thermometer. Meanwhile, lightly beat the egg in a shallow dish, and spread the bread crumbs on a shallow plate. Dip each piece of fish into the egg, letting the excess drain off, then in the bread crumbs, pressing firmly to ensure they stick. When the oil is ready, gently slip a few pieces into it. Do not crowd the pan. Fry until golden brown, about 3 minutes. Using a slotted spoon, transfer to paper towels to drain. Keep warm in a low oven while you make the remaining fritters in the same way. Serve with the chutney, if desired.

BOMBAY DUCK

Bombay duck is a favorite delicacy of the people of Maharashtra, a state on the west-central coast of India. It is not poultry, as its name implies, but a variety of tropical fish, *Harpodon nehereus*, which is abundant in Bombay's coastal waters. Each fish is about 16 inches (40 cm) long, with a silver-white, semitranslucent body.

To catch its prey, the Bombay duck swims near the surface of the water.

In the opinion of the local people, the fish's shiny appearance creates the illusion of a diving duck, hence its name.

Also called *bombil* or *bomla*, Bombay duck is sometimes eaten fresh but is more often dried before cooking. Geometric rows of these fish, gutted, salted, and hung to dry, are a spectacular sight along the beaches. Fresh or dried, Bombay duck has a strong, distinct flavor that is an acquired taste for most. Parsis (followers of the Zoroastrian religion, most of whom live in Maharashtra) are particularly fond of Bombay duck. Parsis cook the fish in curries and fritters. To appreciate its flavor, crisp-fry the dried fish and serve it like bacon.

Savory Pastries with Vegetable Stuffing

Aloo Samosa • Punjab • India

Anyone who has ever eaten at an Indian restaurant has most likely tried—and fallen in love with—*samosas*. Generally served as an appetizer, *samosas* are crisp, flaky-crusted, fried pastries with fragrant fillings. The most popular are filled with potatoes and peas, although it is not unusual to find others stuffed with lamb, chicken, lentils, or nuts. Their seductive shape and flavor make them perfect finger food for cocktail parties. For variety, replace half of the baking potatoes with sweet potatoes or yams.

FILLING

3–4 baking potatoes, about 1¼ lb (625 g) total weight, unpeeled and quartered

1 tablespoon ground coriander

1 teaspoon cayenne pepper

2 teaspoons fresh lemon juice

½ teaspoon ground turmeric

2 teaspoons salt, or to taste

2 tablespoons canola oil

1 cup (5 oz/155 g) cooked fresh or thawed frozen green peas

1 teaspoon dried mint, crushed

PASTRY

2 cups (10 oz/315 g) all-purpose (plain) flour, plus more for dusting

1 teaspoon salt, or to taste

½ teaspoon baking powder

¼ cup (2 fl oz/60 ml) canola oil

⅔ cup (5 fl oz/160 ml) water

¼ cup (1 oz/30 g) cornstarch (cornflour) dissolved in ½ cup (4 fl oz/125 ml) water

Canola oil for deep-frying

Tamarind Chutney (page 77; optional) or Mint Chutney (page 77; optional)

Makes 16 pastries; serves 8

1 To make the filling, boil the potatoes until very soft, about 15 minutes. Drain and, when cool enough to handle, peel and place in a bowl. Using a potato masher, mash until finely crushed. (Do not use a food processor, as this will make the potatoes gluey.) Add the ground coriander, cayenne pepper, lemon juice, turmeric, salt, and oil. Mix well.

2 Preheat a large nonstick frying pan over high heat until very hot. Add the potato mixture, reduce the heat to low, and dry-fry, stirring, until the spices are fragrant and the potatoes are lightly fried, about 8 minutes. Return the potato mixture to the same bowl. Fold in the peas and mint and set aside to cool completely.

3 To make the pastry, in a large bowl, combine the flour, salt, and baking powder. In a measuring cup, stir the oil into the water. Add the liquid to the flour, a little a time, until the dough comes together in a mass that can be kneaded. (Do not add more liquid than necessary; you might have up to 2 tablespoons of oiled water left over.) Turn out onto a floured work surface and knead for 1 minute. Cover with a cloth or wrap in plastic wrap and let rest at room temperature for 30 minutes.

4 On a floured surface, roll the dough into a rope about 18 inches (45 cm) long, and cut into 8 equal pieces. Form each piece into a ball and then flatten it into a patty. Working with 1 patty at a time, roll out into a 6-inch (15-cm) circle, dusting often with flour. Cut the circle in half. Brush half of the straight edge of 1 semicircle with the cornstarch mixture. Form a cone by bringing the halves of the straight edge together; pinch the seam to seal. Holding the cone with the open end toward you, stuff it with 3 heaping teaspoons of the filling. Brush the edges of the open end of the cone with the cornstarch mixture and pinch the edges together to enclose the filling. Repeat with the remaining semicircle and then with the patties.

5 In a *karhai* (page 72), deep-fryer, or large, deep pan, pour oil to a depth of 3 inches (7.5 cm) and heat to 350°F (180°C) on a deep-frying thermometer. When the oil is ready, gently slip the pastries, a few at a time, into the oil. Do not crowd the pan or the *samosas* will not fry evenly. Fry, turning often, until golden, about 5 minutes. Using a slotted spoon, transfer to paper towels to drain. Keep warm in a low oven while you fry the remaining pastries in the same way.

6 Serve the *samosas* warm or at room temperature, either by themselves or with the chutneys, if desired.

FRANCE

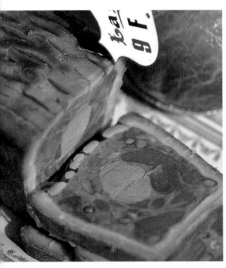

In France, the transition from the work world to the private, pleasurable world of the table is an important one. It starts with the aperitif as well as the first course that accompanies it. These preludes to the main course let the participants relax and ease into a slower pace. Food is eaten leisurely, with time and emphasis given to conversation and conviviality. Business and work are put aside, and politics, theater, or other subjects take their place. It is not only good for the digestion, but, as the French will tell you, it is also part of the good life of the French table.

So what begins a French meal? The choices are varied. One might have a plate of *charcuterie*, a composed salad, a selection of shellfish, an omelet, a seasonal vegetable dish, a tart, crepes, a quiche, or a soup. Beginning with *charcuterie* usually means tasting the local meat products. Terrines, pâtés, rillettes, hams, sausages—all prepared in dozens of different ways, sometimes wrapped in a flaky crust or glossed with aspic—are constructed using duck, pork, wild game, rabbit, vegetables, even fish. In small family-run restaurants and bistros or traditionally minded households, these are often prepared from recipes handed down through the generations, providing a taste of both *terroir* and the gastronomic history of the region. In Rouen, the house specialty might be duck pâté with Armagnac; in the

south, *pâté maison* with juniper berries and marc; in the Basque country a *jambon du pays* rubbed with the hot pepper of Espellete; and in the Southwest, a foie gras terrine, made from the livers of locally raised geese.

Many restaurants along the coasts of France are known for their fresh *coquillage*, proudly displayed near their entrances on beds of crushed ice. Oysters, shrimp, crab, tiny clams, sea urchins, and whelks all figure among the choices, depending on the season. Some of the signature seafood dishes include mussels steamed in a splash of white wine and sautéed clams perfumed with garlic. In Burgundy, far from the sea, there is nevertheless a specialty akin to shellfish— the renowned Burgundian escargots, tender snails served in melted butter laden with minced garlic and parsley. The same region

is home to the country's famed cheese puffs, rich *gougères* made with *choux* pastry.

Served hot or at room temperature, tarts, crepes, and quiches are among the most tempting of French appetizers. A favorite tart of the south, pizza-like *pissaladière*, is thickly spread with a golden confit of onions and topped with anchovy fillets and locally produced olives. In the north, a comparable tart is filled with a buttery mass of leeks dotted with cheese. In both regions, the simple principle is the same: bread dough is rolled flat, spread with vegetables that contain enough natural sugars to caramelize slightly, finished with a complementary toppings. Other tarts are more like pies, shaped in a tin and spread with a local cheese—Cantal in the Auvergne, Beaufort in Savoy, goat cheese in the Indre—then topped with vegetables, such as sliced tomatoes. Quiches combine a savory milk-and-egg custard with ham, cheese, shellfish, or vegetables in nearly infinite variations.

Along the seacoasts and hillsides of Provence, simple combinations are among the most loved: an appetizer plate of air-cured sausage, a few olives, hard-boiled eggs, roasted red peppers, and artichokes, for example, or a slice of rabbit or hare pâté with vinegary cornichons and crusty bread. Equally popular is a plate of grated or sliced raw vegetables (*crudités*) with either vinaigrette or a small bowl of creamy *aïoli*, the pungent, garlic-rich, olive oil–based

mayonnaise that is one of the treasures of this region. Provence also cultivates some of the country's most dazzling produce, showcased in cooked vegetable dishes such as tarts dotted with cherry tomatoes, ripe goat cheese, and fresh basil. Delicate, yellow zucchini flowers, which remain fresh for only a few hours after being picked, are quickly fried and eaten hot with just a sprinkle of sea salt. Heartier starters such as fried mushrooms, zucchini, and eggplants are common as well.

However, the Provençal vegetable starters par excellence are *les petits farcis*, served primarily in the Alpes-Maritimes, the Var, and the Bouches-du-Rhône. Little hollowed-out rounds of eggplant, zucchini, and tomato are mounded with stuffings of diced vegetables and meat finished with a drizzle of olive oil and sprinkle of fresh parsley.

Numerous dips are also part of the southern appetizer menu, including the mouthwatering purée of roasted eggplant known as *caviar d'aubergines* and *anchoïade*, the Niçoise version of the anchovy-laced Italian *bagna cauda*. Alongside these dips can often be found a sheet of the tender, crepelike *socca*, a thin flatbread made from chickpea flour that is fried on large griddles at every outdoor market near Nice. From north to south, French tables display the flavors of the season, a respect for the region's culinary history, and a national passion for dining.

Left: Gothic ornamentation frames a casual café in Aix-en-Provence. Such anachronistic scenes are commonplace in this city, whose history spans twenty-two centuries. Today, Roman ruins mix with Romanesque splendor, and medieval mingles with modern. **Above, left:** Colorfully printed table linens, in profuse array at a market in Arles, are bordered with motifs inspired by two eminent elements of the landscape, the olive and the sunflower. **Above, right:** Vine-ripened tomatoes, popular throughout France, are particularly prevalent in Provençal cooking, where any dish described as *à la provençale* comes with the promise of tomatoes, garlic, and olive oil.

Raw Vegetables with Dips

Crudités • Provence • France

A large platter of attractively arranged raw vegetables is found on dining tables throughout France, but the vegetables are often treated only to a simple bath of oil and vinegar or a bland mayonnaise. In Provence, the lively dips of the region, most notably aioli—garlic mayonnaise—and *anchoïade*—anchovy sauce—elevate this simple array to something extraordinary. This classic dish evokes at a rustic wooden table in the shade of an olive tree under the vivid blue sky of the Mediterranean overhead.

AIOLI

3–6 cloves garlic

3 egg yolks (see page 221)

2 teaspoons Dijon mustard

1¼–1¾ cups (10–14 fl oz/310–430 ml) olive oil

Salt and freshly ground white pepper to taste

White wine vinegar or fresh lemon juice to taste

ANCHOÏADE

1 cup (8 fl oz/250 ml) olive oil

6 salt-packed anchovies, about 4 oz (125 g) total weight, filleted and rinsed (page 219)

3 cloves garlic, crushed

1 tablespoon Dijon mustard

2 tablespoons red wine vinegar

12 baby artichokes, no more than 1½ inches (4 cm) in diameter, trimmed (page 219) and halved lengthwise

16 baby carrots, peeled

3 heads Belgian endive (chicory/witloof), leaves separated

3 celery stalks, halved lengthwise, then cut crosswise into 2-inch (5-cm) pieces

1 small head cauliflower, divided into florets

1 bunch baby radishes, trimmed

2 red and/or green bell peppers (capsicums), seeded and cut lengthwise into strips ½ inch (12 mm) wide

18–20 fresh white button mushrooms, brushed clean and stem ends trimmed

Serves 6–8

1 To make the aioli with a handheld electric mixer or a wire whisk, mash the garlic, using the smaller amount for a lighter flavor and cutting away any green sprout visible at the center of each clove. Place the garlic in a small bowl and add the egg yolks and mustard. Beat for a few moments until blended. Begin adding the oil drop by drop, beating continuously. Once an emulsion forms, add the oil in a very fine, steady stream, continuing to beat until the aioli has thickened to the desired consistency. It should be thick enough to cling to the vegetables. The more oil used, the thicker the result. Season with salt, white pepper, and vinegar or lemon juice, then cover and refrigerate until serving. You should have 1½–2 cups (12–16 fl oz/375–500 ml).

2 To make the aioli in a food processor, coarsely chop the garlic, place in the food processor, and pulse to chop as finely as possible. Add the egg yolks and mustard and pulse again briefly. With the motor running, add the oil in a very fine, steady stream, then proceed as directed for mixer method above.

3 To make the *anchoïade*, in a small saucepan over low heat, combine ½ cup (4 fl oz/125 ml) of the olive oil and the anchovies and cook slowly for 15 minutes to blend the flavors. Remove from the heat and let cool. To make the *anchoïde* by hand, using a whisk, beat the mixture until a paste forms. Add the garlic, mustard, and vinegar and whisk to combine. Add the remaining ½ cup (4 fl oz/125 ml) olive oil slowly at first, then in a fine stream, whisking continuously. Cover and refrigerate until needed. You should have about 1½ cups (12 fl oz/375 ml).

4 To make the *anchoïde* in a food processor, transfer the cooled anchovy-oil mixture to the work bowl and process to a paste, then proceed as directed for the hand method above, adding the second half of the oil with the processor running.

5 Arrange the vegetables on 1 or more large platter(s). Place the bowls of *anchoïade* and aioli in the center of the platter(s) or alongside. Serve at once.

Little Olive Pastries

Petits Pâtés aux Olives • Provence • France

This dressy puff pastry appetizer is modeled after one served in the sophisticated beach resort of Saint-Tropez, with its clutch of great restaurants.

1⅓ cups (6½ oz/200 g) large, brine-cured black olives, plus chopped olives for garnish (optional)

3 tablespoons olive oil

1 small round of mature goat cheese, about 3½ oz (105 g), grated

1 tablespoon finely chopped fresh rosemary, plus 6 small sprigs

1 lb (500 g) good-quality purchased puff pastry, thawed if frozen

1 egg, lightly beaten

Serves 6

1 Pit the olives, then finely mince the flesh. Place in a bowl and stir in the olive oil with a fork. Add the goat cheese and stir to mash the mixture lightly. Add the chopped rosemary and mix well. Preheat the oven to 375°F (190°C). Lightly oil a baking sheet.

2 On a lightly floured work surface, roll out the pastry about ¼ inch (6 mm) thick. Using a sharp knife and small plates as templates, cut out six 5-inch (13-cm) rounds, then cut out six 4¼-inch (10.5-cm) rounds. Transfer the small rounds to the prepared baking sheet.

3 Divide the olive mixture among the pastry rounds on the baking sheet, spooning it into the center of each round. Brush the edges of the small rounds with the beaten egg, and then cover each with a large pastry round, pressing the edges together firmly with your fingers. Brush the tops with the remaining egg.

4 Bake the pastries until golden brown, about 20 minutes. Transfer to a wire rack and let cool slightly. Serve warm. Garnish each with the chopped olives, if desired, and a small rosemary sprig.

OLIVES

With its gnarled, twisted trunk and its narrow silver leaves blowing in the wind, the olive tree is a prevailing image of the Provençal landscape. It lives in backyards, in the wild, in hillside pastures, and in commercial groves, particularly in the Var, the Vaucluse, and the Bouches-du-Rhône.

Its fruit, bitter at birth, yields first the green olive, then the black. The unripe green olives, harvested around November, must be taken from the tree, and then bathed in lye and cured in salt to render them palatable. Ripe, black olives eventually fall from the tree, but in December and January, farmers can be seen manning small tractors fitted with large rubber "arms" that grasp and shake the trunks, releasing the fruits onto large cloths spread beneath the branches. Black olives need no alkaline treatment. They can be simply sun-dried or salt-cured for the table.

At farmers' markets in olive country, you will see dozens of varieties. Green, fleshy *picholines* sit next to green, pointed *lugnes*. You may find black Kalamatas, large *violettes* from Tunisia, green Sévillanes, and the aptly named huge *mamouths*. Some, like the *tanche*, are better known by their place of origin (Nyons), as are the Niçoise, their tiny shape and succulent flesh perfect for topping salads and tarts.

Often there are also pitted, smashed, bruised, and cracked olives on display, suitable for both eating and for cooking in classic daubes and ragouts. Then there are those with flavorings, strictly destined for the aperitif or buffet table. These olives are variously marinated in oil; peppered or mixed with chopped chile or minced herbs; tossed with garlic and capers, garlic and orange peel, or thyme, red peppers, onion, and capers; or even "smeared with anchovy."

Also offered to tempt the palate are large bowls of much-loved local specialties: olives *à la façon grecque* (braised with stock and lemon juice), *à la camarguaise* (with *crème d'anchois* and garlic), and *à la sicilienne* (mixed with lemon).

Salad of Oven-Dried Tomatoes

Salade de Tomates Séchées au Four • Provence • France

Traditionally the work of the sun, drying tomatoes in the oven yields a softer, moister product. Store the tomatoes, covered and refrigerated, for up to 1 week.

OVEN-DRIED TOMATOES

12–15 plum (Roma) tomatoes

2 teaspoons sugar

Salt and freshly ground pepper to taste

¼ cup (2 fl oz/60 ml) olive oil

3 shallots, finely chopped

2 cloves garlic, finely chopped

3–4 tablespoons olive oil

About 2 teaspoons red wine vinegar

8–10 fresh basil leaves

Salt and freshly ground coarse pepper to taste

Makes 24–45 tomato pieces; serves 6

1 To dry the tomatoes, oil a large baking sheet. Halve the tomatoes lengthwise. If they are large, make the first cut off center, then cut the larger piece in two. Trim away the cores. Place the pieces, cut side up, on the prepared baking sheet.

2 Sprinkle the sugar evenly over the tomatoes, and then season with salt and pepper and drizzle with the olive oil. Place in the oven, turn on the oven to 150°F (65°C), and leave in the oven for 8–9 hours or up to overnight. The tomatoes will be semidried. If you are short of time, set the oven at 225°F (110°C) and reduce the cooking time to 3–4 hours. Check occasionally to make sure that the tomatoes are not baking but drying.

3 Time the tomatoes to come out of the oven 30 minutes before the salad is to be served. Place in a large bowl and add the shallots and garlic. Moisten with olive oil and drizzle with vinegar. Tear or coarsely slice the basil leaves and toss in gently. Add salt, if needed, and pepper and serve.

Swiss Chard Omelet

La Trouchia • Provence • France

La trouchia is a style of vegetable omelet unique to the Nice area, where it is always made with Swiss chard. It is similar to the Italian frittata and the Provençal *tian*.

6 tablespoons (3 fl oz/90 ml) olive oil

1 yellow onion, finely chopped

1 lb (500 g) Swiss chard, stems removed and leaves coarsely shredded

7 eggs

1 scant cup (3½ oz/105 g) grated Parmesan cheese

1 clove garlic, finely chopped

2 tablespoons chopped fresh flat-leaf (Italian) parsley

Salt and freshly ground pepper to taste

8–10 small black olives

Serves 4–6

1 In a nonstick frying pan over medium heat, warm 3 tablespoons of the olive oil. Add the onion and sauté until softened, about 1 minute. Add the Swiss chard and cook, stirring, just until the chard has wilted. Reduce the heat to low and cook, stirring often, until tender, 5–6 minutes total. Set aside to cool.

2 In a bowl, using a fork, beat the eggs until blended. Stir in half of the Parmesan cheese and all of the garlic and parsley. Season with salt and pepper, then add the cooled chard mixture and stir briefly to mix.

3 Wipe out the frying pan with a paper towel and return to low heat. Add the remaining 3 tablespoons olive oil. When the oil is hot, add the egg mixture and stir gently with the fork. Stop stirring as soon as the eggs start to set, then allow the pan to rest on the heat until the eggs start to become firm, 3–4 minutes. Place a plate over the pan and, holding the plate and pan together, invert them and lift off the pan. Slip the omelet back into the pan and return to low heat. Sprinkle the remaining Parmesan evenly over the top and cook, without disturbing, for 2–3 minutes.

4 Slide the omelet from the pan onto a serving plate and dot the top with the olives. Cut into wedges and serve at once.

Upside-Down Tart with Oven-Dried Tomatoes

Tarte Renversée aux Tomates Séchées • Provence • France

This tart, a variation on the Norman specialty *tarte Tatin*, exploits the marvelously intense flavor of fresh tomatoes that have been dried in the oven.

10 oz (315 g) good-quality purchased puff pastry, thawed if frozen

3 tablespoons unsalted butter

1 tablespoon olive oil

1 tablespoon sugar

15 shallots, peeled

½ cup (4 fl oz/125 ml) water

Leaves from 1 fresh thyme sprig

Salt and freshly ground pepper to taste

10–12 oven-dried tomato halves (page 121)

Serves 6

1 On a lightly floured work surface, roll out the puff pastry to an even ⅛ inch (3 mm) thickness. Cut into a round about 10½ inches (26.5 cm) in diameter. Place in the freezer for 15–20 minutes.

2 Preheat the oven to 400°F (200°C). Select an ovenproof frying pan 10 inches (25 cm) in diameter. Place over high heat and melt the butter with the olive oil. Add the sugar and stir for 40–50 seconds. Add the shallots and toss for 30 seconds. Add the water, cover, reduce the heat to low, and simmer until evaporated, about 5 minutes. Let cool completely.

3 Distribute the shallots evenly in the pan. Sprinkle with the thyme, salt, and pepper. Place the tomatoes, skin side down, among the shallots. Remove the pastry round from the freezer and lay it over the pan. Quickly trim the edges to the size of the pan. Make 4 knife slits in the pastry and bake until browned, 20–25 minutes.

4 Remove from the oven, cover with a round serving plate slightly larger than the diameter of the pan, and invert the plate and pan together, releasing the tart onto the plate. Carefully lift the pan off the tart. Cut into wedges to serve.

Zucchini Flower Fritters

Beignets de Fleurs de Courgettes • Provence • France

Delicate fritters made with zucchini flowers are associated with Provence. A visit to the region during the spring would be incomplete without sampling them.

1 cup (5 oz/155 g) all-purpose (plain) flour

2 eggs, separated

1 tablespoon olive oil

1 cup (8 fl oz/250 ml) milk

30 zucchini (courgette) flowers

Peanut oil or grapeseed oil for deep-frying

Salt to taste

3 cups (24 fl oz/750 ml) Tomato Sauce (page 139), heated (optional)

Serves 6

1 Place the flour in a bowl. Make a well in the center and add the egg yolks, the olive oil, and 3 tablespoons of the milk. Whisk the ingredients in the well until blended. Stirring constantly, incorporate the flour a little at a time. Add the remaining milk, a little at a time, continuing to stir until the batter is smooth. Let stand for 1 hour.

2 Remove the pistils from the zucchini flowers. Rinse the flowers if needed, then pat dry.

3 In a bowl, whisk the egg whites until firm peaks form. Carefully fold the egg whites into the batter.

4 Pour oil to a depth of 3 inches (7.5 cm) in a deep saucepan and heat to 325°F (165°C) on a deep-frying thermometer. Dip the flowers, two at a time, into the batter and lower gently into the hot oil. Fry in batches, 4–6 at a time, until golden, 1½–2 minutes. Using a wire skimmer or slotted spoon, transfer to paper towels to drain. Keep warm in a low oven while you fry the remaining fritters.

5 Arrange the fritters on a platter, sprinkle with salt, and serve at once. Alternatively, spread a small pool of the tomato sauce on warmed individual plates. Arrange the fritters on top of the sauce, sprinkle with salt, and serve.

Wild Mushroom Omelet

Omelette aux Champignons Sauvages • Southwestern • France

In the Périgord, as in other areas of France, the fall mushroom season is eagerly awaited. When it arrives, locals can be spotted with baskets on their arms, even in the rain, carrying home their forest finds. At least once, usually early in the season, wild mushrooms, such as the cèpes and chanterelles that are particularly abundant in the region, are made into a simple and enticingly savory omelet.

3½ tablespoons unsalted butter

½ shallot, minced

½ lb (250 g) fresh cèpe mushrooms or a mixture of cèpes and chanterelles, brushed clean and thinly sliced

½ teaspoon fresh thyme leaves

¾ teaspoon salt

¾ teaspoon freshly ground pepper

6 eggs

1 tablespoon minced fresh flat-leaf (Italian) parsley

Serves 3 or 4

1 In a small frying pan over medium heat, melt 2 tablespoons of the butter. Add the shallot and sauté until translucent, 1–2 minutes. Add the mushrooms and thyme and sauté until soft, 2–3 minutes. Sprinkle with ¼ teaspoon *each* of the salt and pepper. Set aside. In a bowl, whisk the eggs with the remaining ½ teaspoon *each* salt and pepper until frothy.

2 In a 12-inch (30-cm) frying pan over medium heat, melt the remaining 1½ tablespoons butter. Add the eggs and stir until they begin to thicken, just a few seconds. Reduce the heat to low. As the eggs set along the sides of the pan, lift the edges with a spatula and tip the pan to let the uncooked egg run underneath. Cook until the omelet is set and the bottom is lightly golden, 30–40 seconds longer.

3 Using a slotted spoon, transfer the mushrooms to the omelet, covering half of it to within about 1 inch (2.5 cm) of the edge. Sprinkle with half of the parsley. Pulling the pan up and toward you, and using a spatula, flip the uncovered half over the covered half. Cook until the inner edges are slightly firm, another 30–40 seconds. Transfer to a warmed platter and sprinkle with the remaining parsley. Cut into wedges and serve at once.

BEGINNING THE MEAL WITH CHEESE

We tend to think of cheese coming at the end of a French repast, but it is surprising how often it is used to begin (*pour commencer*) a meal, either with aperitifs or as an element of the first course. From a long habit of convenience, goat herders in Provence who made their own cheese from their milk would put bits left over from larger rounds into a jar of olive oil. They were then spread on toasts for aperitif time. Today one now sees little individual cheeses at the market packed in olive oil, labeled *pour l'apéro*— "for the aperitif." *Gougères*, cheese-flavored puffs made with *pâte à choux*, are another way cheese is presented as a partner to aperitifs. Cubes of a special local cheese may also be served.

A favorite first course on the French menu is a disk of warm goat cheese served atop a well-dressed salad of frisée, a perfect marriage of flavors and textures. Cheese appears in tarts and quiches, too, as an element in composed salads, and in sauces napping elegant first-course crepes or quenelles.

Fresh Tomato Tart with Roquefort

Tarte au Roquefort et Tomates • Southwestern • France

Roquefort is an excellent melting cheese, and here it complements the sweetness of a buttery crust and fresh tomatoes with its tangy bite.

PASTRY

1 cup (5 oz/155 g) all-purpose (plain) flour

½ teaspoon salt

⅓ cup (3 oz/90 g) chilled unsalted butter, cut into ½-inch (12-mm) chunks

3 tablespoons ice water

FILLING

6 oz (185 g) Roquefort cheese, at room temperature

2 tablespoons half-and-half (half cream) or milk

2 tomatoes, sliced ¼ inch (6 mm) thick

½ teaspoon freshly ground pepper

½ teaspoon minced fresh thyme

1 teaspoon extra-virgin olive oil

Serves 6–8

1 To make the pastry, in a bowl, stir together the flour and salt. Using a pastry blender or 2 knives, cut in the butter until pea-sized balls form. Add the ice water 1 tablespoon at a time while turning the dough lightly with a fork and then with your fingertips. (Do not overwork, or it will become tough.) Gather the crumbly dough into a ball, wrap in plastic wrap, and refrigerate for 15 minutes.

2 Preheat the oven to 400°F (200°C). On a floured work surface, roll out the dough into a round about 10½ inches (26.5 cm) in diameter and about ¼ inch (6 mm) thick. Carefully transfer to a 9-inch (23-cm) tart pan with a removable bottom and ½-inch (12-mm) sides. Pat into the bottom and sides and trim the edge even with the rim.

3 To make the filling, in a small bowl, using a fork, mash the cheese together with the half-and-half or milk. Spread evenly over the bottom of the pastry. Cover with the tomato slices in a tightly packed single layer. Sprinkle with the pepper, thyme, and olive oil.

4 Bake until the crust is lightly golden and the tomatoes have collapsed, 20–25 minutes. Transfer the tart to a wire rack and let stand for about 30 minutes. Serve warm or at room temperature.

Sautéed Garlic Clams

Tellines à l'Arlésienne • Provence • France

On a stretch of sandy Mediterranean beach near Arles, *tellines*, tiny clams not much larger than the nail on one's little finger, are found. Sautéed in olive oil with garlic and parsley and served in their shells, they are an aperitif tradition at cafés and homes throughout the area, and they may also appear in larger quantities as a first course.

1 lb (500 g) small clams
or 2 lb (1 kg) mussels

¼ cup (2 fl oz/60 ml) extra-virgin olive oil

4 cloves garlic, minced

¼ cup (⅓ oz/10 g) minced fresh flat-leaf
(Italian) parsley

Serves 3 or 4 as an appetizer,
2 as a first course

1 Rinse the clams or mussels thoroughly under running cold water to remove any grit, sand, or dirt, scrubbing with a brush if necessary. If using mussels, clip any beards that are evident with scissors. Discard any clams or mussels that do not close to the touch. Roughly dry the shellfish with a towel.

2 Select a frying pan large enough to hold all the clams or mussels in no more than 2 scant layers. Place over medium heat and add the olive oil. When hot, add the garlic and sauté for a minute or two, but do not let it brown. Add the clams or mussels and the parsley to the pan, turning the shellfish with a spoon to coat them with the oil. Cook just until the shells open, 2–3 minutes.

3 Transfer the clams or mussels and their juices to a platter or individual plates. Discard any shellfish that failed to open. Serve at once.

Snails with Garlic, Butter, and Parsley

Escargots à la Bourguignonne • Burgundy and Lyon • France

Large or small, the snails of France are a unique delicacy, though for some fans, the snails are really an excuse to eat lots of melted garlic and parsley butter, scooped up with bread. Canned snails and packages of large shells are readily available, as are special dishes with indentations for each snail, where the butter pools as it melts. Special tongs for holding shells and a small two-pronged fork for digging out snails are provided for each diner.

1 cup (8 oz/250 g) salted butter, at room
temperature

6 cloves garlic, minced

½ cup (¾ oz/20 g) minced fresh flat-leaf
(Italian) parsley

1 teaspoon freshly ground pepper

4 dozen canned snails, drained

4 dozen snail shells

Serves 4

1 Preheat the oven to 450°F (230°C).

2 In a bowl, combine the butter, garlic, parsley, and pepper and mix thoroughly with a wooden spoon.

3 Slip a snail into each shell, pushing it toward the back with a small spoon. Then tuck in a plug of the seasoned butter, about 2 teaspoons, pushing it deep into the shell and smoothing it at the opening.

4 Arrange the snails, the butter facing up, on snail plates with individual indentations, and place the plates on a baking sheet. Alternatively, pack them snugly together in a shallow baking dish.

5 Bake until the snails are hot and the butter is beginning to melt, 10–12 minutes. If using snail plates, put them on individual serving plates. If the snails have been cooked in a baking dish, transfer them to small plates or shallow bowls, being careful not to lose any of the garlicky butter. Serve at once.

Artichokes with Shrimp

Artichauts aux Crevettes • Brittany • France

In Brittany, the huge, round Camus variety of artichoke is used for this dish. It is meaty, intensely flavorful, and, because of its size, an excellent candidate for stuffing.

4 large artichokes

1 teaspoon sea salt

4 teaspoons Dijon mustard

1 teaspoon extra-dry vermouth

½ cup (4 fl oz/125 ml) mayonnaise, homemade or good-quality purchased

1 teaspoon minced fresh rosemary

½ teaspoon salt

½ teaspoon freshly ground pepper

1 lb (500 g) bay shrimp or other small cooked peeled shrimp

1½ tablespoons minced fresh flat-leaf (Italian) parsley

Serves 4

1 Trim off the stem of each artichoke even with the bottom and snap off any damaged outer leaves. Put the artichokes in a large pot and add water to a depth of 4 inches (10 cm). Sprinkle with the sea salt and bring to a boil over high heat. Cover, reduce the heat to low, and simmer until the base of the artichokes can be easily pierced with the tines of a fork, about 45 minutes. Using tongs, transfer the artichokes to a colander and invert to drain. Let stand until cool enough to handle.

2 Cut off the upper one-fourth of each artichoke and discard the prickly trimmings. Using a spoon, scoop out the center leaves and the furry choke from each artichoke to create a bowl. Wrap each artichoke in plastic wrap and chill for about 2 hours.

3 In a bowl, combine the mustard and vermouth and stir until well blended. Add the mayonnaise, rosemary, salt, and pepper and stir to combine. Add all but 12 of the shrimp and turn gently to coat evenly. Fill the center of each artichoke, dividing the mixture evenly. Rewrap in plastic wrap and chill for at least 1 hour or for up to 3 hours.

4 Garnish each artichoke with 3 of the reserved shrimp and sprinkle with the parsley. Serve chilled.

SEA SALT

In France, the ancient practice of gathering salt from the sea (*sel marin*) continues. *Le sel de Guérande*, harvested from the salt basins in the area of Guérande in Brittany, is made up of medium-to-large, irregularly shaped crystals, grayish ivory and still slightly moist from the sea. Sometimes called *sel gris* because of its color, the salt has a light, briny taste. Sea salt is also gathered from the salt basins of Ile de Ré, off the Atlantic coast near La Rochelle, and in Provence from the basins of the Camargue and Aigues-Mortes.

The most valued of all the natural sea salts is *fleur de sel*, which forms on the surface of the sea only on certain very dry, hot days when the wind is blowing in a particular fashion. It is scraped up by hand using a special raking tool called a *lousse*. The tiny crystals of *fleur de sel* are very fine and delicate, as is its flavor. One of the most popular uses of this rare salt is as a finishing salt sprinkled on completed dishes for its tiny burst of flavor and texture.

Veal Pâté with Dried Apricots and Hazelnuts

Terrine de Veau aux Fruits Confits • Provence • France

The *charcuteries* of France tend to make similar pâtés no matter where the shop, whereas restaurant chefs like to tamper with the classics to make their own creative variations. This recipe captures the style of *pâté de campagne*, a very moist pork-and-veal terrine studded with apricots, found in a tiny restaurant near Apt.

1 large or 2 small pork tenderloins, about ½ lb (250 g) total weight

1½ lb (750 g) pork fatback

3 shallots, sliced

2 or 3 cloves garlic, sliced

½ cup (4 fl oz/125 ml) Madeira, equal parts Madeira and port, or equal parts Madeira and brandy

1½ lb (750 g) ground (minced) pork

1½ lb (750 g) ground (minced) veal

1 lb (500 g) pork or veal liver, cut into cubes

Leaves from 3 large fresh thyme sprigs or ½ teaspoon dried thyme

1 egg

2 tablespoons salt

Freshly ground pepper to taste

4 bay leaves

Handful of pistachios, hazelnuts (filberts), or a combination

About 15 dried apricots

Boiling water, as needed

Cornichons, for serving

Coarse country bread, sliced, for serving

Makes 1 terrine; yields 15–18 slices

1 Cut the pork tenderloin(s) into long, thin pieces about ¼ inch (6 mm) wide and the length of the tenderloin. Cut about 3 oz (90 g) of the pork fatback in the same manner. Place all the batons in a dish, scatter the shallots and garlic over the top, and add the wine or wine and brandy. Cover and marinate for 2 hours at room temperature or up to overnight in the refrigerator.

2 Drain the meat, reserving the liquid. Retrieve the shallots and garlic from the sieve. Set the meat and the liquid aside separately. Pass the shallots, garlic, remaining pork fatback, ground pork and veal, and liver through a meat grinder fitted with the medium disk, capturing them in a large bowl. Add the thyme, egg, salt, and pepper and pour in the reserved liquid. Mix well with your hands.

3 Position a rack in the middle or lower third of the oven and preheat to 375°F (190°C).

4 Select a lidded earthenware or porcelain terrine with a capacity of about 2 quarts (2 l). Place 2 of the bay leaves on the center of the bottom of the terrine. Working your way up the height of the terrine, assemble the pâté by beginning with a ¾-inch (2-cm) layer of the ground meat mixture. Continue adding the ground meat mixture, interspersing it with the batons of meat and pork fatback and scattering the nuts and apricots here and there as you proceed. End with a ¾-inch (2-cm) layer of ground meat, mounding it attractively.

5 Press the remaining 2 bay leaves onto the top of the ground meat, placing them at a diagonal. Cover the terrine with aluminum foil, prick the foil all over with the tip of a knife, and place the lid on the terrine.

6 Place the terrine into a large, deep baking dish. It should fit snugly. Fill the baking dish three-fourths full with boiling water. Carefully transfer to the oven rack, then pour in additional boiling water to fill the dish as full as possible. Bake for 1½–1¾ hours. Turn off the oven, leave the oven door ajar, and let the terrine cool in the oven until the water is no longer too hot to handle. If you prefer the top of your pâté caramelized, remove the lid and aluminum foil for the last 20 minutes of cooking, replacing it before leaving the terrine in the oven to cool.

7 When the pâté has cooled, remove the lid and foil and sponge the side and bottom of the vessel to remove any grease. Rinse the lid and then re-cover the terrine. Refrigerate for 2–3 days before serving.

8 Remove the pâté from the refrigerator. Set out the cornichons in a small bowl. Cut the pâté into slices about ½ inch (12 mm) thick and serve with the bread slices.

Chickpea Flour Crepe

La Socca • Provence • France

In Provence in the past, chickpea flour was more common than it is today, and this pancakelike snack was once a greater part of the family diet. Today, *socca* lives on in street stalls and marketplaces as a favorite early-morning food of the fishermen, laborers, and shoppers who regularly purchase a hearty piece of it, wrapped in a paper napkin. The chickpea flour gives *socca* its unique flavor and texture, while the sizzling-hot surface on which the crepes are cooked delivers the appetizing bubbles and charred spots.

1⅔ cups (8 oz/250 g) chickpea (garbanzo bean) flour

3 tablespoons olive oil

1 teaspoon salt

Freshly ground pepper to taste

Serves 4

1 Put 2 cups (16 fl oz/500 ml) water in a bowl, then whisk in the chickpea flour, olive oil, and salt, continuing to whisk until no lumps remain. Let stand for 30 minutes.

2 Place a 12-by-16-inch (30-by-40-cm) heavy-duty baking sheet in the oven. Preheat the oven to 500°F (260°C).

3 Remove the baking sheet from the oven, brush with oil, then quickly pour the batter onto the sheet. It should be about ⅛ inch (3 mm) thick.

4 Burst any bubbles in the batter with the tip of a knife. Turn the oven setting to broil (grill) and slip the baking sheet under the broiler (grill) about 5 inches (13 cm) from the heat source.

5 Cook until the entire surface of the crepe is golden and is lightly charred in places, 2–3 minutes. Quickly transfer to a cutting board and cut into squares or rectangles. Dust generously with pepper and serve at once.

Eggplant and Goat Cheese Sandwiches

Sandwiches d'Aubergine et Chèvre • Provence • France

This colorful starter combines the Provençal love for two local products, eggplant and goat cheese. Look for semimature goat cheese, as it slices easily.

3 globe eggplants (aubergines), each 2–3 inches (5–7.5 cm) in diameter

Salt

About ¾ cup (4 oz/125 g) all-purpose (plain) flour

Olive oil for frying and brushing eggplant

6 very firm, very round tomatoes

20–24 fresh basil leaves, shredded, plus 6 sprigs for garnish

10 oz (315 g) semimature goat cheese (see note), cut into slices ⅓ inch (9 mm) thick

Extra-virgin olive oil for serving

Serves 6

1 Cut the unpeeled eggplants lengthwise into slices about ⅓ inch (9 mm) thick. You will need 18 slices in all. Place the slices in a colander, sprinkle with salt, and let stand for about 30 minutes to drain off the bitter juices. Pat the slices dry with paper towels. Spread the flour on a plate and coat the eggplant on both sides with the flour, tapping off the excess.

2 Pour olive oil to a depth of about 1 inch (2.5 cm) in a wide frying pan and heat to 325°F (165°C) on a deep-frying thermometer. Add 2 or 3 eggplant slices and fry, turning once, until golden, about 4 minutes total. Transfer to paper towels to drain. Repeat with the remaining slices.

3 Preheat the oven to 300°F (150°C). Oil a large baking sheet.

4 Set aside 6 eggplant slices with the peels intact on one side. Arrange 6 of the remaining slices on the baking sheet. Slice the tomatoes into thin, uniform slices. Place 3 or 4 slices of tomato on top of each eggplant slice, overlapping the tomato slices slightly. Scatter some shredded basil and some slices of goat cheese over the tomatoes. Top with a second layer of eggplant slices and more tomato slices, basil, and cheese. Finish with the reserved eggplant slices, so each stack resembles a whole eggplant. Brush the tops lightly with olive oil.

5 Bake the sandwiches until slightly softened and warmed through, 5–8 minutes. Transfer to warmed individual plates. Garnish with the basil sprigs and drizzle with extra-virgin olive oil. Serve at once.

Stuffed Cèpes

Cèpes Farcis • Southwestern • France

Cèpes, *Boletus edulis*, are the royalty of the mushroom world, greatly esteemed for their firm texture, aromatic flesh, and intense flavor. During the fall, hunters seek them in the forests from the Dordogne to the Basses-Alpes. In a good year, a sizable number of full baskets can be amassed by a single individual. They are often presented stuffed, to accompany a main dish such as roast duck, veal, or pork, or for serving as a first course. The stuffing can be used for other mushrooms as well, although the unique flavor of the cèpes will be absent.

8 fresh cèpe mushrooms, about 1 lb (500 g) total weight, brushed clean

3 oz (90 g) thinly sliced *jambon cru* or prosciutto, minced

2 oz (60 g) roulade, pancetta, or bacon, minced

1 egg, lightly beaten

2 tablespoons fresh goat cheese

1 clove garlic, minced

1 shallot, minced

2 tablespoons minced fresh flat-leaf (Italian) parsley

1 teaspoon fresh thyme leaves, minced

½ teaspoon freshly ground pepper

2 tablespoons extra-virgin olive oil

Serves 4

1 Preheat the oven to 400°F (200°C).

2 Remove the stems from the mushrooms and mince the stems. In a bowl, combine the minced stems, *jambon cru* or prosciutto, roulade (or pancetta or bacon), egg, goat cheese, garlic, shallot, parsley, thyme, and pepper. Mix well to form a stiff paste.

3 Rub the mushroom caps with all but 1 teaspoon of the olive oil. Using a small spoon, stuff each mushroom cap to heaping with the minced-stems mixture. Place stuffed side up in a baking dish just large enough to accommodate them without crowding. Drizzle the remaining 1 teaspoon olive oil evenly over the tops. Bake until the cheese melts, the stuffing is lightly browned, and the mushroom caps can be easily pierced with the tip of a knife, 20–25 minutes.

4 Transfer to a warmed serving platter and serve at once.

CUISINE WITH CHEESE

When you cook with cheese (*cuisiner avec fromage*), you can bring a complexity of flavors to a dish with just that single ingredient. The great range of tastes and textures present in the myriad of French cheeses—nearly 400 varieties—form a vast pantry available to the French cook. Since many of the cheeses are local, you'll find different types being used for a vegetable gratin in the Auvergne than you'll find in the Basque country or in Gascony. Goat's milk cheese, of which the French consume more than any other European country, is excellent for cooking because the butterfat and solids don't separate when heated, unlike many cow's milk cheeses. Soft fresh goat cheese melts to make a creamy liaison for stuffings or a smooth sauce or topping. Hard cheeses are typically first grated and then added as a garnish to the dish at the end of cooking.

Stuffed Vegetables

Les Petits Farcis • Provence • France

One common French method for adding flavor is with a bundle of herbs called a *bouquet garni*. The herb sprigs must be perfectly fresh or they will diminish the flavor of the dish.

TOMATO SAUCE

2½ tablespoons olive oil

2 yellow onions, chopped

2 lb (1 kg) tomatoes, peeled, seeded, and chopped

2 cloves garlic, finely chopped

Bouquet garni (page 219), with the addition of 1 fresh summer savory and 1 fresh basil sprig

1 orange zest strip, preferably dried, about 1 inch (2.5 cm) wide

Salt and freshly ground black pepper to taste

Pinch of cayenne pepper (optional)

2 tablespoons chopped fresh basil or flat-leaf (Italian) parsley (optional)

12 small tomatoes, each about 2 inches (5 cm) in diameter

Salt to taste

3 zucchini (courgettes), each about 7 inches (18 cm) long and 1¾ inches (4.5 cm) in diameter

⅔ cup (5 fl oz/160 ml) olive oil

1 large yellow onion, finely chopped

¾ lb (375 g) spicy bulk pork sausage meat

1 teaspoon dried herbes de Provence

3 tablespoons chopped fresh flat-leaf (Italian) parsley

2 cloves garlic, finely chopped

1½ cups (3 oz/90 g) fresh bread crumbs

¼ cup (1 oz/30 g) grated Parmesan cheese

1 or 2 eggs, lightly beaten

2 tablespoons fine dried bread crumbs

1 cup (8 fl oz/250 ml) hot water

Serves 6

1 To make the tomato sauce, in a large, heavy frying pan over medium heat, warm the olive oil. Add the onions and sauté for about 10 minutes. Do not allow to color. Add the tomatoes and cook, uncovered, stirring occasionally, until they have rendered their juice, about 15 minutes. Add the garlic, bouquet garni, and orange zest and season with salt. Stir once, reduce the heat to low, and simmer, uncovered, stirring occasionally, until the liquid is reduced by about one-third, 20–30 minutes. Discard the bouquet garni and zest and season with salt and black pepper. If desired, add the cayenne and stir in the basil or parsley, if using. Set aside and cover to keep warm.

2 Meanwhile, cut a thin slice off the stem end of each tomato. Using a teaspoon, scoop out the center, discarding the seeds and juice and reserving the tomato flesh. Salt the inside of each tomato, then place upside down on a wire rack to drain. Trim the ends of the zucchini. Slice each zucchini crosswise into 4 equal lengths. One at a time, stand the pieces upright on an end. Using a melon baller, scoop out their centers, leaving the bottom intact and forming walls about ⅜ inch (1 cm) thick. Be careful not to cut through the walls. Reserve the zucchini flesh.

3 Fill a large saucepan three-fourths full with salted water and bring to a boil. Slip the zucchini pieces into the boiling water, bring the water back to a boil, reduce the heat to low, and simmer, uncovered, until just softened, about 4 minutes. Using a slotted spoon, lift out the zucchini pieces and plunge into a bowl of ice water. When the pieces are cool, place them, hollowed side down, on a kitchen towel to drain.

4 Preheat the oven to 350°F (180°C). Oil a baking dish large enough to hold the vegetables in a single layer without touching.

5 Chop the reserved zucchini and tomato flesh. In a small frying pan over low heat, warm 3 tablespoons of the olive oil. Add the onion and sauté for about 10 minutes. Do not allow to color. Add the chopped zucchini and tomato, season with salt, and continue to cook, stirring and tossing, until softened, about 15 minutes. Transfer the zucchini-tomato mixture to a bowl. Add the sausage meat, herbes de Provence, parsley, garlic, fresh bread crumbs, and Parmesan cheese and stir to mix well. Add 1 egg and drizzle in 2 tablespoons of the remaining olive oil. Using your hands, mix together thoroughly. If the stuffing seems too dry, mix in another egg.

6 Arrange the tomato and zucchini shells in the prepared baking dish. Sprinkle the cavity of each with a little salt and drizzle with some of the remaining olive oil. Using a teaspoon, distribute the stuffing evenly among the vegetables, pressing gently with the back of the spoon. Sprinkle with the dried bread crumbs, then drizzle with the remaining olive oil. Pour the hot water into the bottom of the dish.

7 Bake the stuffed vegetables until the stuffing is golden brown, about 30 minutes. Gently warm the tomato sauce over low heat, if necessary. Spoon some of the sauce on individual plates. Arrange the vegetables on top and serve.

Rabbit Terrine

Terrine de Lapin • Southwestern • France

Rabbit terrines are among the most striking in the panoply of French terrines. When sliced, a mosaic of delicate white meat, interlaced with layers of darker sausage meat, is revealed. In this version, pistachios add notes of green, and the livers bring yet another element of pattern to the design. Have your butcher bone the rabbits, leaving the meat in fillets and the chunks as large as possible. Request the bones and the livers as well. Serve the terrine as a perfect first course for a summer night along with a chilled Bandol rosé wine.

MARINADE

¼ cup (2 fl oz/60 ml) Cognac

6 juniper berries, crushed

4 fresh thyme sprigs

1 bay leaf

1 teaspoon salt

1 teaspoon freshly ground pepper

2 rabbits, 2 lb (1 kg) each, boned, bones and livers reserved (see note)

⅓ lb (5 oz/155 g) pork fatback, sliced into 9 strips, each about ¼ inch (6 mm) thick and ½ inch (12 mm) wide

1 lb (500 g) bulk pork sausage

1 egg

6 juniper berries, ground

3 teaspoons Cognac

½ cup (2 oz/60 g) shelled pistachios

Serves 8–10

1 To make the marinade, in a large bowl, combine the Cognac, crushed juniper berries, thyme, bay leaf, salt, and pepper.

2 Add the rabbit meat and the strips of fatback to the marinade. Turn the meat several times, then cover and refrigerate overnight.

3 Preheat the oven to 350°F (180°C).

4 To construct the terrine, remove the rabbit meat and fatback from the marinade. Discard the marinade. In a bowl, mix together the sausage and egg. Pack a 5-cup (40–fl oz/1.25-l) lidded terrine with one-third of the sausage mix. (Alternatively, use a heavy baking dish of the same size and aluminum foil.) Top with one-fourth of the rabbit meat in an even layer. Lay 3 rows of fatback strips the length of the terrine. Sprinkle with a little ground juniper and 1 teaspoon of the Cognac. Arrange 2 long rows of pistachios on top. Lay the livers in the middle. Repeat the same layering, without the livers, two more times, ending with a layer of rabbit. Fit some of the bones across the top. (The small foreleg bones fit nicely.) Cooking with the bones on top will help the terrine to jell.

5 Place the lid on the terrine, (or cover the baking dish with foil) making sure it fits snugly. Set in a baking dish with 3-inch (7.5-cm) sides and pour hot water into the baking dish to reach halfway up the sides of the terrine.

6 Bake until the rabbit meat is opaque, firm, and cooked through, 1½–2 hours.

7 Remove from the oven and, while still hot, uncover and remove and discard the bones. Cut a piece of aluminum foil slightly larger than the surface of the terrine and place it on top of the cooked meat, pressing it down and into the corners to make a snug fit. Wrap a brick or similar weight with foil and place it on top. Refrigerate the weighted terrine for 24 hours.

8 To serve, remove the weight and foil. Heat a knife under hot tap water, wipe dry, and run the hot knife along the edges of the terrine to loosen it. If possible, use a flexible icing spatula to reach beneath and loosen the bottom. (Alternatively, place the base of the mold in very hot water for 5 minutes.) Invert a platter on top of the terrine. Holding both the mold and the platter, invert them together. Lift off the mold. If it does not come free, repeat the loosening process and try again.

9 To serve, cut into slices 1 inch (2.5 cm) thick.

APPELLATION D'ORIGINE CONTRÔLÉE (AOC)

Appellation d'Origine Contrôlée (AOC) appears on numerous French products. Nîmes black olives, Le Puy lentils, Grenoble walnuts, Bresse poultry, over thirty different cheeses (including Camembert, Roquefort, and Saint-Nectaire), and wines and liqueurs are recipients of the AOC designation. It is a guarantee that the items are of a certain quality and were produced in a particular region under specified conditions.

To win this coveted status, producers present detailed documentation about the uniqueness of their regional product based on its production in a *terroir*. This means that

not only are the standards for manufacturing, harvesting, handling, and packaging very strict and very specific to the product, but also that the item must come from a precisely defined territory. These criteria are the purchaser's assurance of a certain level of quality. Belon oysters, Banon cheese, and Périgord foie gras are some of the products that have recently been considered by the French government for an AOC designation.

Goat Cheese and Tomato Tarts

Galette au Chèvre et aux Tomates • Provence • France

To give the dish a lightness—and the cook the option of using purchased pastry dough—this little galette is made with puff pastry rather than the olive oil–based shortcrust pastry that is traditionally used. However, the rustic nature of the original still shines through in the combination of potatoes, tomatoes, and cheese made from the milk of myriad goats that roam the hillsides of Haute Provence. The basil oil can be stored in a cool, dark place for up to 2 months. It is also excellent in salads and drizzled over lamb or seafood.

BASIL OIL

1 bunch fresh basil

About 1½ cups (12 fl oz/375 ml) peanut oil or grapeseed oil

1 cup (8 fl oz/250 ml) olive oil

1 lb (500 g) good-quality purchased puff pastry, thawed if frozen

4 round yellow-fleshed potatoes, about 2 inches (5 cm) in diameter

5 very round, very red tomatoes, about 2 inches (5 cm) in diameter

Sugar for sprinkling (optional)

10 oz (315 g) fresh goat cheese

4 fresh basil leaves, torn into small pieces

Olive oil for brushing

Serves 6

1 To make the basil oil, pluck the basil leaves from their stems. Place the stems and about ½ cup (½ oz/15 g) of the leaves in a small saucepan. Add enough peanut oil to cover. Heat the oil and basil slowly over low heat, then remove and let stand for 10 minutes.

2 Transfer the contents of the pan to a blender and purée until smooth. Pour the purée through a fine-mesh sieve placed over a pitcher, then transfer to a clean bottle. Let cool completely and then add the olive oil. You should have about 2½ cups (20 fl oz/625 ml) basil oil.

3 Preheat the oven to 400°F (200°C).

4 On a lightly floured work surface, roll out the puff pastry ⅛ inch (3 mm) thick. Using a sharp knife and a small plate as a template, cut out six 5-inch (13-cm) rounds and place the rounds on a lightly oiled large baking sheet. Prick them with a fork to prevent them from rising, cover with a second baking sheet, and place an ovenproof weight on top. Bake until brown and crisp, 18–20 minutes, pressing down twice on the top sheet to expel any air from the rounds. Remove from the oven, lift off the weight and top baking sheet, and set the pastry rounds aside to cool.

5 In a saucepan, combine the potatoes with salted water to cover. Bring to a boil over high heat, reduce the heat to medium-high, and boil until tender, about 10 minutes. Drain and let cool completely, then peel and slice ¼ inch (6 mm) thick. Set aside at room temperature. Slice the tomatoes to the same thickness as the potatoes. If you like a slightly caramelized flavor, cut them thicker (⅓ inch/9 mm), sprinkle lightly with sugar on one side, and panfry on the sugared side for a moment to brown, then remove quickly. Carefully transfer to parchment (baking) paper to cool. Thinly slice the cheese.

6 Preheat the broiler (grill).

7 Alternating the tomato, potato, and cheese slices, arrange them in a spiral pattern to cover each pastry round. Distribute the basil evenly among the pastries, placing the pieces in the gaps between the vegetables and cheese. Brush the surface of each tart lightly with olive oil.

8 Slip the baking sheet under the broiler 5 inches (13 cm) from the heat source and broil (grill) until the tarts are glazed and warmed through, 2–3 minutes.

9 Carefully transfer each tart to the center of a warmed plate. Drizzle a line of basil oil around and over each tart and serve at once.

LE POTAGER

No matter where you travel in France, you'll find *potagers*. These year-round kitchen gardens, like the open markets, are the source of the fresh vegetables and herbs that make even the simplest French food exquisite. Freshly dug potatoes; haricots verts; firm eggplants; crisp, white heads of cauliflower; slender green asparagus stalks; and solid, purple-topped turnips all commonly travel from the *potager* to the table within hours. The gardens are rarely very large. Their purpose is to supply the kitchen with fresh vegetables on a daily basis, and they succeed admirably. *Potagers* are so important in French life that they are often detailed in deeds. Even as late as the mid-twentieth century, having a *potager* was considered necessary in many parts of France to ensure fresh vegetables of good quality throughout the year. The tradition continues to be strong.

Layered Terrines with Raspberry Sauce

Terrines de Légumes au Coulis de Framboise • Loire Valley • France

The distinct flavor of each vegetable is retained in this colorful layered dish. Raspberry sauce, slightly tart, brings out the sweetness in the vegetables.

1 lb (500 g) celery root (celeriac), peeled and cut into slices ⅜ inch (1 cm) thick

1 lb (500 g) young, sweet carrots, peeled and quartered lengthwise

1 lb (500 g) fresh English peas, shelled

1 whole egg, plus 2 egg yolks

1 cup (8 fl oz/250 ml) heavy (double) cream

¼ cup (2 oz/60 g) unsalted butter

RASPBERRY SAUCE

½ cup (2 oz/60 g) fresh raspberries

2 tablespoons sugar

½ cup (4 fl oz/125 ml) *vin doux* such as Banyuls or Beaumes-de-Venise, or port

⅓ cup (3 fl oz/80 ml) raspberry vinegar

Serves 2–4

1 Bring a saucepan three-fourths full of water to a boil over high heat. Add the celery root, reduce the heat to medium, and cook until very tender when pierced with a fork, about 15 minutes. Drain well and set aside.

2 Meanwhile, bring another saucepan three-fourths full of water to a boil over high heat. Add the carrots, reduce the heat to medium, and cook until very tender when pierced with a fork, 5–7 minutes. Drain well and set aside.

3 Bring a third small saucepan three-fourths full of water to a boil over high heat. Add the peas, reduce the heat to medium, and cook until very tender, 5–7 minutes. Drain well and set aside.

4 Purée each vegetable separately in a blender, rinsing the blender container between uses and putting the purées in separate bowls. Each purée should measure about 1½ cups (12 fl oz/375 ml).

5 In a separate bowl, whisk together the whole egg, egg yolks, and cream just until blended. Spoon ¼ cup (2 fl oz/60 ml) of the egg mixture into each of the vegetable purées. Stir each until well mixed.

6 Preheat the oven to 350°F (180°C). Using the butter, generously grease 2 terrines each 6 inches (15 cm) long and 3¼ inches (8 cm) wide (or use small loaf pans of the same size).

7 Fill a pastry bag fitted with a plain tip with the puréed carrots and squeeze an even layer of carrots into each terrine, filling each vessel about one-third full. Using a clean pastry bag, repeat the process, first with the puréed peas, filling the middle one-third of each terrine, and then with the celery root, filling the top one-third.

8 Place the terrines in a large, ovenproof pot with a tight-fitting lid. Carefully pour water into the pot to reach about ½ inch (12 mm) below the tops of the terrines. Remove the terrines from the pot and bring the water to a boil over high heat. Remove the pot from the heat, put the terrines back into the pot, and cover the pot tightly.

9 Bake until the mixture is firm to the touch, 50–60 minutes. Remove the terrines from the pot and let stand for 10–15 minutes.

10 Meanwhile, make the raspberry sauce: In a saucepan over medium heat, combine the raspberries, sugar, *vin doux*, and vinegar. Cook, stirring, until the sugar thoroughly dissolves, 4–5 minutes. Remove from the heat and pour through a fine-mesh sieve placed over a bowl, pressing it through with the back of a spoon.

11 To unmold, invert a serving plate on top of a terrine. Holding both the plate and the terrine, invert them together. Gently shake the terrine and lift it off. Repeat with the other terrine. To serve 4, cut each terrine into slices and, using a spatula, transfer each half to another plate.

12 To serve, spoon the raspberry sauce around each serving.

Trio of Crudités

Les Crudités • Île-de-France • France

This preparation offers a dressier version of the typical raw crudités cut for dipping. Be sure to toss the beets separately so that they do not stain the other vegetables.

3 beets

5 carrots, peeled and finely grated

3 tomatoes, sliced

6 tablespoons (3 fl oz/90 ml) extra-virgin olive oil

1 teaspoon Dijon mustard

4 tablespoons (2 fl oz/60 ml) red wine vinegar

¾ teaspoon salt

¾ teaspoon freshly ground pepper

8 butter (Boston) lettuce leaves

2 tablespoons minced fresh flat-leaf (Italian) parsley

Serves 4

1 Trim off the beet greens, leaving 1 inch (2.5 cm) of the stems. Place the beets in a saucepan, add water to cover, and bring to a boil over medium-high heat. Reduce the heat to medium-low, cover, and cook until tender when pierced with a fork, about 1 hour. Drain and, when cool enough to handle, peel the beets. Cut into ½-inch (12-mm) cubes. Place in a bowl and set aside.

2 Place the carrots and tomatoes in separate bowls. In another bowl, using a fork, stir together 4 tablespoons (2 fl oz/60 ml) of the olive oil and the mustard until thickened. Mix in 3 tablespoons of the vinegar and ½ teaspoon *each* of the salt and pepper to form a vinaigrette.

3 Pour half of the vinaigrette over the beets and turn to coat. Pour the other half over the carrots and turn. Sprinkle the remaining 2 tablespoons oil, 1 tablespoon vinegar, and ¼ teaspoon *each* salt and pepper over the tomatoes and turn them.

4 Arrange the lettuces leaves on a platter or individual plates. Spoon separate piles of the seasoned vegetables on top of the lettuce. Sprinkle everything with the parsley and serve.

Basil-Scented Savory Cookies

Palmiers au Basilic • Provence • France

These small, very Provençal cookies, ideally partnered with an aperitif, can also be spread with tapenade or topped with shredded Gruyère cheese.

20 fresh basil leaves

4 cloves garlic, roughly chopped

¼ cup (2 fl oz/60 ml) olive oil, plus extra for brushing

½ lb (250 g) good-quality purchased puff pastry, thawed if frozen

Sea salt

Makes 20–22 pastries

1 Preheat the oven to 400°F (200°C).

2 In a small food processor, combine the basil and garlic cloves and process until a paste begins to form. With the motor running, add the ¼ cup (2 fl oz/60 ml) olive oil in a slow, steady stream, processing until a smooth paste forms.

3 On a lightly floured work surface, roll out the puff pastry into a rectangle about 15 by 12 inches (38 by 30 cm). Spread the basil paste thinly over the pastry surface. Make a small imprint on the long side at the top of the rectangle, positioning it at the midpoint. Make a second imprint in the same position at the bottom of the rectangle, indicating an imaginary line down the center. Roll the 2 narrow ends of the pastry sheet inward, not too tightly, brushing with a little olive oil to help it hold together. When the rolls meet at the center, press together very lightly, then place in the freezer for 20 minutes.

4 Lightly oil a baking sheet. Remove the pastry roll from the freezer, place on a work surface, and cut crosswise into pieces about ⅜ inch (1 cm) thick. Transfer each piece to the prepared baking sheet, laying it on a cut side. When the baking sheet is full, sprinkle the pastries with the sea salt, then pass a rolling pin very lightly over each piece to spread the salt a little and to help it adhere.

5 Bake until golden, about 15 minutes. Using a spatula, transfer the pastries to a rack and let cool completely before serving.

Onion Confit Pizza

Pissaladière • Provence • France

This is the pizza of Provence, rich with onions that have been cooked down with herbs, butter, and olive oil to make a thick, golden confit.

ONION CONFIT

¼ cup (2 oz/60 g) unsalted butter

3½ lb (1.75 kg) yellow onions, sliced ¼ inch (6 mm) thick

2 fresh bay leaves or 1 bay leaf

4 large fresh thyme sprigs

4 fresh winter savory sprigs

1 teaspoon freshly ground pepper

½ teaspoon salt

4 tablespoons (2 fl oz/60 ml) extra-virgin olive oil

DOUGH

5 teaspoons (2 packages) active dry yeast

1 cup (8 fl oz/250 ml) warm water (105°F–115°F/41°C–46°C)

1 teaspoon sugar

1 teaspoon salt

2 tablespoons extra-virgin olive oil

About 3½ cups (17½ oz/545 g) all-purpose (plain) flour

20 anchovy fillets

20 oil-cured black olives

2 teaspoons olive oil

2 tablespoons minced fresh marjoram

Serves 10

1 Preheat the oven to 300°F (150°C).

2 To make the onion confit, cut the butter into several pieces and place in a shallow baking dish large enough to hold the onions in a heaping layer 1–1½ inches (2.5–4 cm) deep. If the onions are spread too thinly, they will fry rather than "melt" into a confit. Put in the oven to melt, about 5 minutes. Remove the dish and place half the sliced onions in it. Tear the bay leaves into 2 or 3 pieces and scatter half of the pieces over the onions. Then add 2 *each* of the thyme and winter savory sprigs, ½ teaspoon of the pepper, and ¼ teaspoon of the salt. Drizzle with 2 tablespoons of the oil. Repeat with the remaining onions, seasonings, and oil, piling them on top. Return the dish to the oven and continue to bake, turning the onions every 10–15 minutes, until they are a light golden brown and have reduced in volume by nearly half, 1–1½ hours. Remove from the oven and discard the thyme, winter savory, and bay.

3 Meanwhile, make the dough: In a small bowl, dissolve the yeast in the warm water. Add the sugar and let stand until foamy, about 5 minutes.

4 In a food processor, combine the yeast mixture, the salt, 1 tablespoon of the olive oil, and 3 cups (15 oz/470 g) of the flour. Process until the ingredients come together into a ball. If the dough is too wet, add as much of the remaining ½ cup (2½ oz/75 g) flour, a little at a time, as needed to form a smooth, firm ball. If the dough is too dry, add dribbles of warm water until the ball forms. Continue to process after the ball has formed until the dough is silky but firm, 3–4 minutes. Turn out the dough onto a well-floured work surface and knead until the dough is smooth and elastic, 4–5 minutes.

5 Oil a large bowl with the remaining 1 tablespoon olive oil. Place the dough ball in the bowl and turn the ball to coat the surface with oil. Cover with a clean, damp kitchen towel and let stand in a warm place until the dough doubles in size, 1–1½ hours. Punch down the dough, re-cover the bowl with the towel, and let rest for another 30 minutes.

6 Position a rack in the upper third of the oven and preheat to 500°F (260°C).

7 Punch down the dough and turn out onto a floured work surface. Roll out the dough into a rectangle about 13 by 19 inches (33 by 48 cm). Sprinkle a little flour on the bottom of a 12-by-18-inch (30-by-45-cm) rimmed baking sheet. Lay the dough on it, patting it up the sides to make a crust. Spread the surface with the onion confit, then arrange the anchovies and olives evenly over the surface.

8 Bake until the bottom surface of the crust is crisp and the edge is lightly browned, 12–15 minutes. Remove from the oven. While hot, drizzle with the 2 teaspoons olive oil, then sprinkle with the marjoram.

9 To serve, cut the *pissaladière* into rectangles about 3 by 3½ inches (7.5 by 9 cm) and serve warm or at room temperature.

APERITIFS

In France, *l'apéritif* is both a beverage and a social activity that encompasses the entire breadth of the society. Twice a day throughout the year, in cafés, restaurants, and homes, people share the ritual of having a drink together with a few nuts, olives, or perhaps a square or two of cheese, before sitting down to a meal. The drink is usually not strong spirits, which would dull the appetite, but a fortified wine such as a sweet vermouth or a spirit-based drink like Campari and water.

Different regions have their specialties, too. In the south, it is pastis, a rather bitter anise-flavored drink served with ice and water, but for which one develops a taste. Suze, Aveze, and Salers, flavored with the bitter gentian root, are specialties of the Auvergne. Kir, a mixture of white wine and *crème de cassis* that originated in Dijon and takes its name from a former mayor, is quite popular all over the country, but there are variations. In Brittany, one is offered *kir Bretagne* made with cider, while in the Cevennes *crème de cassis* is added to red wine to make a *camisard*.

Fortified *vins maisons*, based on local fruits and nuts, are homemade and proudly produced at aperitif time. Crisp, refreshing *vin d'orange* is made with white wine and bitter oranges, and the dark, spicy *vin de noix* gets its flavor and color from green walnuts. Champagne, of course, is the aperitif of choice everywhere for celebratory occasions, and *vins doux*, sweet fortified wines, find a local following in the southwest where Banyuls and Rivesaltes are made.

Gratinéed Mussels on the Half Shell

Moules Farcies · Languedoc · France

In the coastal regions of France that border Spain, both on the Mediterranean and Atlantic, mussels are commonly prepared by packing a savory stuffing into the shells on top of the already-cooked mollusks.

48 mussels, scrubbed and debearded

1¼–1½ cups (5–6 oz/155–185 g) fine dried bread crumbs

3 tablespoons minced fresh flat-leaf (Italian) parsley

2 tablespoons minced fresh thyme

4 cloves garlic, minced

½ teaspoon salt

½ teaspoon freshly ground pepper

2 small tomatoes, peeled and seeded (page 225), minced, and drained

1½–2 tablespoons extra-virgin olive oil

Serves 8 as an appetizer, 4 as a first course

1 Preheat the oven to 500°F (260°C). Arrange the mussels in a baking dish in one layer, discarding any that do not close to the touch. Bake just until the shells open, 8–10 minutes.

2 Remove from the oven and let cool for about 15 minutes. Discard any mussels that failed to open. Reserve the collected juice in the bottom of the dish. Pull apart the shells of each mussel, holding it over the dish to capture the juices. Using a knife, cut through the muscles that attach the meat to the shell, discarding one shell and leaving the meat resting in the other. Reduce the oven temperature to 450°F (230°C).

3 In a bowl, combine the bread crumbs, captured mussel juices, parsley, thyme, garlic, salt, and pepper. Mix in the tomatoes. Add enough olive oil to hold the stuffing together. Cover the mussels in their half shells with about 1 tablespoon of the filling, mounding it to the rim of the shell and packing it tightly. Place the filled shells on a baking sheet.

4 Bake until the filling is golden brown, 12–14 minutes. If still pale, slip the mussels under a broiler (grill) for 1–2 minutes. (Watch closely to prevent burning.) Transfer to a platter and serve hot or at room temperature.

Warm Black Olives

Olives Sautées • Provence • France

Only occasionally are olives served warm, but this quick method of heating them to transform their flavor results in an ideal appetizer.

1 lb (500 g) large, fleshy black olives

3 tablespoons olive oil

3 slices air-cured ham, torn into bite-sized pieces

8 fresh sage leaves

3 bay leaves, broken up if large

2 red bird's-eye chiles, sliced

1 tablespoon sea salt

Serves 8–10

1 Drain the olives, rinse, and pat dry. Warm the olive oil in a frying pan over medium heat. Add the olives and fry, stirring constantly, until heated through, about 2 minutes. Add the ham, the sage and bay leaves, and lastly the chiles. Mix briefly, add the salt, and stir to mix evenly without dissolving the salt.

2 Transfer to a serving bowl and serve at once.

Marinated Olives

Olives en Marinade • Provence • France

For serving with aperitifs or as part of an array of hors d'oeuvres, locals in Provence like to marinate cured olives with oil, garlic, and herbs.

10 oz (315 g) brine-cured black olives

6 oz (185 g) brine-cured green olives

2 cloves garlic

3 or 4 peppercorns

3 or 4 fresh thyme sprigs

Leaves from 1 long fresh rosemary or fennel sprig

1 bay leaf

1 red bird's-eye chile (optional)

Olive oil to cover

Serves 8–10

1 Drain the olives. Place in a preserving jar with a glass lid attached with a wire and bales; select a jar at least one-third larger than the volume of the olives. Intersperse among the olives the garlic, peppercorns, thyme, rosemary or fennel, bay leaf, and chile (if using).

2 Add olive oil just to cover the olives, then cap the jar. Store in a cool, dark place, allowing the olives to marinate for at least 3 weeks before serving. If stored submerged in olive oil and tightly capped, the olives will keep indefinitely.

Vegetables with Hot Anchovy Sauce

Bagna Cauda · Provence · France

Given its history under the Houses of Savoy and Sardinia—the County of Nice was finally ceded to France in 1860—Nice has many connections with the cooking just across the Italian border. The Niçois, with their plentiful supply of anchovies, consider this dish as much their own as do the Piedmontese or the Ligurians. *Bagna cauda*, meaning "hot bath," is served in much the same way as an aioli. Since the sauce needs to be kept warm, it is best made in a fondue pot or similar saucepan with a burner placed under it.

1 In a saucepan, combine the potatoes with water to cover. Bring to a gentle boil over medium-high heat and cook, uncovered, until tender, 12–15 minutes. Drain and set aside to cool completely.

2 If the beet greens are attached, cut them off, leaving about ½ inch (12 mm) of the stems intact. Do not peel. In a saucepan, combine the beets with water to cover. Bring to a gentle boil over medium-high heat and cook, uncovered, until tender, 10–12 minutes. Drain and, when cool enough to handle, trim off the stems and root ends and slip off the peels. Set the beets aside.

3 Bring a saucepan three-fourths full of water to a boil. Add the leeks and blanch for about 1 minute if using whole baby leeks, or for 2 minutes if using sliced large leeks. Drain, immerse under running cold water to stop the cooking, and drain again. Cut whole leeks on the diagonal into 2-inch (5-cm) lengths. Set aside.

4 Arrange all the vegetables on large platters. About 20 minutes before serving, begin making the sauce: In a fondue pot or similar saucepan, combine the anchovies, garlic, and olive oil. Place over low heat and stir constantly with a wooden spatula, mashing the anchovies until they are reduced to a purée, for 15–20 minutes. Be careful not to let the mixture boil. The garlic should become translucent but never brown, and the anchovies must not be allowed to become crisp. Season with pepper.

5 Transfer the pan holding the sauce to a tabletop burner. Bring the platters of vegetables to the table. Let diners help themselves to vegetables and drizzle them with the warm anchovy sauce.

15–18 small boiling potatoes, peeled

12 baby beets

12 whole baby leeks, or 2 large leeks, including tender green tops, sliced

3 or 4 celery stalks, halved lengthwise, then cut into 4-inch (10-cm) pieces

12 baby carrots, peeled, or 3 large carrots, peeled and quartered lengthwise

1 small cauliflower, cut into florets

6 baby artichokes, trimmed (page 219) and quartered lengthwise

12 green (spring) onions, including 2–2½ inches (5–6 cm) of the green tops, trimmed

1 large bunch radishes, trimmed

2 large red bell peppers (capsicums), seeded and cut lengthwise into strips about ½ inch (12 mm) wide

30–35 cherry tomatoes

3 heads Belgian endive (chicory/witloof), leaves separated

SAUCE

15 salt-packed anchovies, about 7 oz (220 g), filleted and rinsed (page 219)

6 cloves garlic, sliced

Scant 1 cup (7 fl oz/220 ml) olive oil

Freshly ground pepper to taste

Serves 8

Foie Gras Terrine

Terrine de Foie Gras • Southwestern • France

1 fresh foie gras of duck (page 221), about 1 lb (500 g), chilled

2 cups (16 fl oz/500 ml) water or milk, at room temperature

½ cup (4 fl oz/125 ml) Cognac

1 teaspoon salt

1 teaspoon freshly ground pepper

½ teaspoon sugar

Serves 8

1 Place the chilled liver in a bowl with the water or milk. Let it soften for about 5 minutes. It should be pliable but not melting.

2 Remove the liver from the bowl. Separate the large lobe from the small lobe with your fingers. Remove the small exposed nerves that run two-thirds of the way down the liver, pulling very gently to remove them whole. Then, use a small, sharp knife to slit both the small and large lobes two-thirds of the way through the center and two-thirds of the length. Using your fingers or the tip of the knife, remove the remaining network of nerves. Put the liver in a bowl and pour the Cognac over it. Sprinkle with the salt, pepper, and sugar, then turn the liver once to coat it evenly. Cover the bowl and refrigerate overnight.

3 Preheat the oven to 275°F (135°C).

4 Uncover the liver; most of the Cognac will have been absorbed. Transfer the liver to a baking dish. Cover the dish and place in a larger baking dish with 3-inch (7.5-cm) sides. Pour hot water into the larger dish to reach halfway up the sides of the covered dish.

5 Bake until the liver releases a good amount of bright yellow fat and is warmed through, about 35 minutes. Put out a small bowl to collect the fat, then position a colander over it. Place the liver in the colander and let drain for 10 minutes. Then pack the liver into a terrine just large enough to accommodate it. Pour the collected fat over the top to cover the liver and lay a piece of aluminum foil on top of the fat. Cut a piece of cardboard to fit the top of the terrine and place it atop the foil. Then place a 1-lb (500-g) weight on the cardboard. Make sure the weight is evenly distributed.

6 Refrigerate, keeping the weight on the terrine for at least 24 hours. Remove the weight, but keep the terrine refrigerated for at least 4 days or for up to 2 weeks before serving. The layer of fat seals the foie gras, but once it is broken, the foie gras should be eaten within 2–3 days. To serve, scoop away the outer fat and cut into ½-inch (12-mm) slices.

Stuffed Flat Bread

Fougasse • Provence • France

The town of Carpentras in Provence is home to a group of proud bakers devoted to upholding the tradition of making *fougasse*. Nearly every bakery window is filled with this regional flatbread. When you pull the bread apart at its trademark slits, the morsels inside are revealed. If desired, use a combination of anchovies, olives, and ham for the filling.

SPONGE

⅔ cup (3½ oz/105 g) bread (hard-wheat) flour

½ cup (4 fl oz/125 ml) lukewarm water

1 cake (1 oz/30 g) fresh yeast, or 2½ teaspoons (1 package) active dry yeast

DOUGH

2¾ cups (14 oz/400 g) bread (hard-wheat) flour

1 teaspoon salt

1 cup (8 fl oz/250 ml) lukewarm water

2 tablespoons olive oil

20 olive oil–packed anchovy fillets, drained and patted dry; or ½ lb (250 g) large, fleshy black olives, pitted and coarsely chopped; or 2 cups (12 oz/375 g) coarsely chopped cooked ham

Salt and freshly ground pepper to taste

Olive oil for brushing

Makes 1 loaf

1 To make the sponge, place the flour in a small bowl. Place the lukewarm water in a cup, crumble in the yeast, and stir to dissolve. Pour the dissolved yeast into the flour and stir until blended. Cover the bowl with oil-coated plastic wrap and let rise in a warm place until doubled in bulk, 30–40 minutes.

2 To make the dough by hand, place the flour on a lightly oiled work surface and make a large well in the center. Sprinkle in the salt and add the sponge, lukewarm water, and olive oil. Using a fork, blend the liquid with the sponge, gradually breaking down the wall of flour until the flour is incorporated. Then knead the dough until it is light and elastic, 8–10 minutes. The dough will be fairly wet, but do not add more flour; instead, dust your hands with flour and continue kneading. Form the dough into a ball, place in a lightly oiled bowl, turn to coat with oil, cover the bowl with a damp kitchen towel, and let the dough rise until doubled in bulk, 45–60 minutes.

3 To make the dough in a food processor, use a plastic blade and, if possible, reduce the speed of the processor as needed to prevent the dough and the machine from overheating. Combine the flour and salt in the processor. Add the sponge, lukewarm water, and olive oil. Process until the mixture comes together and begins to form a ball at the top of the blade. Turn out the dough onto a lightly floured work surface and knead until it is light and smooth, 2–4 minutes. Form the dough into a ball, place in a lightly oiled bowl, turn to coat with oil, cover the bowl with a damp kitchen towel, and let the dough rise until doubled in bulk, 45–60 minutes.

4 Preheat the oven to 450°F (230°C). Have ready a fine-nozzled mister filled with water.

5 Turn out the dough onto a lightly floured work surface. Punch it down and roll out into a 20-by-8-inch (50-by-20-cm) rectangle. Spread the anchovies, olives, or ham over half of the rectangle, leaving a ¾-inch (2-cm) border uncovered. If not using anchovies, season with salt and pepper. Fold the rectangle in half to form a loaf 10 inches (25 cm) long and 8 inches (20 cm) wide, then transfer to a baking sheet. Using a knife, make 7 or 8 slits, spacing them about 2 inches (5 cm) apart and extending them through to the work surface. Pull the slits open well, so that they do not close during baking. Here and there, lightly press the exposed edges of the dough to the bottom layer, so some stay closed during baking. Brush with olive oil, cover with a damp kitchen towel or oiled plastic wrap, and let rest for 30 minutes.

6 Remove the towel or plastic, place the flat bread in the oven, and quickly spray 3 gusts of water into the top and bottom of the oven. Bake until the bread is golden brown, about 25 minutes, misting the oven again 5 minutes before removing the bread. (The misting ensures a crisper result.)

7 Remove the bread from the oven, transfer to a rack to cool, and immediately brush with olive oil. Serve warm or at room temperature.

LES FOUGASSES

In central-south Provence, especially in the Lubéron and south to the Camargue, bakers' windows feature a unique style of flat bread, *la fougasse*, immediately recognizable from the irregularly spaced slits that mark its surface. Normally radiating out from an imaginary center like veins from the spine of an oak leaf—or sometimes trellislike in their patterning—these slits contribute to the crustiness of the breads by cutting across their doughy centers, effectively clamping the top and bottom together at intersections along the surface.

Fougasses are made in many forms, from fan-shaped loaves to small rolls that look like hands, fingers extended. The sixth-generation Fassy family bakery in Maillane, near Saint-Rémy, makes such a specialty of *fougasses* that they offer twenty-five varieties, all of them sourdough leavened.

Perennial favorites are the rectangular loaves into which the baker folds a stuffing, such as chopped pungent black olives, crispy fried duck or goose skin bits called *grattons*, ham, anchovies, or even Roquefort cheese from Aveyron. Copiously garnished within, these loaves make an ideal picnic lunch with little more than a bottle of wine. In Nice, a sweetened version of the bread, *fougassette*, is a Christmas tradition.

Parsleyed Salt-Cured Ham

Jambon Persillé • Burgundy and Lyon • France

This is a traditional preparation of Burgundy, but now it is found all over France. It makes a beautiful charcuterie first course, with the bright green parsley and deep red ham glistening in the wine-scented jelly. Serve it with mustard and cornichons on the side, along with a chilled white wine. *Jambon cru,* or "raw ham," is ham that has been cured in salt. It is a popular charcuterie item throughout France, with each region using different breeds of pigs and customizing its curing technique.

1 piece boneless *jambon cru* or prosciutto, about 2 lb (1 kg)

3 whole cloves

5 yellow or white onions

1 veal shank, about ½ lb (250 g)

1 calf's foot, about 1½–2 lb (750 g–1 kg; optional)

2 fresh chervil sprigs

2 fresh tarragon sprigs

2 fresh thyme sprigs

2 shallots

1 clove garlic

1 bottle (24 fl oz/750 ml) dry white wine

¼ cup (2 fl oz/60 ml) plus 5 tablespoons (2½ fl oz/75 ml) Cognac

2 tablespoons powdered pectin

2 tablespoons white wine vinegar

1 teaspoon freshly ground pepper

½–⅔ cup (¾–1 oz/20–30 g) minced fresh flat-leaf (Italian) parsley

Serves 15

1 Place the ham in a large pot, add water to cover, and let soak overnight to remove some of the salt.

2 The next day, pour off the water. In the same large pot, combine the ham with water to cover and bring to a boil over medium-high heat. Reduce the heat to low, cover, and cook for 1 hour.

3 Pour off the cooking water and rinse the ham in cold water. Wash the pot and return the ham to it. Stick the 3 cloves in 1 onion and then add all 5 onions to the pot along with the veal shank, calf's foot (if using), chervil, tarragon, thyme, shallots, garlic, 4 cups (32 fl oz/1 l) water, the wine, and the ¼ cup (2 fl oz/60 ml) Cognac.

4 Place over medium-high heat, bring to a boil, skim off any foam that collects on the surface, and reduce the heat to low. Cover and simmer, occasionally skimming off any foam, until the ham can be separated with a fork, about 1 hour.

5 Remove the ham and the other meats from the cooking liquid and set aside. Discard the calf's foot, if using. Pour the liquid into a bowl through a sieve and discard the vegetables and herbs. Then line the sieve with several layers of cheesecloth (muslin), place over a clean saucepan, and pour the liquid through it again. Set aside.

6 Using a fork, tear the ham, including any fat, into chunky pieces. Strip the veal from the shank bone and tear the meat into small pieces, discarding any fat. Pack half of the ham and the veal into a 2-qt (2-l) glass or ceramic bowl.

7 Bring the liquid to a simmer over medium heat. Pour one-fourth of the hot liquid into another bowl and add the pectin, stirring until completely dissolved. Stir the liquid-pectin mixture into the liquid remaining in the pan and remove it from the heat.

8 Sprinkle the ham and veal in the bowl with 1 tablespoon of the vinegar, 2 tablespoons of the Cognac, and ½ teaspoon of the pepper. Pour half of the liquid over the ham, then sprinkle with about half of the parsley. Add the remaining meats and then sprinkle with the remaining 1 tablespoon vinegar, 3 tablespoons Cognac, ½ teaspoon pepper, and the parsley. Pour the remaining liquid over all. The ham may float to the surface, but it will eventually settle.

9 Cover and refrigerate overnight to set the jelly and chill thoroughly. It will keep refrigerated for up to 2 weeks. To serve, using a very sharp knife, cut into slices ½ inch (12 mm) thick and carefully remove them from the bowl.

Egg, Onion, and Tomato Gratin

Oeufs à la Tripe • Provence • France

Before modern transportation made a variety of foods readily available year-round, the rural people of Alpes-de-Haute-Provence fed themselves as much as possible from what they could grow. The cows provided milk, and the vegetable plot at the back of the house yielded Swiss chard, cardoons, fennel, and other produce. In turn, the local ingredients were combined with a white sauce, dusted with cheese, and baked into gratins such as this one.

1 Oil an oval or rectangular baking dish measuring about 9 by 14 inches (23 by 35 cm).

2 In a large frying pan over medium heat, warm the olive oil. Add the onions and sauté, stirring constantly, until softened, about 2 minutes. Cover with parchment (baking) paper cut to fit the diameter of the pan, reduce the heat to low, and simmer, stirring occasionally, until tender, about 20 minutes longer. Transfer to the prepared dish. Set aside.

3 To make the tomato sauce, in a frying pan over medium heat, warm the olive oil. Add the tomatoes and sauté until they start to soften, about 2 minutes. Add the oregano or basil and season with salt and pepper. Reduce the heat to low and cook, uncovered, until a thick, sauce forms, about 15 minutes. If there is too much liquid, raise the heat to high and cook briskly to evaporate it, stirring to prevent scorching. Stir in the tomato paste and parsley and spoon the tomato sauce evenly over the onions.

4 Arrange the egg halves, cut sides down, over the tomato sauce, placing them so that they are evenly spaced over the surface.

5 Preheat the oven to 450°F (230°C).

6 To make the béchamel sauce, pour the milk into a small saucepan and place over medium heat just until it starts to boil. In a deep saucepan over medium heat, melt the butter. Whisk in the flour and cook, stirring, for about 2 minutes. Stir in the hot milk and bring to a boil, stirring constantly, until thickened and smooth. Remove from the heat and season with salt, pepper, and nutmeg. Stir in the 1 tablespoon Gruyère cheese. Pour the sauce evenly over the eggs.

7 Sprinkle the surface of the gratin with the ¼ cup Gruyère cheese and dot with the butter. Bake until the cheese is melted and the top is golden brown, 5–8 minutes. Bring to the table and serve at once.

6 tablespoons (3 fl oz/90 ml) olive oil

6 large yellow onions, thinly sliced

TOMATO SAUCE

¼ cup (2 fl oz/60 ml) olive oil

8 large tomatoes, peeled and seeded (page 225), then coarsely chopped

3 fresh oregano sprigs or 12 fresh basil leaves, shredded

Salt and freshly ground pepper to taste

1 heaping tablespoon tomato paste, or to taste

3 tablespoons chopped fresh flat-leaf (Italian) parsley

6 hard-boiled eggs, peeled and halved lengthwise

BÉCHAMEL SAUCE

3 cups (24 fl oz/750 ml) milk

5 tablespoons (2½ oz/75 g) unsalted butter

3 tablespoons all-purpose (plain) flour

Salt and freshly ground pepper to taste

Freshly grated nutmeg to taste

1 tablespoon shredded Gruyère cheese

¼ cup (1 oz/30 g) shredded Gruyère cheese

4 teaspoons unsalted butter

Serves 8

Bacon-Wrapped Prunes

Brochettes de Pruneaux • The Pyrenees and Gascony • France

In southern France, rosemary grows wild, and the stiff branches, stripped of all but their uppermost leaves, are often used as skewers. Here, skewered prunes (such as those from Agen in Touraine) and bacon become lightly infused with the flavor of rosemary and the delightful smokiness of the fire. Dried figs may be substituted for the prunes.

16 pitted prunes

8 slices bacon, cut in half crosswise

4 sturdy rosemary branches, leaves removed and tips whittled to a point

Serves 4–6

1 Prepare a fire in a charcoal grill with a cover.

2 Wrap each prune with a half slice of bacon and fasten it with a toothpick. Thread 4 wrapped prunes onto each of 4 rosemary skewers, being careful not to pack them together too tightly.

3 When the coals are hot, push them to the sides of the fire pan and place a drip pan in the bottom of the grill. Place the skewers on the grill rack and grill, uncovered, until the bacon is golden on the first side, 2–3 minutes. Turn the skewers and grill 2–3 minutes longer to brown the second side lightly.

4 Cover the grill and close the vents. Cook for 2–3 minutes longer. Lift the cover and turn the skewers to check the bacon. It should be very crisp.

5 Divide the skewers among individual plates and serve hot or warm.

ROSÉ WINES OF FRANCE

Nothing goes better with the brash, pungent flavors of Provençal food than the local rosé wines. The Provençaux have made the production of rosés an art form, turning out young, fresh, crisp, evocative, and, for the most part, drier wines than any of their many counterparts. Arguably the best rosé in the world, Tavel, a wine of deep, rich hue and a full finish, claims the title of premier rosé of France. It comes from the town of the same name, which lies just north of Avignon.

Tavel vintners have made rosé since the tenth century, as have vintners in nearby Lirac, another rosé name of renown. Among the other top producers of

red wine in Provence, only Gigondas and Domaine Tempier in Bandol make rosé.

Most other rosés are generic wines, made and served locally with neither fuss nor pretension. Drunk young, fresh, and dry as an aperitif or with an appetizer, fish, or a light white-meat course, even the unheralded ones are trustworthy enough to be ordered by the carafe in most restaurants. The chalky gray-pink rosé of the Camargue, *gris de gris de Listel* is one of the least expensive rosés on the market, and also one of the driest. This intriguing wine sits beautifully with the strongly flavored, garlic-infused and oil-drenched food with which it was intended to be served.

Olive and Anchovy Choux Puffs

Gougères du Soleil • Bouches-du-Rhone • France

Here, classic *gougères*—small, cheese-flavored choux puffs from Burgundy—are enlivened with the rich flavors of olives, anchovies, and sun-dried tomatoes. The dough for *choux* pastry is made by mixing flour into boiling water, then adding eggs. It is easy to prepare, but the ratio of water and flour is crucial. Be sure to measure both ingredients carefully. Sifting the flour onto parchment (baking) paper allows the flour to be poured quickly into the water just after it comes to a boil.

CHOUX PASTRY

1 cup (5 oz/155 g) all-purpose (plain) flour

1 cup (8 fl oz/250 ml) water

5 tablespoons (2½ oz/75 g) unsalted butter, cut into small dice

Pinch of salt

4 eggs

3 tablespoons finely diced Gruyère cheese

4 olive oil–packed anchovy fillets, drained, patted dry, and diced

5 oil-cured black olives, pitted and chopped

3 sun-dried tomatoes, drained and patted dry if oil packed, diced

1 clove garlic, finely chopped

Salt and freshly ground pepper to taste

Serves 6

1 If using an electric oven, position a rack in the center. If using a gas oven, position a rack in the upper third. Preheat to 400°F (200°C). Line 2 baking sheets with parchment (baking) paper.

2 To make the *choux* pastry, sift the flour onto a sheet of parchment paper and set aside. Pour the water into a saucepan that is deep rather than wide and add the butter and salt. Bring to a boil over high heat, stirring to ensure that the butter has melted completely by the time the water reaches a boil.

3 Reduce the heat to medium and add the reserved flour all at once, stirring briskly with a wooden spatula rather than a spoon (the bowl shape tends to trap the flour). Continue stirring until the flour rolls off the walls of the saucepan and clings in a ball to the spatula, 30–40 seconds, evaporating as much water as possible without scorching the pastry. Remove from the heat. Transfer the pastry to a bowl and let cool for 3 minutes. Add the eggs, one at a time, stirring to blend completely before adding the next egg.

4 Fold the Gruyère cheese, anchovies, olives, tomatoes, garlic, salt, and pepper into the pastry. Using 2 spoons, scoop up portions of the pastry and form into balls about 1¼ inches (3 cm) in diameter, spacing them about 2 inches (5 cm) apart on the prepared baking sheets. You should have about 30 puffs.

5 Bake the puffs until golden brown, about 20 minutes. Turn off the heat, open the door, and let the puffs dry in the oven for 5–10 minutes (if not allowed to dry, the puffs will be soft rather than crispy). Remove the baking sheets from the oven and tap gently on a countertop to release the puffs.

6 Transfer the hot puffs to a bread basket lined with a napkin and serve at once.

THE MEDITERRANEAN

The bounty of choices available on a classic Italian antipasto table are enough to whet even the most jaded palate. Contrary to their often casual atmosphere, many trattorias offer a stunning array: tomatoes stuffed with herbed rice, a golden frittata laced with cheese and greens, a salad of lemony seafood and crunchy celery, white anchovy fillets marinated with vinegar and garlic, salami of various types and sizes, a whole leg of prosciutto on a special stand, a bowl of fresh mozzarella balls, and an enormous wedge of Parmigiano-Reggiano.

The character of the antipasti changes as you travel from one region to another and pass from one season to the next. Piedmont, in northwestern Italy, is arguably the capital of antipasto. Typical Piedmontese dishes are *carne cruda*, lean, tender veal chopped and mixed with garlic, oil, and lemon; *bagna cauda*, literally a "hot bath" of anchovies, garlic, butter, and olive oil served as a dip for cardoons, bell peppers, celery, and other vegetables; and *salame de la duja*, a soft pork sausage preserved in a covering of lard. Another favorite is *fonduta*, a creamy blend of fontina cheese and eggs. When you arrive at the table, you may also find long, crisp *grissini* (bread sticks) laid across the center.

To the south of Piedmont, Ligurians favor antipasti from the garden. Dishes made with mushrooms or stuffed vegetables tend to predominate, along with marinated anchovies and a variety of savory *torte* and focaccia. Here, one of the most popular versions is simply made with fresh herbs added to the dough and then topped with olive oil and coarse salt.

In Tuscany, a typical *antipasto toscano* will include a platter of assorted cured meats (*affettato misto*): prosciutto, fennel sausage, perhaps a few slices of piquant *salsicce di cinghiale* (dried wild boar sausages). Scattered alongside the meats will usually be an assortment of vegetables preserved in vinegar or olive oil—crunchy pearl onions and spears of wild asparagus steeped in wine vinegar, or baby artichoke hearts and porcini mushrooms marinated in olive oil with peppercorns and herbs. Inevitably, there will also be a selection of *crostini e*

bruschetta. In the fall, after the olives have been harvested and pressed, thick slices of country bread are toasted on the grill, rubbed with garlic, and bathed in *olio nuovo*, or covered with tender *fagioli bianchi* (white beans) or boiled *cavolo nero* (Tuscan black cabbage) and the new oil.

In the Marches, *olive all'ascolana*, large pitted green olives stuffed with ground meat and seasonings, coated with bread crumbs, then deep-fried, are a favorite antipasto, the flavorful, fleshy local olives ensuring their fame. Heading south, the antipasti begin to focus more on seafood, from grilled shrimp, stuffed clams, and mussels steamed in white wine to seafood salads made with octopus, calamari, and shrimp.

These regions offer excellent vegetables, too, either fried, stuffed, or in salads. Eggplants are commonly marinated raw, dusted with crumbs and fried, or layered in a gratin with tomatoes and cheese. Roasted pepper salad is often served with anchovies or sharp provolone. Fresh mozzarella, particularly extra-fine *mozzarella di bufala*, is served Capri style, with slices of ripe tomatoes, basil, and olive oil, or baked on pizza. Indeed, pizza, the ultimate snack food, is one of the most common antipasti in Neapolitan restaurants.

In Iberia, the snacks sampled alongside a before-dinner drink have been elevated to an art form. The Spanish word *tapa* comes from *tapar*, to cover, and it originated with a barkeep's habit of placing a little plate or slice of bread on top of a glass of wine to keep out flies. Soon a tidbit of food was set on the plate or bread—a slice of ham, a piece of cheese—and thus an enduring tradition was born. In Portugal, these appetizers, called *acepipes*, remain simple— olives, almonds, a few *bolinhos de bacalhau* (salt cod fritters), or a few slices of ham and cheese, consumed with a tumbler of red wine. But in Spain, *el tapeo*, the custom of traveling from bar to bar and sampling just a dish or two—the bar's specialties—at each one is a popular and lengthy ritual, especially in lovely Andalusia, the home of the tapa.

Tapas fall into three major categories: *cosas de picar*, *pinchos*, and *cazuelas*. *Cosas de picar*, the biggest group, are essentially finger foods—a bowl of marinated olives or fried almonds, a wedge of cheese, or slices of sausage. *Montaditos*, spreads on bread; *bocadillos*; *empanadillas*, foods encased in a crust; *tartaletas*, tiny filled pastry shells; slices of tortilla; and deviled eggs all fall under this banner, as do *fritos* (fried foods) and *buñuelitos* (small fritters), both of which are served with aioli. *Pinchos*, including *banderillas* (named for the dart thrust into the bull at a bullfight) and *palillos*, are skewered foods, whether on toothpicks or larger rods. *Cazuelas* or *cazuelitas*, dishes cooked in earthenware pots of the same names, require utensils. All tapas, of course, are usually accompanied with wine.

Left: Elegantly austere, the campanile of the Abbey of Sant'Antimo, near Montalcino, Italy, encloses a bell dating to 1219. **Above, left:** Tuscans are reputed to have an exquisite eye for composition and color, apparent in even the simplest aspects of everyday life, like these vibrant hydrangeas framed in an archway. **Above, right:** Eminent among the widespread Mediterranean taste for winter squashes is the formidible pumpkinlike *zucca*.

Fresh Tomato Toasts

Bruschetta di Pomodori • Tuscany • Italy

Bruschetta can be made with different toppings, the simplest being a rub of garlic and a drizzle of extra-virgin olive oil. This version, which demands summertime's finest vine-ripened tomatoes, is one of the best. A bit of balsamic vinegar brings out the sweetness of the tomatoes. You can also add some chopped garlic, if you like. A thin slice of ricotta salata laid on top of the tomatoes is a nice addition and can turn this antipasto into a light lunch.

2 tomatoes, chopped

6 fresh basil leaves, torn into small pieces

¼ cup (2 fl oz/60 ml) extra-virgin olive oil

1 teaspoon balsamic vinegar

Coarse salt to taste

8 slices coarse country bread, each about ½ inch (12 mm) thick

2 large cloves garlic

Serves 4

1 Preheat the broiler (grill) or prepare a fire in a charcoal grill.

2 In a bowl, combine the tomatoes, basil, olive oil, vinegar, and salt. Toss well.

3 Place the bread on a baking sheet or grill rack and broil or grill, turning once, until lightly toasted on both sides, about 2 minutes total. Remove from the broiler or grill and immediately rub one side of each slice with the garlic cloves.

4 Arrange the grilled bread, garlic side up, on a platter and spoon on the tomatoes, dividing evenly. Serve at once.

BREAD

Fresh bread, *pane*, is on the table at all Italian meals, a venerable symbol of sustenance and prosperity. It is always served alone, without butter or olive oil, and leftovers are rarely wasted. Instead they are made into crumbs for stuffings or a pasta topping, or sliced and toasted for *crostini* (croutons) for soups or salads. Every region has its own versions, and most holidays are celebrated with special loaves. In Sicily, for example, intricately shaped *pani* are baked to celebrate St. Joseph's Day. Some, fashioned into birds or flowers, are used for decorations. Others, like the *bastone di San Giuseppe*, a long, twisted loaf that is thought to resemble the saint's walking staff, are blessed by the village priest and eaten by nearly everyone. Tuscans always bake *pani coi santi* for All Saints' Day, which is on November 1. Traditionally served for breakfast or snacks, *pani coi santi* are made from a basic yeast dough to which sugar, raisins, walnuts, and black pepper are added.

Dipping Vegetables and Olive Oil

Pinzimonio • Siena • Italy

Tuscans are always looking for ways to highlight that most precious of all local ingredients, olive oil. The word *pinzimonio* doesn't actually refer to the confetti of colorful raw vegetables, which should always be the freshest, most tender available, but to the seasoned oil in which they are dipped. Although the vegetables are presented on a single large platter, everyone at the table gets his or her own ramekin to fill with oil and season with salt and pepper.

2 baby artichokes, trimmed (page 219)

1 lemon, sliced into quarters

2 fennel bulbs

4 carrots

1 head celery

4–6 radishes

4–6 green (spring) onions

1 head Belgian endive (chicory/witloof)

Extra-virgin olive oil

Salt and freshly ground pepper to taste

Serves 4–6

1 Cut each of the trimmed artichokes into quarters lengthwise. Fill a large bowl with cold water, squeeze the lemon quarters into the water, and then add the rinds to the bowl. Place the artichoke quarters in the bowl with the lemons and set aside.

2 Remove the feathery leaves and the tough outer layers from the fennel and cut the bulbs into medium-sized wedges. Peel the carrots and, if large, cut in half lengthwise and then into serving-sized pieces. Trim the celery head, separate into stalks, and slice the heart lengthwise into medium-sized pieces. Trim the tops from the radishes, leaving a small section of stem, and then slice off the root ends. Cut an X into the bottom of each radish. Trim the green tops and the root end from each green onion, then make a few lengthwise slices in the bulb. Finally, separate the leaves of the endive.

3 Put a small ramekin at each place setting. Drain the artichoke pieces well, pat them dry, and arrange on a large serving platter along with the fennel wedges, carrot pieces, celery stalks and pieces, radishes, green onions, and endive leaves. Bring to the table along with a cruet of olive oil, salt, and a pepper grinder. Let each diner season his or her own oil.

PECORINO

Walk into any cheese shop in Tuscany and you will find among the lovely straw-colored wedges of Parmesan from the north and the soft, milky mozzarella balls from the south round upon round of the local sheep's milk cheese known as *pecorino*. This specialty seems to come in as many varieties as there are producers.

As with most things Tuscan, nothing is wasted in the cheese-making process. From the whey is made a delicate, light ricotta that can be eaten fresh with olive oil, salt, and pepper, or incorporated into a variety of pasta dishes. The pecorinos themselves range from the soft, almost sweet fresh pecorinos to piquant, flavorful ones aged for varying lengths of time and more or less dense, salty, and rich in taste and smell.

Some producers lace their pecorino with various herbs, garlic, chile, parsley, spicy arugula, or slivers of wild truffles. Others are returning to the medieval technique of aging their cheeses in earthen pits to re-create the famous *pecorino di fossa*, a hard, yet moist cheese with a texture similar to that of a fine Parmesan and a ripe, spicy flavor. Still others are combining traditional pecorino-making techniques with those of other cheeses—Gorgonzola, for example—with spectacular results.

Green Vegetable Tart

Torta di Erbe Pontremolese • Tuscany • Italy

This savory *torta* comes from the small village of Pontremoli in the Lunigiana, a small, little-visited area in the northwestern part of Tuscany, just below Liguria. It uses a mixture of greens, including cucumber-scented borage, which grows wild in the area. Since it is as delicious at room temperature as it is warm, the *torta* is often served as part of a buffet at large gatherings. Make one to bring to a friend's house to start off a simple dinner—you'll find that it will be as well received as the most luscious homemade sweet.

PASTRY

2 cups (10 oz/315 g) all-purpose (plain) flour

½ teaspoon salt

½ cup (4 oz/125 g) chilled unsalted butter, cut into ½-inch (12-mm) pieces

About 6 tablespoons (3 fl oz/90 ml) water

FILLING

1 lb (500 g) Swiss chard

2 tablespoons extra-virgin olive oil

1 clove garlic, crushed

2 oz (60 g) borage or 1 head Belgian endive (chicory/witloof), chopped

1 leek, including tender green top, chopped

2 eggs, beaten

⅔ cup (5 oz/155 g) ricotta cheese

2 tablespoons grated Parmesan cheese

½ teaspoon salt

Freshly ground pepper to taste

1 egg lightly beaten with 1 tablespoon water

Serves 6

1 To make the pastry, in a large bowl, combine the flour and salt. Add half of the butter and, using your fingers, work the butter into the flour. Add the remaining butter and continue to work into the flour until the mixture resembles coarse crumbs. Slowly incorporate the water into the flour-butter mixture, stirring lightly with a fork and adding only enough to make a dough that holds together. Shape into a ball, wrap in plastic wrap, and refrigerate while you make the filling.

2 To make the filling, trim away the ribs and any battered or tough leaves from the chard. Bring a large saucepan three-fourths full of salted water to a boil. Add the chard and boil until the chard is wilted, about 3 minutes. Drain well and let cool. Squeeze out the excess water, then chop coarsely.

3 In a large, heavy frying pan over medium heat, warm the olive oil. Add the garlic to the pan and sauté until fragrant, about 2 minutes. Remove and discard the garlic.

4 Add the chard, the borage or endive, and the leek to the pan and sauté until the borage or endive is wilted, about 5 minutes. Remove from the heat.

5 In a large bowl, combine the eggs, ricotta and Parmesan cheeses, and salt. Season with pepper, add the sautéed vegetables, and mix well.

6 Position a rack in the lower third of the oven and preheat to 375°F (190°C).

7 To assemble the *torta*, divide the dough in half. On a lightly floured work surface, roll out half of the dough into an 11-inch (28-cm) round ⅛ inch (3 mm) thick. Drape the round over the rolling pin and carefully ease it into a 9-inch (23-cm) tart pan with a removable bottom, pressing it into the bottom and sides. (Alternatively, roll out the dough between 2 sheets of plastic wrap, peel off the top sheet, and use the other sheet for transferring the pastry round to the pan.)

8 Spoon the filling into the pastry-lined pan. Roll out the remaining dough half into a 10-inch (25-cm) round. Lay the dough round over the filling and trim the edges. Crimp lightly to form an attractive rim. Brush the top crust with the egg mixture.

9 Bake the *torta* until the crust is golden brown, about 45 minutes. Transfer to a rack and let cool for 10 minutes. Cut the *torta* into slices and serve warm or at room temperature.

Sweet-Tart Eggplant and Peppers

Caponata · Sicily · Italy

In this well-known Sicilian dish, eggplants, bell peppers, celery, and onions are cooked separately so that they retain their individual character, then simmered together with tomatoes in a sweet-and-sour sauce. The sweet and sour flavors of the dish reflect its Arabic heritage. Serve hot or cold, as an antipasto or a side dish. Caponata tastes best the day after it is made, once the flavors have had a chance to blend and mellow. It keeps well in the refrigerator, but should be brought to room temperature before serving.

1 In a deep, heavy frying pan, pour in oil to a depth of ½ inch (12 mm). Place over medium heat and heat until a piece of the eggplant dropped into the pan sizzles and swims around in the oil.

2 Dry the eggplant well with paper towels. Working in batches, and adding additional oil to the pan as needed, carefully arrange the eggplant pieces in the pan in a single layer. Cook, stirring occasionally, until the eggplant is tender and browned on all sides, 7–8 minutes. Using a slotted spoon, transfer to paper towels to drain.

3 When all of the eggplant has been cooked, fry the bell peppers in the same way until tender and lightly browned, 4–6 minutes, then drain on paper towels. Finally, fry the onions and celery together in the same way until tender and golden, 7–8 minutes, and drain on paper towels.

4 In a large saucepan over low heat, combine the tomatoes, olives, raisins, capers, sugar, and vinegar. Stir well and add the fried vegetables and salt. Cover and cook over low heat, stirring occasionally, until thickened, about 20 minutes. Add a little water if the mixture begins to dry out. Remove from the heat, transfer to a serving dish, and let cool. If time permits, cover and refrigerate overnight to allow the flavors to marry.

5 Bring to room temperature before serving. Just before serving, sprinkle with the toasted pine nuts.

Canola oil for frying

2 eggplants (aubergines), about
1 lb (500 g) each, cut into 1-inch
(2.5-cm) cubes

2 red or yellow bell peppers (capsicums),
seeded and cut into ¾-inch (2-cm) cubes

2 large yellow onions, cut into
¾-inch (2-cm) cubes

3 tender celery stalks, sliced

3 tomatoes, chopped

1 cup (5 oz/155 g) chopped pitted
green olives

⅓ cup (2 oz/60 g) raisins

2 tablespoons capers

2 tablespoons sugar

2 tablespoons red wine vinegar

Pinch of salt

¼ cup (1 oz/30 g) pine nuts,
lightly toasted (page 223)

Serves 6

Little Spinach Pies

Empanadillas Rellenas de Espinacas • Catalonia • Spain

Empanadillas, or "little pies," have been made in Spain since medieval times. This Catalan recipe calls for spinach, which is cultivated in the region's extensive market gardens, located around the lower Ebro River delta, a fertile expanse that also produces grains, olives, and wine grapes. Other popular fillings include tuna, chorizo, onion, or anchovy.

PASTRY

2 cups (10 oz/315 g) all-purpose (plain) flour

¼ cup (2 fl oz/60 ml) olive oil

2 tablespoons solid vegetable shortening

¼ cup (2 fl oz/60 ml) milk or water

1 teaspoon salt

½ teaspoon baking soda (bicarbonate of soda)

FILLING

⅓ cup (3 fl oz/80 ml) olive oil

4 cloves garlic, minced

1½ cups (9 oz/280 g) peeled, seeded (page 225), and chopped tomato

1½ lb (750 g) spinach (tough stems removed) and chopped

½ cup (2 oz/60 g) pine nuts

2 hard-boiled eggs, peeled and coarsely chopped

Salt and freshly ground pepper to taste

1 egg, beaten

Serves 4–6

1 To make the dough, put the flour into a bowl and make a well in the center. Add the oil, shortening, milk or water, salt, and baking soda to the well. Mix with a wooden spoon until the dough comes away from the sides of the bowl. Turn out onto a lightly floured work surface and knead briefly. Cover with a kitchen towel and let rest for 20–30 minutes.

2 Meanwhile, make the filling: In a frying pan over low heat, warm the olive oil. Add the garlic and sauté until softened, 2–3 minutes. Add the tomato and simmer, uncovered, until the tomato is soft and some of the liquid has been absorbed, about 10 minutes. Add the spinach and pine nuts and cook until the spinach is wilted, 3–5 minutes longer. Remove from the heat. Pour off the excess oil from the filling, then fold in the chopped eggs and season with salt and pepper. Let cool to room temperature. Set aside.

3 Preheat the oven to 350°F (180°C). Lightly oil a baking sheet.

4 Divide the dough into 2 equal pieces. On a lightly floured work surface, and working with 1 piece at a time, roll out the dough about ⅛ inch (3 mm) thick or less. Cut out rounds 4–5 inches (10–13 cm) in diameter. You should have about 12 rounds in all. Place a tablespoon of filling in the center of each round, fold in half, and seal, turning up the edges to make a narrow rim. Place on the prepared baking sheet and brush with the beaten egg.

5 Bake until golden, 20–30 minutes. Serve warm or at room temperature.

Salt Cod Fritters

Bolinhos de Bacalhau • Douro • Portugal

Although they originated in northern Portugal, these golden fritters are now served throughout the country. Accompany with few lemon wedges.

½ lb (250 g) boneless salt cod, soaked (page 225)

2 boiling potatoes, about 10 oz (315 g) total

2 tablespoons olive oil

1 small yellow onion, minced

2 cloves garlic, finely minced

2 eggs, lightly beaten

3 tablespoons *each* chopped fresh flat-leaf (Italian) parsley and fresh cilantro (fresh coriander)

Pinch of cayenne pepper

Freshly ground black pepper to taste

Milk, if needed

Olive oil or canola oil for deep-frying

Serves 6–8

1 Drain the cod and place in a saucepan with water to cover. Bring to a simmer over medium heat and cook until tender, 10–15 minutes. Drain and, when cool enough to handle, flake the cod, removing any bits of skin and small bones. Pulse in a food processor until finely shredded, then place in a bowl.

2 Meanwhile, in a saucepan, combine the potatoes with water to cover, bring to a boil, and boil until tender, 20–30 minutes. Drain and, when slightly cooled, peel and mash until smooth. Add to the salt cod.

3 In a small sauté pan over medium heat, warm the olive oil. Add the onion and sauté until tender, about 8 minutes. Add the garlic and sauté for 2 minutes. Add the contents of the sauté pan to the cod mixture and mix well. Fold in the eggs, parsley, and cilantro. Season with cayenne pepper and black pepper. The mixture should be the consistency of firm mashed potatoes. If it is too stiff, beat in a little milk. Form into balls 1 inch (2.5 cm) in diameter.

4 In a deep, heavy frying pan, pour oil to a depth of 2 inches (5 cm) and heat to 375°F (190°C) on a deep-frying thermometer. Add the balls, a few at a time, and fry until golden, about 4 minutes. Using a slotted spoon, transfer to paper towels to drain. Serve at once.

SHERRY

The Andalusian towns of Jerez de la Frontera, Sanlúcar de Barrameda, and Puerto de Santa Maria lie at the three points of a triangle ribboned with vineyards. According to Spanish law, the Palomino Fino grapes harvested from these vines are the only ones that can be used to make the product labeled Spanish sherry. Jerez de la Frontera harbors most of the area's bodegas, the warehouses in which the legendary wines are fermented, aged, and bottled.

To make sherry, the pressed grapes are first allowed to ferment in open casks. Then the wine is graded, fortified with brandy, and aged for a year or two. Finally, the critical *solera* process begins: Casks of sherry are arranged in a pyramid, with the oldest wines on the bottom and the youngest at the top. As the immature wines are slowly moved down the stack, they are blended with the older wines at each level, inheriting important characteristics as they age.

Fino and *oloroso* are the primary types of sherry. Both should be drunk from a tulip-shaped *copita*, its top just wide enough to appreciate the wine's heady aroma.

Toasted Bread with Garlic and Olive Oil

Fettunta · Florence · Italy

More than anything, the food of Tuscany is defined by its ingredients. Recipes rely much more on raw materials than on complex culinary techniques. So while bread and oil might sound like the humblest of dishes, when you use heavy, unsalted Tuscan bread (page 216) and jewel-green olive oil from the countryside, simplicity becomes sublime.

1 lb (500 g) coarse country bread (see note), thickly sliced

2 cloves garlic, halved

Extra-virgin olive oil for drizzling

Salt to taste

Serves 6

1 Prepare a fire in a charcoal grill, or preheat a broiler (grill).

2 Place the bread slices on the grill rack or a broiler pan and grill or broil, turning once, until golden, about 4 minutes total; do not allow the slices to scorch. Transfer the slices to a work surface and rub the cut sides of the garlic over one side of each piece of toast.

3 Arrange the slices on a serving platter, garlic-rubbed side up. Drizzle liberally with olive oil and sprinkle with salt. Serve at once.

Chickpeas with Salt Cod

Baccalà con i Ceci · Tuscany · Italy

Chickpeas, which hold their shape beautifully during cooking, are a wonderful match for the salty flavor and firm texture of salt cod.

6½ oz (200 g) salt cod

⅔ cup (4 oz/125 g) dried chickpeas (garbanzo beans)

1 small carrot, peeled and cut into pieces

1 small yellow onion, quartered

1 small celery stalk, cut into pieces

1 clove garlic, crushed

Salt to taste

⅓ cup (3 fl oz/80 ml) extra-virgin olive oil

Juice of ½ lemon

Freshly ground pepper to taste

4 large cupped lettuce leaves

2 tablespoons finely chopped fresh flat-leaf (Italian) parsley

Serves 4

1 In a bowl, combine the cod with water to cover. Refrigerate for 48 hours; change the water 8 times during that time.

2 Pick over the chickpeas, discarding any grit or misshapen beans. Rinse well and place in a saucepan. Add water to cover by 3 inches (7.5 cm) and bring to a boil. Reduce the heat to low, cover partially, and simmer until tender, 1½–2½ hours. Drain well.

3 Drain the salt cod. In a saucepan, bring water to a depth of 3–4 inches (7.5–10 cm) to a boil. The water must be deep enough to submerge the fish. Add the carrot, onion, celery, and salt cod, reduce the heat to low, cover, and simmer until the cod is tender, about 10 minutes. Drain, discarding the vegetables. Peel away the skin from the fish, then flake the fish, removing any bones. Place in a bowl and add the chickpeas.

4 Place the garlic clove in a small bowl, sprinkle with salt, and mash with a spoon or pestle. Whisk in the olive oil and then the lemon juice to make a dressing. Pour over the fish and beans, season with pepper, and toss gently but thoroughly.

5 Place a lettuce leaf on each individual plate. Top with the cod and beans, and garnish with the parsley. Serve warm or at room temperature.

Chicken and Ham Croquettes

Croquetas de Pollo y Jamón • Andalusia • Spain

Spaniards are fond of these bite-sized morsels with a crunchy, golden crust enclosing a creamy filling. Look for dry-cured imported *jambón serrano* in specialty-food stores.

¼ cup (2 fl oz/60 ml) olive oil, plus more for deep-frying

2 boneless, skinless chicken breast halves, about ¾ lb (375 g) total weight

1 small yellow onion, minced

⅓ cup (2 oz/60 g) all-purpose (plain) flour

2½ cups (20 fl oz/625 ml) milk

¼ lb (125 g) serrano ham, chopped

Salt and freshly ground pepper to taste

Pinch of ground cinnamon

1 egg, separated

Fine dried bread crumbs for coating

Serves 4–6

1 In a frying pan over medium-low heat, warm the ¼ cup (2 fl oz/60 ml) olive oil. Add the chicken, cover, and cook, turning once, until opaque throughout, about 10 minutes total. Transfer to a cutting board, let cool, and then chop finely.

2 Add the onion to the oil remaining in the pan and sauté over medium heat until golden, 12–15 minutes. Add the flour and stir until the mixture thickens, 3–4 minutes. Slowly pour in the milk, stirring constantly, and then cook, stirring, until very thick and creamy, about 5 minutes. Add the ham and chicken and season with salt, pepper, and cinnamon. Remove from the heat and let cool slightly. Lightly beat the egg yolk, then stir well into the mixture. Let cool.

3 In a shallow bowl, beat the egg white until frothy. Place the crumbs in another shallow bowl. Using 1 or 2 spoons, scoop up an egg-shaped ball of the chicken mixture. Dip it into the egg white and then into the crumbs, coating evenly each time. Place on a rack or on a baking sheet lined with parchment (baking) paper. Repeat until all the mixture is used.

4 In a deep frying pan, pour oil to a depth of 3 inches (7.5 cm) and heat to 375°F (190°C) on a deep-frying thermometer. Working in batches, fry the croquettes until golden, about 4 minutes. Transfer to paper towels to drain; keep warm. Place on a platter and serve hot.

Eggplant Salad with Onions and Peppers

Escalivada • Catalonia • Spain

Although *escalivar* means "to grill," many restaurant cooks in Spain roast their vegetables, as it is easier and requires less maintenance; that technique is used here.

2 yellow or red onions, unpeeled

Olive oil for rubbing on onions, plus 1 cup (8 fl oz/250 ml)

3 eggplants (aubergines)

3 tomatoes

2 red bell peppers (capsicums), seeded (page 219) and halved

½ cup (4 fl oz/125 ml) fresh lemon juice

3 cloves garlic, minced

Salt and freshly ground pepper to taste

Chopped fresh flat-leaf (Italian) parsley for sprinkling

Serves 6–8

1 Preheat the oven to 400°F (200°C). Put the onions in a small baking pan and rub with olive oil. Roast until tender when pierced, at least 1 hour. Let stand until cool enough to handle, then peel and slice ½ inch (12 mm) thick.

2 Meanwhile, prick the eggplants a few times with a fork and place them in a separate baking pan. Add the tomatoes to the pan and place in the oven along with the onions. Roast the tomatoes until the skins blacken, about 15 minutes. Let stand until cool enough to handle, then peel and cut into cubes. Continue to roast the eggplants until soft, about 45 minutes. Let cool, then peel and tear into large strips. Place in a colander to drain.

3 Turn the oven to broil (grill). Place the bell peppers, cut sides down, on a baking sheet. Broil (grill) until the skins blacken and blister. Remove from the broiler (grill), drape the peppers with aluminum foil, let cool for 10 minutes, and then peel away the skins. Cut into long, narrow strips. Combine the onions, eggplants, tomatoes, and peppers in a large bowl. In a small bowl, whisk together the 1 cup olive oil, the lemon juice, and the garlic. Season with salt and pepper. Pour over the eggplant mixture and toss to coat well. Taste and adjust the seasoning. Sprinkle the salad with parsley and serve.

Cheese Wafers

Frico • Friuli–Venezia Giulia • Italy

In the Friuli–Venezia Giulia region, in Italy's far northeast, crisp cheese wafers are made from a combination of aged and young montasio cheese. When young, montasio is mild and springy; with aging, it turns hard and brittle. Aged montasio is difficult to find outside of Italy; if it is unavailable, substitute Parmesan cheese, which has a similar dry texture.

½ lb (250 g) aged montasio or Parmesan cheese (see note)

2 oz (60 g) young montasio cheese

Canola oil

Makes about 2 dozen wafers

1 Grate the cheeses on the finest holes of a cheese grater into a bowl. Stir together.

2 Lightly rub a heavy griddle or frying pan with oil and place over medium heat. When a drop of water sprinkled onto the surface sizzles, the pan is ready.

3 Spread about 2 tablespoons of the grated cheese into a 2-inch (5-cm) round in the pan. Cook until the cheese melts and the underside is golden, about 1 minute. Using a thin spatula, turn the wafer over and cook the second side until golden, about 30 seconds longer. Carefully transfer to paper towels to drain. Let cool completely. Repeat with the remaining cheese.

4 When completely cool, the wafers are ready to serve. You can transfer the wafers to an airtight container and store at cool room temperature for up to 1 week.

Sage Bread Sticks

Grissini alla Salvia • Liguria • Italy

Thin, crunchy bread sticks turn up in many Italian breadbaskets. When flavored with sage or other herbs, they become a lovely accompaniment to a glass of wine. Or you might wrap them with thin slices of prosciutto and place them on an antipasto platter.

2½ teaspoons (1 package) active dry yeast

1 cup (8 fl oz/250 ml) warm water (105°–115°F/40°–46°C)

3½–4 cups (17½–20 oz/545–625 g) unbleached all-purpose (plain) flour

2 teaspoons salt

2 teaspoons dried sage, finely crumbled

⅓ cup (3 fl oz/80 ml) olive oil

Makes about 6 dozen bread sticks

1 In a small bowl, sprinkle the yeast over the warm water and let stand until creamy, about 5 minutes. Stir until dissolved. In a large bowl, using a wooden spoon, stir together 3½ cups (17½ oz/545 g) of the flour, the salt, and the sage. Add the yeast mixture and the olive oil. Stir until a soft dough that holds its shape forms, about 2 minutes. Turn out onto a lightly floured work surface and knead until smooth and elastic, about 10 minutes. If the dough feels sticky, knead in flour as needed.

2 Oil a large bowl, place the dough in it, and turn it once to coat the top. Cover the bowl with plastic wrap and let the dough rise in a warm, draft-free place until doubled in bulk, about 1 hour.

3 Preheat the oven to 400°F (200°C). Turn out the dough onto a lightly floured work surface. Punch down, then cut into 4 equal quarters. Working with one quarter at a time, cut the dough into 18 pieces. Keep the remaining quarters covered with plastic wrap. Using your palms, and working with one piece at a time, roll out the dough to form a rope 10 inches (25 cm) long. Place the ropes 1 inch (2.5 cm) apart on ungreased baking sheets.

4 Bake until crisp and browned, about 10 minutes. Transfer to a wire rack to cool completely. Repeat with the remaining dough quarters. Store in an airtight container at room temperature for up to 2 weeks.

APERITIFS AND DIGESTIFS

While Italians seldom drink hard liquor or cocktails, they do enjoy *aperitivi* before meals and *digestivi* after meals. The former stimulate the appetite and prepare the digestion for the food to come. Light, low in alcohol, and not too sweet, they are often accompanied with olives or *salatini*, little salted things like pretzels, nuts, or crackers.

Typical *aperitivi* are Aperol, flavored with oranges and often served with an orange slice in a glass with a sugared rim; Campari, which is cherry red and flavored with bitter herbs, orange zest, and quinine, served with soda or on the rocks; and vermouth, red or white wine flavored with sugar, roots, and bitter herbs.

As their name suggests, *digestivi* are known to aid digestion, and many have a toniclike medicinal quality. Every region has its own favorite, with Fernet-Branca the most famous. It has an extremely bitter taste and many people never get accustomed to it, but there are those who swear by its benefits after a big meal. Averna, from Sicily, is a less harsh alternative that is equally effective.

Asparagus Omelet

Tortilla de Espárragos • Catalonia • Spain

This omelet comes from Casa Leopoldo in Barcelona, where it appears in spring, along with the season's first asparagus and green garlic, at La Boquería market. If you cannot find green garlic, a combination of garlic chives and garlic cloves will capture a similar aroma.

½ lb (250 g) pencil-thin asparagus, tough ends removed

6 tablespoons (3 fl oz/90 ml) olive oil

8 green (spring) onions, including tender green tops, finely chopped

½ cup (1½ oz/45 g) coarsely chopped green garlic shoots, or 2 or 3 cloves garlic, minced

12 garlic chives, if using garlic cloves

7 large eggs

Salt and freshly ground pepper to taste

Serves 6

1 Bring a saucepan three-fourths full of water to a boil. Add the asparagus and boil for 3–4 minutes. Drain and place under cold running water to halt the cooking. Drain again and cut into 1-inch (2.5-cm) lengths. Set aside.

2 In a frying pan over low heat, warm 3 tablespoons of the olive oil. Add the green onions and the green or regular garlic and sauté until tender, about 8 minutes. Add the chives, if using, and the asparagus and sauté to warm through, about 2 minutes. Remove from the heat. In a bowl, lightly beat the eggs until blended. Add the asparagus mixture. Season with salt and pepper.

3 In an omelet pan or a frying pan over high heat, warm the remaining 3 tablespoons olive oil until very hot. Pour in the egg mixture and reduce the heat to medium. Cook until the underside is golden, about 6 minutes. Run a spatula around the edges of the pan a few times during cooking to loosen the eggs. Invert a large plate on top of the pan, invert the pan and plate together, and lift off the pan. Slide the omelet back into the pan and return it to low heat. Cook until pale gold and just set, 2–3 minutes longer.

4 Slide the omelet onto a serving plate, let cool slightly, and then cut into wedges to serve.

Garlicky Fried Mushrooms

Champiñones al Ajillo • Basque Country • Spain

Mushrooms grow wild in the abundant forests of the Basque country and Catalonia, and the people of both regions are crazy for wild mushrooms. *Boletus edulis* (porcini or cèpes), *girolles* (chanterelles), and *rabassoles* (morels) are among the most prized. Chanterelles, portobellos, and cremini combined with white cultivated mushrooms make a flavorful dish.

5 tablespoons (2½ fl oz/75 ml) olive oil

2 tablespoons minced garlic

¼ cup (½ oz/45 g) diced bacon or ham (optional)

1 lb (500 g) assorted fresh mushrooms (see note), brushed clean and halved if small or sliced ¼ inch (6 mm) thick

¼ cup (2 fl oz/60 ml) dry white wine or dry sherry, if needed

¼ cup (⅓ oz/10 g) chopped fresh flat-leaf (Italian) parsley

Salt and freshly ground pepper to taste

Serves 4–6

1 In a large frying pan over medium heat, warm the olive oil. Add the garlic and the bacon or ham, if using, and sauté until warmed through, about 2 minutes.

2 Raise the heat to high, add the mushrooms, and sauté briefly, stirring occasionally, until tender, 4–6 minutes, depending upon the type of mushrooms and the thickness of the slices. If the mushrooms haven't given off much juice, add the wine or sherry and continue to cook until the liquid is absorbed. Add the parsley and stir well.

3 Sprinkle with salt and pepper, transfer to a serving dish, and serve at once.

AN ITALIAN BAR

Every Tuscan town or village, no matter how small or grand, has a *bar*, or more likely several. This is where the Tuscan day begins, and where the life of the town hovers until the evening. Newspapers are read; politics and soccer are loudly debated; cigarettes are lit.

In the morning, glass counters are filled with brioches and sandwiches, which together with an espresso or a cappuccino constitute the average Tuscan breakfast. Locals tend to spend their time *in piedi* (standing up) at the long counter. Anyone who doesn't have to rush off to work or run errands lingers at a table, although there is sometimes a price for such privilege, indicated by menus that list two prices next to each item. Another flurry of activity occurs in midmorning, when workers abandon their offices to quickly gulp down an espresso.

The aperitivo hour begins sometime between 6:00 and 7:00 in the evening. In a small *bar*, a couple of bowls filled with *salatini* (little salted crackers) and olives will be set on the counter, to nibble on while drinking a Campari soda, a glass of wine or spumante, or some other lightly alcoholic drink. An exception to the "lightly alcoholic" category is the Negroni, a concoction of Campari, gin, and sweet vermouth purported to have originated in Florence.

Fancier places will usually offer more elaborate choices during the *aperitivo* hour—one can almost always find a platter of crisp raw fresh vegetables such as radishes, carrots, celery, and fennel; little bowls of olives, brine-cured capers, sweet gherkins and pickled onions; and slivers of hard cheese and various cured meats. You could make a meal out of these offerings, but restraint is advised.

The *aperitivo* is simply meant to tease every appetite, to help begin the slow descent from the bustle of the day's activities to the leisurely pace of the evening meal.

Mushrooms in Olive Oil

Funghi Sott'olio · Tuscany · Italy

Not long ago, preserving vegetables was the only way to eat them once their brief, glorious seasons had passed. Even though the circumstances that necessitated preservation have changed, the tradition itself remains. Serve these mushrooms as part of an antipasto plate, or chop them coarsely, mix with a mild, soft cheese, and use as a spread for crostini.

2 cups (16 fl oz/500 ml) red wine vinegar

1 lb (500 g) fresh button mushrooms, brushed clean, with stems intact

1 tablespoon salt

3 whole cloves

1 small cinnamon stick

2 bay leaves

4 peppercorns

About 1½ cups (12 fl oz/375 ml) extra-virgin olive oil

Makes 1 pt (16 fl oz/500 ml)

1 In a nonaluminum saucepan over high heat, combine 2 cups (16 fl oz/500 ml) water and the vinegar and bring to a boil. Add the mushrooms, the salt, 2 of the cloves, the cinnamon, and 1 of the bay leaves. Reduce the heat to medium and simmer, uncovered, for 20 minutes. Drain the mushrooms, discarding the seasonings, and spread on a kitchen towel to dry for 6 hours.

2 Spoon the mushrooms, peppercorns, and remaining clove and bay leaf into a sterilized 1-pt (16–fl oz/500-ml) glass jar. Pour in enough olive oil to cover the mushrooms. Let the jar rest, uncovered, for a couple of hours while the contents settle. Add more oil if necessary to cover the mushrooms, then cap the jar tightly. Set in a dark, dry place for at least 5 days before serving.

3 Serve the mushrooms with toothpicks. Once the jar is opened, refrigerate it; return the mushrooms to room temperature before serving.

Grilled Polenta with Mushrooms

Crostini di Polenta con Funghi • Piedmont • Italy

The cooking of the Piedmont is divided into two distinct cuisines, one of the cities and lowlands and one of the higher altitudes. Polenta, well known for its rib-sticking properties, holds a place of honor on the mountain table. Here, grilled slices are topped with sautéed mushrooms, but other toppings such as sautéed peppers, pesto sauce, or Gorgonzola would also be good. In fact, polenta crostini can be a wonderful substitute for bread crostini in nearly any recipe, especially as a base for stews.

1 To make the polenta, bring 4 cups (32 fl oz/1 l) water to a boil in a large saucepan. Add the polenta in a slow, steady stream, whisking constantly to prevent lumps from forming. Add the salt. Reduce the heat to low and cook, stirring often, until the polenta thickens and begins to pull away from the sides of the pan, 30–40 minutes.

2 Meanwhile, oil a 12-by-9-inch (30-by-23-cm) baking pan.

3 When the polenta is ready, pour it into the prepared pan, spreading it evenly with a spatula dipped in cold water. Let the polenta cool at room temperature until firm, about 1 hour, or cover with plastic wrap, place in the refrigerator, and chill overnight.

4 In a large frying pan over medium heat, melt the butter with the 1 tablespoon olive oil. Add the garlic and cook, stirring, until lightly golden, about 30 seconds. Stir in the mushrooms, thyme or rosemary, salt, and pepper. Cook, stirring often, until the mushrooms are browned, about 10 minutes.

5 Add the tomato and cook until the juices have evaporated, about 10 minutes more. Stir in the 1 tablespoon parsley and remove from the heat. Cover and keep warm.

6 Preheat a broiler (grill).

7 Cut the polenta into 8 squares and brush on both sides with olive oil. Arrange on a heavy baking sheet.

8 Broil (grill) 4 inches (10 cm) from the heat source, turning once, until crisp and golden on both sides, about 3 minutes on each side.

9 Place 2 polenta crostini on each plate. Top with the mushroom mixture, dividing evenly, and sprinkle with parsley. Serve hot.

POLENTA

1 cup (5 oz/155 g) polenta (coarse yellow cornmeal)

1 teaspoon salt

3 tablespoons unsalted butter

1 tablespoon olive oil, plus more as needed

1 clove garlic, finely chopped

¾ lb (375 g) fresh white mushrooms, brushed clean and halved or quartered if large

1 teaspoon chopped fresh thyme or rosemary

Salt and freshly ground pepper to taste

1 tomato, chopped

1 tablespoon chopped fresh flat-leaf (Italian) parsley, plus extra for garnish

Serves 4

Baked Asparagus Bundles

Fagottini di Asparagi al Forno • Emilia-Romagna • Italy

This dish of slender asparagus spears wrapped in creamy mozzarella cheese and sweet local prosciutto is a favorite in the fertile region of Emilia-Romagna. To transform it into a light meal, serve the bundles alongside a couple of fried eggs or a few slices of frittata. If pencil-thin asparagus are in the market, you will need the larger number of spears.

16–24 asparagus spears

Salt to taste

4 thin prosciutto slices

4 fresh mozzarella cheese slices

1 tablespoon unsalted butter, cut into bits

Salt and freshly ground pepper to taste

Serves 4

1 Preheat the oven to 375°F (190°C). Butter a 9-inch (23-cm) square baking dish.

2 Trim off any tough ends from the asparagus, cutting at the point at which they begin to turn white. Thicker asparagus spears benefit from a light peeling to within about 3 inches (7.5 cm) of the tips.

3 Bring a large saucepan three-fourths full of water to a boil. Add the asparagus and salt, reduce the heat to medium, and simmer until the spears are just beginning to bend when they are lifted by the stem end, 4–8 minutes; the timing will depend on the thickness of the asparagus. Using tongs, transfer to a platter and pat dry with paper towels.

4 Divide the asparagus evenly among the prosciutto slices, centering the spears across the end of each slice. Roll up the prosciutto, encasing the asparagus inside, to form 4 bundles.

5 Place the bundles in the prepared dish. Lay a mozzarella slice on top of each bundle. Dot the ends and tips of the asparagus with the butter.

6 Bake until the cheese is melted, about 10 minutes. Sprinkle with salt and pepper. Transfer to warmed individual plates and serve hot.

Pizza with Onion, Prosciutto, and Mozzarella

Pizza di Cipolle, Prosciutto e Mozzarella • Veneto • Italy

This inspired combination is typical of the lively pizzerias in Verona. Since it is made without tomatoes, it's considered a *pizza bianca*, or "white pizza." If you like, scatter a handful of arugula leaves on top of the hot pizza as it emerges from the oven.

Pizza dough (page 214)

2 tablespoons olive oil

1 red onion, thinly sliced

Salt to taste

¼ lb (125 g) mozzarella cheese, preferably fresh, thinly sliced

2 or 3 thin prosciutto slices

Serves 2–4

1 Prepare the pizza dough as directed through step 4. Place a pizza stone or a baking sheet on the lowest rack of the oven and preheat the oven to its hottest setting (500° or 550°F/260° or 290°C) 30–60 minutes before baking.

2 Meanwhile, in a frying pan over medium heat, warm the olive oil. Add the onion and sauté until tender and golden, about 5 minutes. Sprinkle lightly with salt and remove from the heat. Set aside to cool.

3 Uncover the dough and, using your fingers, stretch and flatten it into a 12-inch (30-cm) round, turning the round over once or twice as you work. Dust a baker's peel or the back of a baking sheet with flour. Place the dough round on the peel and shake the peel once or twice to be sure the dough isn't sticking. If it is, lift the round and dust the peel or baking sheet with more flour.

4 Spread the onion on the dough. Immediately slide the pizza onto the baking stone. Bake for 3–4 minutes. Remove from the oven and arrange the mozzarella on top. Bake until the edges are puffed and the crust is crisp and golden brown, 4–5 minutes longer. Remove from the oven and arrange the prosciutto slices on top. Transfer the pizza to a cutting board. Cut into wedges to serve.

LA VERA PIZZA NAPOLETANA

Although pizza is available in nearly every corner of the world, nowhere does it achieve the status that is grandly bestowed upon it in Naples, where the modern pie was born. A few years ago, Neapolitan pizza makers, alarmed at what they saw as the degradation of their culinary art, established La Vera Pizza Napoletana, an organization that is dedicated to defining and defending all genuine Neapolitan pizza recipes and preparations.

The classic pizza is a subtle masterpiece—a no-frills pie that showcases only a handful of the very best ingredients available. It is always thin crusted, but never too thin, and always crisp and chewy at the same time.

Seasonal crushed vine-ripened tomatoes, fresh mozzarella, a thread of high-quality fruity green olive oil, and several bright leaves of fresh basil crown the popular Margherita pizza, named after a beloved queen. *Pizza marinara*, another ubiquitous traditional pie, is topped with nothing but tart tomatoes, tangy garlic, a bit of oregano, and a dash of olive oil. Both of these simple recipes respect the legacy of simplicity that separates the true Neapolitan pie from its competitors.

Savory Pie with Greens

Coca de Verduras • Balearic Islands • Spain

Most visitors to the Balearics arrive by overnight ferry from Barcelona or Valencia. The three largest islands of the chain, Majorca, Minorca, and Ibiza, each have a distinctive character and culture, but cooks on all of them are well known for their sweet rolls and savory pastries, including *cocas*. Similar to pizzas, *cocas* feature toppings as varied as caramelized onion, anchovies, and pine nuts or this simple combination of greens and onions.

DOUGH

1 tablespoon active dry yeast

½ cup (4 fl oz/125 ml) warm water (105°–115°F/40°–46°C)

3½ cups (17½ oz/545 g) unbleached all-purpose (plain) flour

¾ cup (6 fl oz/180 ml) cold water

2 tablespoons olive oil

1½ teaspoons salt

TOPPING

1 lb (500 g) spinach

1 lb (500 g) Swiss chard

3 tablespoons olive oil

6 green (spring) onions, including tender green tops, chopped

Salt to taste

Sweet paprika to taste

1 large tomato

Cornmeal for dusting

Serves 8–10

1 To make the dough, in a large bowl, dissolve the yeast in the warm water. Add ½ cup (2½ oz/75 g) of the flour and stir to combine. Cover and let stand for about 30 minutes.

2 Add the remaining 3 cups (15 oz/470 g) flour, the cold water, the olive oil, and the salt and stir with a wooden spoon until the dough comes away from the sides of the bowl. Turn out onto a lightly floured work surface and knead until smooth and elastic, about 10 minutes. (You can also make the dough in a stand mixer, mixing it with a paddle attachment and then kneading it on low speed with the dough hook for 10 minutes.) Transfer the dough to an oiled bowl, cover the bowl with plastic wrap, and let stand in a warm place until the dough has doubled in size, about 1 hour.

3 Turn out the dough onto a lightly floured work surface, punch down, and shape into 1 large ball or divide in half and shape into 2 balls. Place on a floured baking sheet, cover, and let rest in the refrigerator for about 30 minutes.

4 Meanwhile, make the topping: Remove the tough stems from the spinach and Swiss chard leaves and cut the leaves into narrow strips. Set aside. In a large frying pan over medium heat, warm the olive oil. Add the green onions and sauté until softened, about 3 minutes. Then add the spinach and chard and cook, stirring occasionally, until wilted, about 3 minutes longer. Transfer to a sieve and drain off any excess liquid. Season with salt and paprika. Set aside.

5 If you are using a pizza stone, place it in the oven and preheat to 475°F (245°C) for at least 30 minutes. Meanwhile, chop the tomato and set aside.

6 If making a single, rectangular crust, dust a baking sheet with cornmeal. On a lightly floured work surface, roll out and stretch the dough into a rectangle large enough to line the baking sheet. Transfer the rectangle to the baking sheet, top evenly with the greens mixture, and then scatter the tomato on top.

7 If making 2 round crusts, roll out and stretch each ball into a 9-inch (23-cm) round, forming a slight rim at the edges. If using a pizza stone, place 1 round on a cornmeal-dusted baker's peel or rimless baking sheet. If not using a pizza stone, place the round on a cornmeal-dusted baking sheet. Top evenly with half of the greens mixture and then half of the tomato. Place the *coca*-topped baking sheet in the oven, or slide the *coca* from the baker's peel or sheet onto the stone.

8 Bake until the crust is golden, about 15 minutes. Remove from the oven and let cool slightly. If making round *cocas*, top the second one with the remaining greens mixture and tomato, place it into the oven, and bake in the same way. Cut the rectangular *coca* into squares or the round ones into wedges. Serve warm.

Herbed Focaccia

Focaccia alle Erbe • Liguria • Italy

Focaccia is so popular in Liguria that it's served all day long. The well-loved flat bread is made in other regions of Italy as well, with a delicious variety of ingredients and shapes.

2½ teaspoons (1 package) active dry yeast

½ cup (4 fl oz/125 ml) warm water (105°–115°F/40°–46°C)

1½ cups (12 fl oz/375 ml) milk

6 tablespoons (3 fl oz/90 ml) olive oil

5 cups (1½ lb/750 g) unbleached all-purpose (plain) flour

2 teaspoons salt

1 teaspoon chopped fresh thyme or ¼ teaspoon dried thyme

1 teaspoon chopped fresh rosemary or ¼ teaspoon dried rosemary

1 teaspoon chopped fresh sage or ¼ teaspoon dried sage

Coarse salt to taste

Serves 8

1 In a small bowl, sprinkle the yeast over the warm water and let stand until creamy, about 5 minutes. Stir until dissolved. Add the milk and 4 tablespoons (2 fl oz/60 ml) of the olive oil and stir to combine.

2 In a large bowl, using a wooden spoon, stir together the flour, salt, thyme, rosemary, and sage. Add the yeast mixture and stir until a soft dough forms, about 2 minutes. Turn out the dough onto a lightly floured work surface and knead until smooth and elastic, about 10 minutes. Shape the dough into a ball.

3 Oil a large bowl, place the dough in the bowl, and turn it once to coat. Cover with plastic wrap and let rise in a warm, draft-free place until doubled in bulk, about 1 hour.

4 Oil a 15-by-10-by-1-inch (38-by-25-by-2.5-cm) jelly-roll pan. Punch down the dough, transfer to the prepared pan, and flatten it out with your hands to cover the bottom completely. Cover with plastic wrap and let rise again in a warm place until doubled in bulk, about 1 hour.

5 Preheat the oven to 450°F (230°C).

6 Using your fingertips, press down firmly into the dough to make dimples about 1 inch (2.5 cm) apart and 1 inch (2.5 cm) deep. Drizzle the entire surface of the dough with the remaining 2 tablespoons olive oil and sprinkle with the coarse salt.

7 Bake until golden brown, 25–30 minutes. Slide the focaccia onto a wire rack to cool completely. Cut into squares to serve.

Fennel Bread Rings

Taralli · Apulia · Italy

Crisp bread rings are popular in Apulia, where bakers shape tiny rounds on the tips of their fingers for bite-sized snacks and fashion large versions for topping with salads for a quick lunch. *Taralli* are great any time with a robust red wine, such as Apulia's Notarpanaro. If you like, vary the flavor by adding black pepper in place of the fennel seeds.

2½ teaspoons (1 package) active dry yeast

½ cup (4 fl oz/125 ml) warm water (105°–115°F/40°–46°C)

3 cups (15 oz/470 g) unbleached all-purpose (plain) flour

1 cup (5 oz/155 g) semolina flour

2 tablespoons fennel seeds

2 teaspoons salt

¾ cup (6 fl oz/180 ml) dry white wine

½ cup (4 fl oz/125 ml) olive oil

Makes 6 dozen

1 In a small bowl, sprinkle the yeast over the warm water and let stand until creamy, about 5 minutes. Stir until dissolved.

2 In a large bowl, using a wooden spoon, stir together the all-purpose flour, semolina flour, fennel seeds, and salt. Add the yeast mixture, wine, and olive oil and stir until a soft dough forms, about 2 minutes. Turn out the dough onto a lightly floured work surface and knead until smooth and elastic, about 10 minutes. Shape the dough into a ball.

3 Oil a large bowl, place the dough in the bowl, and turn it once to coat. Cover with plastic wrap and let rise in a warm, draft-free place until doubled in bulk, about 1 hour.

4 Turn out the dough onto a lightly floured work surface and cut into 8 equal pieces. Work with 1 piece of dough at a time and keep the rest covered.

5 Pinch off a small piece of dough about the size of a grape. Using your palms, roll the piece against the floured work surface until it stretches into a rope 4 inches (10 cm) long. Shape the dough into a ring, pinching the ends together to seal. Repeat with the remaining dough pieces.

6 Bring a large pot three-fourths full of water to a boil. Add the dough rings, a few at a time, and boil until they rise to the surface, about 1 minute. Skim them out with a slotted spoon and place, not touching, on a kitchen towel to drain. Repeat until all the rings are boiled and drained.

7 Preheat the oven to 350°F (180°C).

8 Arrange the boiled rings on baking sheets. Bake until golden brown and crisp all the way through, about 45 minutes. Turn off the oven and open the door slightly. Let cool in the oven for 10 minutes.

9 Transfer to a wire rack and let cool completely. Store in an airtight container for up to 2 weeks.

"Fierce" Potatoes

Patatas Bravas · New Castile · Spain

No one can resist these spicy potatoes. Found all over Spain, they are especially popular in the lively tapas bars of Madrid. Some versions of the recipe omit the stock, cooking the potatoes in a tomato mixture spiked with chiles, while others add aioli to the sauce for a smoother, richer consistency. Pour glasses of cold beer to temper the heat of the peppers.

Olive oil for frying

2 lb (1 kg) new potatoes, cut into 2-inch (5-cm) chunks

2 tablespoons all-purpose (plain) flour

1 teaspoon sweet paprika

1 cup (8 fl oz/250 ml) beef stock

2 tablespoons red wine vinegar

½–1 teaspoon red pepper flakes

¼ cup (2 fl oz/60 ml) tomato sauce

Salt to taste

Serves 8

1 In a large frying pan over medium heat, pour olive oil to a depth of 1½ inches (4 cm). When the oil is hot, add the potatoes and more oil if necessary to cover, reduce the heat to low, and cook until the potatoes are tender, 20–30 minutes. Raise the heat to high and allow them to brown. Using a slotted spoon, carefully transfer the potatoes to a baking dish and keep warm in a low oven.

2 Drain off all but 1 tablespoon of the oil from the pan. Add the flour and paprika and stir over low heat for a few minutes. Slowly add the stock, stirring constantly. Then add the vinegar and red pepper flakes and simmer, uncovered, over low heat for about 10 minutes. Stir in the tomato sauce and salt. Taste and adjust the seasoning.

3 Pour the sauce over the potatoes, toss to coat, and serve warm.

TAPAS BARS

The tapas bar is Spain's most enduring gastronomic icon. The bar itself can go under various names—*tasca*, *taberna*, *mesón*, *bodega*—and its character can vary as well, from Madrid's elegant José Luis, where caviar is on the menu, to Seville's rustic El Rinconcillo, where small plates have been served in an unchanging atmosphere for over three hundred years. Some bars are attached to restaurants, some stand alone. Some have only a handful of choices; others produce scores of different dishes. Some are frequented by bullfight fans; others are the haunts of the intelligentsia. Some display all their culinary wares on a long bar, others have patrons order from a chalkboard list. Tapas bars are found in big cities and in the smallest villages, and a *tapeo*, visiting a number of spots in a single evening before heading off to dinner, is the best way to explore them.

Many Spaniards stop for a quick drink and tapa or two before the midday meal or in the afternoon, but the evening hours, between seven and ten, are when tapas bars are at their busiest and most convivial. Most customers stand at the bar, which is usually topped with wood, tile, or marble and often has sawdust strewn below it.

A tapa is traditionally just a single bite. But if you favor a particular dish, you can order a *ración*, a larger portion. Some people skip dinner altogether, filling up on *tapas* and *raciones* and then wending their way home.

What you drink depends on where you are. In Andalusia, reputedly the birthplace of the tapa, the region's celebrated sherry is drunk. But in Madrid, table wines or beer are more common, and in Asturias, serious cider drinkers don't forsake their local beverage.

Grilled Bread with Tomato

Pa amb Tomàquet • Catalonia • Spain

This classic Catalan tapa is the soulmate of the better-known Italian bruschetta. It is no more than good rustic bread that is grilled, rubbed with garlic, then rubbed with a ripe tomato half and drizzled with a fruity olive oil. The tomatoes can also be very finely chopped, almost to a purée, and rubbed into the bread. If you wish to add a small embellishment, top with a chopped anchovy or a paper-thin slice of serrano ham.

6 slices coarse country bread, each about ⅓ inch (9 mm) thick

Extra-virgin olive oil, preferably Spanish

2 cloves garlic

2 very ripe tomatoes, halved

Salt and freshly ground pepper to taste

Serves 6

1 Preheat the broiler (grill) or prepare a fire in a charcoal or gas grill.

2 Brush both sides of the bread lightly with olive oil. Place on a baking sheet and place under the broiler, or place on the grill rack. Broil or grill, turning once, until golden brown on both sides, 4–6 minutes total.

3 Transfer the bread to a platter. Rub the hot bread on one side with the garlic cloves, and then squeeze the tomato halves as you rub them across the surface. Drizzle with olive oil and season with salt and pepper. Serve at once.

Fried Stuffed Zucchini Flowers

Fiori di Zucca Fritti • Lazio • Italy

One of the pleasures of summer in Rome is being able to eat fried stuffed zucchini flowers to one's heart's content. When you bite into the *fiori fritti*, the cheese and anchovies ooze out with mouthwatering decadence. Serve them immediately so they don't get soggy. Use the blossoms as soon as possible after picking, as they will wilt within a day.

1 cup (5 oz/155 g) all-purpose (plain) flour

1 teaspoon salt

2 eggs

½ cup (4 fl oz/125 ml) cold sparkling mineral water

1 tablespoon canola oil, plus extra for deep-frying

2 oz (60 g) fresh mozzarella cheese

20 large squash blossoms, such as zucchini (courgette) blossoms

10 anchovy fillets, drained (page 219), patted dry, and cut in half crosswise

Makes 20

1 In a small bowl, stir together the flour and salt. Add the eggs, mineral water, and the 1 tablespoon canola oil and whisk just until blended. Cut the mozzarella into sticks 1 inch (2.5 cm) long by ¼ inch (6 mm) wide by ¼ inch (6 mm) thick.

2 In a heavy frying pan at least 3 inches (7.5 cm) deep or in a deep-fat fryer, pour oil to a depth of 1 inch (2.5 cm). Heat to 375°F (190°C) on a deep-frying thermometer or until a bit of the batter sizzles when dropped into the oil.

3 While the oil is heating, gently spread open the petals of each flower and carefully pinch out the filaments inside. Insert a piece of the cheese and the anchovy into each flower. Press the petals closed.

4 One at a time, dip the flowers into the batter, turning to coat completely. Lift out and drain off the excess. Working with a few at a time, slip the flowers into the hot oil and fry until golden brown on all sides, about 4 minutes. Using a slotted spoon, transfer to paper towels to drain. Continue with the remaining flowers. Serve at once.

Gazpacho Cream Dip

Salmorejo Cordobés • Andalusia • Spain

The word *salmorejo* is used to describe a sauce made with water, vinegar, oil, salt, and pepper. *Salmorejo cordobés* adds tomato and garlic to this base, making it essentially a gazpacho without the water. It can be garnished with chopped hard-boiled eggs and diced ham or with pieces of chopped orange. This purée is served in Córdoba and Seville, where it is used as a dip for fresh vegetables such as carrots, celery, pepper strips, and blanched green beans.

½ lb (250 g) day-old coarse country bread, crusts removed and bread sliced

4 ripe tomatoes, peeled, seeded (page 225), and chopped

1 small green bell pepper (capsicum), seeded and coarsely chopped

3 cloves garlic, chopped

2 raw eggs

1 teaspoon salt, plus salt to taste

½ cup (4 fl oz/125 ml) olive oil

¼ cup (2 fl oz/60 ml) red or white wine vinegar

Freshly ground pepper to taste

¼ lb (125 g) serrano ham, chopped (optional)

2 hard-boiled eggs, peeled and coarsely chopped (optional)

Carrots, celery, and bell peppers (capsicums), cut into 2-inch (5-cm) slices, for serving

Serves 8

1 In a bowl, combine the bread with water to cover. Let soak for 15–20 minutes.

2 Squeeze the bread dry and place it in a blender or food processor along with the tomatoes, bell pepper, and garlic. Process until smooth. Add the raw eggs and the 1 teaspoon salt and process to blend. Then, with the motor running, slowly drizzle in the olive oil, processing until it is incorporated and the mixture is emulsified. Mix in the vinegar and season with salt and pepper.

3 Spoon the purée into a shallow bowl. If desired, garnish with the chopped ham and hard-boiled eggs. Serve with a selection of raw vegetables for dipping.

Artichoke Omelet

Tortino di Carciofi • Florence • Italy

This dish is called a *tortino* because it is baked in the oven. If it were cooked on the stove top, it would be called a frittata. Zucchini, cardoons, and eggplant can all be substituted for the artichokes. Serve the *tortino* cut into thin wedges as an appetizer, or with country bread and a small green salad as a light supper.

6 baby artichokes, trimmed (page 219)

1 lemon, sliced into quarters, plus more lemon wedges for serving

½ cup (2½ oz/75 g) all-purpose (plain) flour

1 teaspoon salt, plus salt to taste

½ cup (4 fl oz/125 ml) extra-virgin olive oil

1 clove garlic, minced

6 eggs

2 tablespoons water

Freshly ground pepper to taste

Serves 4

1 Preheat the oven to 350°F (180°C).

2 Cut the artichokes into thin slices, drain the pieces well, and pat dry. Fill a large bowl with cold water, squeeze the lemon quarters into the water, and then add the rinds to the bowl. Place the artichoke quarters in the bowl with the lemons and set aside.

3 Combine the flour and the 1 teaspoon salt on a plate and stir to mix well. In a large ovenproof pan over medium heat, warm the olive oil. Add the garlic and sauté until golden, about 1 minute. Dust the artichoke slices with the flour mixture, shaking off the excess, and add them to the pan. Fry the slices, turning once, until well browned, about 5 minutes.

4 Meanwhile, in a bowl, lightly beat the eggs until blended. Beat in the water and season with salt and pepper. When the artichokes are well browned, pour in the egg mixture. The eggs should sizzle when they hit the pan. Swirl the pan to distribute the eggs evenly, and immediately put into the oven. Bake until the *tortino* is set on the surface, 20–25 minutes.

5 Bring to the table at once, cut into wedges in the pan, and serve with lemon wedges, or slide onto a serving plate and bring the plate to the table.

IL LARDO DI COLONNATA

It isn't every day that a new culinary sensation hits Tuscany. Of course, *lardo di Colonnata*—the hard layer of fat just below the skin of the pig's back, preserved in a brine of salt water, garlic, herbs, and spices—isn't actually new. For centuries, it has been a staple of marble cutters in Colonnata, a quarry town in the white-marbled Apuan Alps above Carrara. Now, however, the secret is out, and restaurants and food shops all over the region are clamoring for pale white *lardo*, with its soft, buttery texture and aromatic spicing.

What makes Colonnata's version so special, and different from its rather unappealing counterpart, common lard, is the way it's preserved and aged. Every winter, vats or troughs built of local marble are filled with slabs of the fat, which are then covered with water, salt, and some combination (every family has its own recipe) of seasonings, such as bay leaves, pepper, juniper berries, thyme, and nepitella.

The vats are stored in cool, dark cellars for at least six months while the *lardo* cures, during which time it soaks up the herbs and turns as white as the marble in which it is aged. Not surprisingly, the best way to eat *lardo* is also the most traditional: in thin slices on warm toasted bread.

Chickpea Fritters

Panelle · Sicily · Italy

In Palermo, these crisp-edged fritters called *panelle* are sometimes tucked into sandwich rolls with fresh ricotta cheese. You could use that option for a memorable but quick lunch.

3½ cups (28 fl oz/875 ml) water

2 cups (8 oz/250 g) chickpea (garbanzo bean) flour

2 teaspoons salt, plus salt to taste

Freshly ground pepper to taste

Canola oil for frying

Serves 8–10

1 Line two 15-by-10-by-1-inch (38-by-25-by-2.5-cm) jelly-roll pans with plastic wrap.

2 Pour the water into a saucepan, then slowly whisk in the chickpea flour, a little at a time, to prevent lumps from forming. Whisk in the 2 teaspoons salt and the pepper. Place over medium-low heat and bring to a simmer, stirring constantly. Reduce the heat to low and cook, stirring, until the mixture is very thick, about 5 minutes. Pour the batter into the prepared pans, dividing evenly. With a rubber spatula dipped in water, quickly spread to a thickness of about ¼ inch (6 mm). Let cool completely to allow the mixture to set.

3 Using a knife, cut the cooled sheets into 3-by-2-inch (7.5-by-5-cm) strips, then peel the strips off the plastic wrap. In a large, deep frying pan, pour canola oil to a depth of ½ inch (12 mm). Place over medium heat and heat until the oil sizzles when a piece of a strip is dropped into it. Carefully lower a few strips into the hot oil; do not crowd the pan. Fry, turning once, until golden brown and slightly puffed, 3–4 minutes. Using a slotted spoon, transfer to paper towels to drain. Keep warm in a low oven while you fry the remaining pieces. Arrange the fritters on a platter, season with salt, and serve at once.

Shrimp in Green Sauce

Gamberi in Salsa Verde · Tuscany · Italy

This dish originates in Viareggio, one of the popular vacation towns along the Tuscan coast. If tomatoes are not at their peak of ripeness, serve this colorful dish in radicchio-leaf cups.

GREEN SAUCE

½ cup (¾ oz/20 g) chopped flat-leaf (Italian) parsley

¼ cup (1½ oz/45 g) chopped yellow onion

2 tablespoons capers, chopped

2 anchovy fillets, drained, patted dry, and chopped

½ cup (4 fl oz/125 ml) extra-virgin olive oil

2 tablespoons fresh lemon juice

½ teaspoon grated lemon zest

Salt to taste

1 lb (500 g) shrimp (prawns), peeled and deveined

4 tomatoes, sliced crosswise

Lemon wedges for serving

Serves 6

1 To make the green sauce, on a cutting board, chop together the parsley, onion, capers, and anchovies until very fine. Transfer to a bowl. Whisk in the olive oil, lemon juice and zest, and salt.

2 Bring a saucepan three-fourths full of water to a boil. Add salt and the shrimp and cook just until they turn bright pink, about 2 minutes. Drain.

3 Arrange the tomato slices, slightly overlapping, on a large platter. Place the warm shrimp on top. Drizzle with some of the sauce and garnish with lemon wedges. Pass the remaining sauce at the table.

Polenta Crisps with Anchovy Sauce

Polenta Fritta con Acciugata • Florence • Italy

The Mugello is the rugged, mountainous area of Tuscany bordering Emilia-Romagna. In the past, economic hardship often forced *mugellani* into seasonal migration to the Maremma, the coastal area of southern Tuscany, for work. This recipe combines anchovies from the sea with polenta, a staple from the mountains. The polenta can be made the day before, refrigerated, and then sliced and fried just before serving. You can also top it with anything from marinated mushrooms to a dollop of tomato sauce and a fresh basil leaf.

POLENTA

Salt

1 cup (5 oz/155 g) coarse-grain polenta

SAUCE

⅓ cup (3 fl oz/80 ml) extra-virgin olive oil

1 clove garlic, minced

4 large olive oil–packed anchovy fillets

2 tablespoons chopped canned tomatoes

1 tablespoon capers, rinsed and finely chopped

1 teaspoon finely chopped fresh flat-leaf (Italian) parsley

Freshly ground pepper to taste

Canola oil for deep-frying

Serves 6

1 To make the polenta, in a deep saucepan over high heat, bring 5 cups (40 fl oz/1.1 l) water to a boil and salt lightly. Pour in the polenta in a thin, steady stream, stirring constantly. Reduce the heat to low and cook, stirring constantly with a wooden spoon, for about 40 minutes. The polenta is ready when it becomes quite thick and pulls away from the sides of the pan as you stir it. Remove from the heat.

2 Oil the bottom and sides of a 9-by-12-inch (23-by-30-cm) baking pan. Pour the polenta into the prepared pan, smoothing the surface with the back of a spoon. Let the polenta cool for a few hours or for up to overnight in the refrigerator.

3 Invert the polenta onto a cutting board. Cut into 2-by-1-inch (5-by-2.5-cm) rectangles.

4 To make the sauce, in a saucepan over low heat, warm the olive oil. Add the garlic and sauté until fragrant, about 1 minute. Add the anchovy fillets and, using a wooden spoon, break them apart in the pan. Cook, stirring occasionally, until the sauce thickens slightly, about 6 minutes. Stir in the tomatoes, capers, and parsley, season with pepper, raise the heat to medium, and cook, uncovered, for 10 minutes. Remove from the heat, cover, and set aside.

5 Lay a few sheets of paper towel near the stove and top with a wire rack. In a large, deep frying pan, preferably of cast iron, pour vegetable oil to a depth of 3 inches (7.5 cm) and heat to 350°F (180°C) on a deep-frying thermometer. Working in batches, fry the polenta, turning once, until crisp and golden on both sides, about 10 minutes total. Using a slotted spoon or spatula, transfer the slices to the wire rack to drain. Keep warm in a low oven until serving.

6 Arrange the hot polenta crisps on a warmed serving platter and top each slice with a teaspoon of the sauce. Serve at once.

Tomatoes Stuffed with Green Rice

Pomodori Ripieni di Riso Verde • Lazio • Italy

During the summer months, ripe red tomatoes bursting with a rice stuffing are a staple antipasto of Roman *trattorie*. They can also be served as a first course.

½ cup (3½ oz/105 g) medium-grain white rice such as Arborio

Salt to taste

4 large tomatoes

2 tablespoons olive oil

¼ cup (¼ oz/10 g) finely chopped fresh basil, plus whole leaves for garnish

2 tablespoons chopped fresh flat-leaf (Italian) parsley

2 tablespoons grated Parmigiano-Reggiano cheese

1 small clove garlic, finely chopped

Freshly ground pepper to taste

Serves 4

1 Bring a saucepan filled with water to a boil. Add the rice and salt and simmer until the rice is about half cooked, 9–10 minutes. Drain, place in a large bowl, and set aside.

2 Preheat the oven to 350°F (180°C). Oil a baking dish just large enough to hold the tomatoes snugly.

3 Cut off a slice ½ inch (12 mm) thick from the top of each tomato and reserve. Using a small spoon, scoop out the tomato seeds and juice and place in a sieve set over a bowl. Arrange the tomatoes in the prepared baking dish.

4 Add the rice, olive oil, chopped basil, parsley, cheese, and garlic to the strained tomato juice and mix well. Season with salt and pepper. Spoon the rice mixture into the hollowed-out tomatoes, dividing evenly. Cover each tomato with its top.

5 Bake until the rice is tender, about 20 minutes. Remove from the oven and serve hot or at room temperature, garnished with the whole basil leaves.

Potato Omelet

Tortilla Española • New Castile • Spain

Unlike most omelets, a *tortilla española* is served at room temperature. It is the classic tapa, prepared all over Spain, but reputed to be best in La Mancha, a forbidding land of parched earth and the legendary, aging windmills from the story of Don Quixote.

½ cup (4 fl oz/125 ml) olive oil, plus 3 tablespoons

2 lb (1 kg) baking potatoes, peeled and sliced ¼ inch (6 mm) thick

Salt and freshly ground pepper to taste

2 yellow onions, thinly sliced

6 eggs, lightly beaten

2–4 oz (60–125 g) serrano ham, diced (optional)

1 large red bell pepper (capsicum), roasted, peeled and seeded (page 219), then cut into strips (optional)

Chopped fresh flat-leaf (Italian) parsley, for garnish

Serves 6–8

1 In a large frying pan over low heat, warm the ½ cup olive oil. Add half of the potato slices and fry, turning occasionally, until tender but not browned, 15–20 minutes. Using a slotted spoon, transfer the potato slices to a plate and season with salt and pepper. Repeat with the remaining potato slices. Leave the oil in the pan.

2 In another frying pan over medium heat, warm the 3 tablespoons oil. Add the onions and fry until soft and golden, about 15 minutes. Remove from the heat and let cool a bit.

3 In a large bowl, whisk the eggs until blended. Mix in the onions and the ham and roasted pepper, if using. Season with salt and pepper. Fold in the cooked potatoes.

4 Heat the oil remaining in the large frying pan over low heat and pour in the egg mixture. Cook until the bottom is set and golden, 8–10 minutes. Invert a plate on top of the pan, invert the pan and plate together, and lift off the pan. Slide the omelet back into the pan and return to low heat. Cook until the second side is set, about 4 minutes. Slide onto a plate, garnish with parsley, and cut into wedges.

TORTILLA

Some French food historians insist that the omelet was the creation of a Gallic monk at work in the kitchen of a Carthusian monastery. But a number of Spanish scholars dismiss the claim, countering with a story set in the court of Louis XIV, where the queen's Spanish cook served what he called *tortilla a la Cartujana*—Carthusian omelet—to a chorus of royal raves.

Whatever the omelet's true origin (nearly everyone else agrees that it dates back to ancient Rome), Spain's *tortilla española*, a large, thick cake of eggs, potatoes, and sometimes onion, is one of the simplest yet best representatives of the omelet world.

This classic *tortilla* is served many ways. Office workers might eat a wedge in the late morning to bridge the wait for lunch. Shepherds and schoolchildren like to slip a square between two slices of crusty bread for a hearty midday meal. In the evening, staffs at tapas *bars* such as Madrid's old, lively Taberna de Antonio Sánchez know that everyone who walks in the door will expect to find a bountiful supply of *tortillas* on top of the bar. The ubiquitous, delicious *tortilla* is even known to turn up on everyday dinner tables, which have been simply set out with bread and salad and usually washed down with a chilled local white wine.

Marinated Anchovies

Boquerones • Cantalonia • Spain

The Costa Brava's Mediterranean waters yield excellent anchovies. Local fleets set out from the small settlements of Palamós, Sant Feliu de Guíxols, and L'Escala, the last an important anchovy center for centuries because of the plankton-rich waters just beyond its port. *Boquerones* appear in nearly every tapas assortment in Catalonia and Andalusia. The small fresh fish are sometimes dipped in seasoned flour and deep-fried, or they are left uncooked to marinate in a tart vinaigrette such as this one.

1 lb (500 g) fresh anchovies (about 16)

Kosher salt and freshly ground pepper to taste

⅔ cup (5 fl oz/160 ml) extra-virgin olive oil

⅓ cup (3 fl oz/80 ml) red wine vinegar

2 cloves garlic, finely minced

1 red onion, sliced paper-thin

3 tablespoons chopped fresh flat-leaf (Italian) parsley

Serves 4

1 Lay the anchovies on a plate, sprinkle with kosher salt, cover, and refrigerate overnight. The next day, using a small, sharp knife, slit each fish along its belly and remove the entrails. Cut off the head in back of the gills and discard. Slip the knife under the backbone near the neck and slide it to the tail, separating the bone from the bottom fillet. Repeat with the top fillet. Discard the bone. Rinse the anchovies.

2 In a bowl, whisk together the olive oil, vinegar, and garlic to make a vinaigrette. Pour just enough of it over the anchovies to cover them. Let stand for 35–45 minutes at room temperature. Place the onion slices in a shallow bowl and spoon the remaining vinaigrette over them. Let stand for 15 minutes.

3 Divide the onion slices among individual plates, then lay the anchovies on top. Sprinkle with the parsley and pepper and serve.

Fried Sage Leaves

Salvia Fritta · Tuscany · Italy

Italy's warm Mediterranean climate is perfect for growing sage. In Tuscany, not only is it one of the most widely used of all culinary herbs, but the leaves are also dipped in batter and fried. Choose especially large, fresh, attractive leaves and serve them plain as appetizers. You can also use them as a dramatic garnish for grilled fish or steaks.

24 large, fresh sage leaves

1 egg

1 cup (5 oz/155 g) all-purpose (plain) flour

½ teaspoon salt, plus salt to taste

Corn oil or soybean oil for deep-frying

Serves 6

1 Rinse the sage leaves well, shake off as much water as possible, and lay them on a clean kitchen towel to dry.

2 In a shallow bowl, beat the egg until blended. Beat in 2 tablespoons water and set aside. Sift the flour onto a plate and mix in the ½ teaspoon salt.

3 Line a tray with paper towels and set a wire cooling rack on top. Place next to the stove.

4 Pour oil to a depth of 1 inch (2.5 cm) into a deep, heavy frying pan, preferably cast iron, and heat to 350°F (180°C) on a deep-frying thermometer.

5 While the oil is heating, gently slip the sage leaves into the egg mixture. Once the proper temperature has been reached, working quickly, take out 1 sage leaf at a time, allowing the excess egg mixture to drain off. Coat with the salted flour, shaking off the excess, and carefully place in the hot oil. Repeat with additional sage leaves, being careful not to crowd the pan. Fry the sage leaves until lightly golden, about 3 minutes. Do not allow them to brown. Using a wire skimmer, transfer the sage leaves to the wire rack to drain.

6 When all the leaves have been fried, sprinkle them with salt. Arrange the leaves in a single layer on a platter and serve at once.

Four Seasons Pizza

Pizza Quattro Stagioni • Campania • Italy

Pizza quattro stagioni is the perfect pie for people who cannot make up their minds. It is one of Italy's most popular pizzas, and every *pizzaiolo* gives it his own special touch. Substitute any toppings you like, such as *prosciutto cotto*, anchovies, salami, sausage, and cheese. For a Neapolitan-style pizza with a crisp crust, bake the pie on a baking stone or tiles (available in cookware stores) as directed here. If you lack these options, bake it on an oiled pizza pan or a heavy baking sheet placed on the oven rack in the lowest position.

PIZZA DOUGH

1¼ teaspoons active dry yeast

½ cup (4 fl oz/125 ml) warm water (105°–115°F/40°–46°C)

1½ cups (7½ oz/235 g) unbleached all-purpose flour

1 teaspoon salt

TOPPING

1 red bell pepper (capsicum), roasted (page 219)

½ cup (4 fl oz/125 ml) tomato sauce

2 fresh white mushrooms, brushed clean and thinly sliced

2 jarred or canned artichoke hearts, drained and thinly sliced

6 black olives, pitted and thinly sliced

2 tablespoons olive oil

2 fresh basil leaves, torn into small pieces

Makes one 12-inch (30-cm) pizza; serves 2–4

1 To make the dough, in a small bowl, sprinkle the yeast over the warm water and let stand until creamy, about 5 minutes. Stir until dissolved.

2 In a large bowl, using a wooden spoon, stir together the flour and salt. Add the yeast mixture and stir until a soft dough forms, about 2 minutes. Turn out the dough onto a lightly floured surface and knead until smooth and elastic, about 10 minutes. Shape the dough into a ball.

3 Place the dough in a floured bowl. Cover the bowl with plastic wrap and let rise in a warm, draft-free place until doubled in bulk, about 2 hours.

4 Punch down the dough and knead briefly on a floured work surface to remove any air bubbles. Leave the ball on the floured surface and invert a bowl over it. Let rise until doubled in bulk, about 1 hour.

5 Place a pizza stone or unglazed quarry tiles on the lowest rack of the oven and preheat the oven to its hottest setting (500° or 550°F/260° or 290°C) 30–60 minutes before baking.

6 To make the topping, cut or tear the roasted bell pepper into narrow strips. Set aside.

7 Uncover the dough and, using your fingers, stretch and flatten it into a 12-inch (30-cm) round, turning the round over once or twice as you work.

8 Dust a baker's peel or the back of a baking sheet with flour. Place the dough round on the peel and shake the peel once or twice to be sure the dough isn't sticking. If it is, lift the round and dust the peel or baking sheet with more flour.

9 Spread the tomato sauce on the dough, leaving a ½-inch (12-mm) border uncovered. Visualize the surface in 4 equal wedges and arrange the mushrooms, artichoke slices, olives, and pepper strips each in their own wedge. Drizzle with the olive oil.

10 Immediately slide the pizza onto the baking stone. Bake until the edges are puffed and the crust is crisp and golden brown, 5–7 minutes.

11 Remove from the oven and transfer to a cutting board. Sprinkle with the basil, cut into wedges, and serve at once.

BREAD

Tuscans are extraordinarily proud of their bread, but at first bite you may wonder why. True, the heavy golden loaves piled one atop the other at the local bakery are gorgeous to look at, their crusts appealingly thick, their pale interiors dense and textured. But at first mouthful, the uninitiated may will say it has no taste. Further consideration reveals that what it lacks is not flavor, but salt.

Some pundits contend that Tuscan bread is saltless (or *sciocco*, meaning "insipid," as it is called there) because historically salt carried a tax, and saltless bread was a way around it. Others say that Tuscan cooking has such strong flavors that it requires a bland but well-textured bread.

There is no doubt, however, that the best Tuscan bread is made from stone-ground flour, uses a natural leavening agent, and is baked in wood-burning ovens, as it was in the old days when meals were made of *pane e companatico*— bread and something to go with the bread. The absence of salt in the bread means that as the

loaf goes stale, it hardens but doesn't mold, so day-old bread is never wasted. It is an ingredient in such Tuscan classics as *acquacotta* (a soup from the Maremma made of vegetables, egg, and bread), *ribollita* (bread-and-vegetable soup), *pappa al pomodoro* (tomato-and-bread soup), and *panzanella* (bread salad with tomatoes, onions, cucumbers, and basil).

Once you get used to it—toasted and drizzled with olive oil, covered with tomatoes and basil, or as a tool for soaking up sauces—it is difficult to imagine a bread more suited to Tuscan food.

That said, the best Tuscan *panifici* use organic flours and filtered spring water to make unsalted loaves of whole wheat, farro, corn, rye, or mixed grains. Some are sprinkled with sesame seeds, others laced with anything from rosemary and walnuts to black olives and fiery peperoncini. Even for the most die-hard of salt lovers, each one of these loaves makes a delicious accompaniment to any meal.

Black Cabbage Bruschetta

Fette col Cavolo Nero • Tuscany • Italy

Cavolo nero, or Tuscan "black cabbage," grows leafy and tall all summer long and throughout the fall, but it isn't ready to eat until after the first frost, which is usually in November. Late fall is also when the olives are pressed and harvested, and the rich taste of the black cabbage is offset beautifully by the sharp, fruity flavor of the new oil.

1 bunch black cabbage (see note) or kale

2 cloves garlic

6 slices coarse country bread, ½ inch (12 mm) thick

Extra-virgin olive oil

Salt and freshly ground pepper to taste

Serves 6

1 Remove the center rib from the black cabbage. If using kale, cut off the heavy bottom stalks. Cut the cabbage or kale leaves into coarse strips. Crush 1 of the garlic cloves.

2 Bring a large saucepan three-fourths full of salted water to a boil over high heat. Add the cabbage or kale and the crushed garlic clove, cover, and boil until the greens are wilted and tender, about 20 minutes. Drain and let cool. When the greens are cool enough to handle, squeeze out the excess liquid, then roughly chop the leaves.

3 Toast the bread. Cut the remaining garlic clove in half and rub 1 side of each piece of toast with a cut side of the garlic.

4 Arrange the bread slices, garlic side up, on a platter or individual plates and divide the greens evenly among them. Drizzle generously with olive oil. Season with salt and pepper and serve at once.

GLOSSARY

AJOWAN SEEDS Ajowan seeds (also known as *ajwain*) come from the thymol plant, a close relative of caraway and cumin. Native to southern India, the plant also thrives in Egypt, Iran, Afghanistan, and Pakistan. The seeds resemble large celery seeds. They have a sharp taste and, when crushed, smell strongly of thyme. Ajowan has been used for centuries in India to flavor vegetable dishes, breads, pickles, and pappadums. It helps control digestive problems, so it is often added to starchy dishes and those containing legumes. If unavailable, thyme imparts a similar flavor.

ANCHOVIES Preserved with salt, which highlights their naturally sharp, briny taste, these tiny, silver-skinned fish are used as a flavor enhancer. For the freshest-tasting best-quality, and meatiest anchovies, look for those sold layered whole in salt. They are available in 1-lb (500-g) tins or sold by weight from larger tins in specialty-food stores and many Italian delicatessens. If salted anchovies are unavailable, use a good brand of anchovy fillets packed in olive oil. Select those sold in glass jars, which permit you to judge more easily their meatiness.

To prepare salted anchovies for use, rinse well under cold running water and scrape off their skins with a small, sharp knife. Split open along the backbone, cutting off the dorsal fins. Then pull out the spines and rinse the fillets well. Pat dry with paper towels, place in a glass or other nonreactive bowl, pour in olive oil just to cover with a thin layer, cover tightly, and refrigerate. Use within 2 weeks.

ARTICHOKES Prickly on the outside but tender within, artichokes are are actually the flower bud of a large-leaved perennial in the sunflower family. If left on the plant, the buds would gradually open to reveal glorious purple blossoms, but harvesters cut them when they are still tightly closed.

To trim artichokes, cut the stem flush with the bottom. Using a serrated knife, cut about 1½ inches (4 cm) off the top of the artichoke. Using scissors, snip off the pointed tips of each leaf. Rub the artichoke with a lemon half to preserve its color while you prepare it.

ASAFETIDA This resinous substance, obtained from two species of the giant fennel, is best known for its strong smell, which is released when the spice is ground but mellows as it is cooked. Asafetida is used in small amounts of ¼–½ teaspoon. It can be replaced with about 1 teaspoon minced garlic, or taste.

AVOCADO LEAVES The long, leathery leaves of the avocado tree are used fresh or dried as a savory, aniselike seasoning to dishes in south-central Mexico.

To toast avocado leaves, heat a heavy frying pan over medium heat. Place the leaves on the pan, press down on them with a spatula, and cook them briefly, turning once, just until they color lightly and give off their fragrance.

BEANS Whether beans are gathered and eaten fresh in spring and early summer or dried for use at other times of the year, enthusiastic eaters value such favorites as speckled, pale pink borlotti, similar to cranberry beans; cannellini, ivory-colored kidney beans of moderate size; and chickpeas (garbanzo beans), large, round, tan beans.

To cook dried beans, first sort through them to eliminate any debris or misshapen specimens. Presoak in cold water, cover, and refrigerate overnight or, to quick-soak, place in a large pot of cold water, bring to a boil, and let stand for 1–2 hours. After soaking, drain the beans, place in a pot with fresh water to cover, bring to a boil, and simmer until tender, 1–2 hours, depending upon the type of bean. In some recipes that do not require long cooking, you can substitute canned beans. A 15-ounce (470-g) can, rinsed and drained, yields about 2 cups (14 oz/440 g) beans, equivalent to the yield of about 3 ounces (90 g) dried beans.

BELL PEPPERS Also known as capsicums and sweet peppers, large and meaty green bell peppers turn red and become sweeter when fully ripened. As attractive as they are versatile, bell peppers add crunch when used raw in appetizers; take on a silky sweetness when cooked slowly; and contribute a distinctive smokiness when roasted.

To roast bell peppers, using tongs or a large fork, hold a whole pepper over the flame of a gas burner for 10–15 minutes, turning it to char and blister the skin evenly. Place in a bowl, cover, and leave for 10 minutes. The steam will loosen the skin and allow for easier peeling. When the pepper is cool, peel and discard the blackened skin, then slit the pepper lengthwise and remove the stem, seeds, and membranes. If you have a large number of peppers to roast or if you have an electric range, broil (grill) the peppers, turning as needed, until charred on all sides.

BLACK SALT Black salt, known in India as *kala namak*, is not a true sodium salt at all but rather a sulfur compound or deposit, which causes it to taste and smell of boiled eggs with onions. The salt is mined from underground deposits in central India, Pakistan, and Afghanistan. It is brownish black in its natural form, hence the name. When ground, however—the form in which it is usually sold—the crystals become light pink. It is usually sprinkled over appetizers, snacks, and starters, and is known for being both a flavor enhancer and an appetite stimulant.

BOUQUET GARNI The classic bouquet garni includes only three herbs: fresh flat-leaf (Italian) parsley sprigs, fresh thyme sprigs, and bay leaves. When a recipe calls for a bouquet garni, use 3 large parsley sprigs, 2 large thyme sprigs, and 1 bay leaf. Lay the thyme and bay on the parsley sprigs, "pleat" the parsley sprigs to hold the other herbs firmly in the center, tightly wind kitchen string around the whole packet, and then tie securely, leaving a tail of string to permit easy removal of the herb bundle from the dish. The sprigs must be fresh, as any mustiness will diminish the flavor.

BREAD, COARSE COUNTRY European-style country bread has a thick and chewy crust enveloping a tender and moist crumb. The classic loaf is white, but darker whole-wheat (wholemeal) versions are also sold. Seek out similar loaves at bakeries, which usually label them country or peasant breads.

BREAD CRUMBS Used to make crisp toppings for oven-baked dishes or to lend body to fillings, bread crumbs should be made from a slightly stale coarse country white loaf.

To make dried bread crumbs, trim the loaf of its crusts and process in a food processor to form crumbs. Dry the crumbs on a baking sheet in a preheated 325°F (165°C) oven for about 15 minutes; let cool, process again until fine, and then bake, stirring once or twice, until pale gold, about 15 minutes longer.

CAPERS Growing wild throughout the Mediterranean, the caper bush yields tiny gray-green buds that are preserved in salt or pickled in vinegar to produce a piquant seasoning or garnish.

CARDAMOM This tall, perennial shrub grows on the Malabar coast of southern India. The pale green, three-sided, oval pods are about ½ inch (12 mm) long, each of which contains up to 20 small, black seeds. When ground, the seeds give off an intense, camphorlike aroma, although the taste is sweet and mild, with lemony and grassy notes. The loose and ground seeds lose flavor quickly, so it is best to buy whole pods and remove and grind the seeds as they are needed.

To toast cardamom: Heat whole pods or seeds in a dry frying pan over medium heat for a few minutes until their aroma develops.

CHAT MASALA In India, various saladlike snacks are known by the generic name *chat*, and *chat masala* (*masala* simply means "blend") is the tart and salty spice mixture commonly used. Every Indian cook has a favorite recipe, but *chat masala* typically contains cumin seeds, red pepper, black pepper, black salt, coarse salt, asafetida, and mango powder; the last gives the blend its sharp, tart flavor.

CHICHARRONES Known in English as fried pork rinds, these are the crisp cracklings made from sheets of air-dried pork skin with just a paper-thin layer of fat. In Mexican markets, they are sold in huge sheets. The more widely available snack variety, sold as bite-sized pieces, may be used in most recipes.

CHILE OIL Chile oil is an infusion of fresh or dried hot red chiles in vegetable oil or sesame oil. The hot, flavored red oil is used sparingly as a condiment and seasoning.

CHILES, DRIED Buy dried chiles with skins that are flexible rather than brittle in texture, and store them in airtight containers, away from both light and moisture.

ANCHO A dried form of the poblano, anchos measure 4½ inches (11.5 cm) long, with wide shoulders and wrinkled, deep reddish brown skin, and have a mild bittersweet chocolate flavor and a slight aroma of prunes.

ÁRBOL This is a smooth-skinned, bright reddish orange chile about 3 inches (7.5 cm) long, narrow in shape and fiery hot

CHIPOTLE The smoke-dried form of the ripened jalapeño is rich in flavor and very hot. Sold in its dried form, it is typically a leathery tan, although some varieties are a deep burgundy. It is available packed in a vinegar-tomato sauce (*chiles chipotles en adobo*) as well as lightly pickled (*en escabeche*)

PASILLA These skinny, wrinkled, raisin-black pasillas are about 6 inches (15 cm) long, with a sharp, fairly hot flavor.

To seed dried chiles, clean them with a damp cloth, then slit them lengthwise and use a small, sharp knife to remove the seeds.

To toast dried chiles, clean them with a damp cloth, then heat a heavy frying pan over medium heat. Add the whole or seeded chiles, press down firmly with a spatula, turn the chiles, and press down once more before removing. The chiles will change color only slightly and start to give off their aroma.

Caution The oils that are naturally present in chiles can cause a painful burning sensation when they come in contact with your eyes or other sensitive areas of your skin. After handling them, be sure to wash your hands thoroughly with warm, soapy water. If you have particularly sensitive skin, wear kitchen gloves or slip plastic bags over your hands before working with chiles.

CHILES, FRESH Choose firm, bright fresh chiles. Smaller chiles are usually hotter. Store them in the refrigerator for up to 1 week.

ANAHEIM This long, green, mild to moderately spicy chile is found in most markets. It is similar to the New Mexican chile variety.

GÜERO A pale yellow to light green chile. Several varieties may be used, including the Fresno, yellow banana, and Hungarian wax, which vary in degree of heat. Most are rather sweet with a pungent punch.

JALAPEÑO This popular chile, measuring 2–3 inches (5–7.5 cm) in length, has thick flesh and varies in degree of hotness. It is found in green and sweeter ripened red forms.

POBLANO Named for the Mexican state of Puebla, this moderately hot chile is usually about 5 inches (13 cm) long and is known for its polished deep green skin.

SERRANO Slender chiles measuring 1–2 inches (2.5–5 cm) long that are very hot, with a brightly acidic flavor. Available in both green and ripened red forms at most markets.

To roast, peel, and seed fresh chiles, using tongs, hold a whole chile over the flame of a gas burner for 10–15 minutes (5–8 minutes for smaller chiles), turning it to char and blister the skin evenly. Place in a bowl, cover, and leave for 10 minutes. The steam will loosen the skin and allow for easier to peeling. When the chile is cool, peel off the blackened skin, then slit the chile lengthwise and remove the stem, seeds, and membranes. If you have a large number of chiles to roast or if you have an electric range, broil (grill) the chiles, turning as needed, until charred on all sides.

CHINESE FIVE-SPICE POWDER The components of this popular southern Chinese spice blend vary, but star anise, fennel seeds or aniseeds, cinnamon, cloves, Sichuan peppercorns, and sometimes ginger are usually part of the mix.

CHORIZO/CHOURIÇO There are countless variations on this spicy sausage, common in Spanish, Portuguese, and Mexican cooking, but lean and fat pork, garlic, herbs, and generous amounts of paprika (the source of its deep red color) are always part of the mix. Depending upon the region and the sausage maker, these sausages are sold fresh, dried to various stages, or slightly smoked.

CREMA Although *crema* translates simply as "cream," Mexican *crema* is a thick, rich, slightly soured product that can be found in jars in Latin American grocery stores. In its place, you can use the more widely available French crème fraîche, which is similar in consistency. A substitute may be made by thinning commercial sour cream slightly with whole milk or half-and-half (half cream).

To make crema, in a small nonaluminum bowl, stir together 1 cup (8 fl oz/250 ml) heavy cream (do not use an ultrapasteurized product) and 1 tablespoon buttermilk or good-quality plain yogurt with active cultures. Cover with plastic wrap, poke a few holes in the plastic, and leave at warm room temperature (about 85°F/30°C) until well thickened, 8–24 hours. Stir, then cover with fresh plastic wrap, and refrigerate until firm and well-chilled, about 6 hours. If the *crema* becomes too thick, thin with a little whole milk or half-and-half (half cream).

COCONUT, SHREDDED The rich, chewy white flesh of the mature fruit of a tropical palm tree is used in sweet and savory recipes. Toasting gives it an even richer, nutlike flavor.

To toast shredded coconut, preheat an oven to 350°F (180°C). Evenly spread the coconut in a thin layer on a baking dish and toast, stirring frequently, until golden brown, 7–10 minutes.

CORNSTARCH Also known as cornflour, cornstarch is a fine-textured powder made from maize, sometimes with wheat flour added. When used in a paste with water as a thickener, it results in a glossy, translucent sauce, and gives a crisp coating to fried foods.

DAIKON Used extensively in Japanese cooking, the daikon is a cylindrical radish that grows up to 20 inches (50 cm) long and 2 inches (5 cm) in diameter. As with most Asian radishes, it is most often cooked, pickled, or eaten raw.

EGG Eggs are sometimes used raw or partially cooked in sauces, dressings, and preparations such as aioli. These eggs run the risk of being infected with salmonella or other bacteria, which can lead to food poisoning. This risk is of most concern to small children, older people, pregnant women, and anyone with a compromised immune system. If you have health or safety concerns, do not consume raw or partially cooked eggs.

To separate an egg, crack the shell in half by tapping it against the side of a bowl and carefully break the shell apart with your fingers. Holding the shell halves over the bowl, gently transfer the yellow yolk back and forth between them, letting the clear white drop away into the bowl. Taking care not to break it, transfer the yolk to another bowl. Alternatively, gently pour the egg from the shell onto the slightly cupped fingers of your clean hand, held over a bowl. Let the whites fall between your fingers into the bowl; the whole yolk will remain in your hand. The same basic function is performed by an egg separator placed over a bowl. The separator holds the yolk intact in its cuplike center and allows the white to drip out into the bowl through slots in its side.

FISH SAUCE In many Southeast Asian kitchens, fish sauce assumes the same seasoning role played by soy sauce in China and Japan. Made by layering anchovies or other tiny fish with salt in barrels or jars and leaving them to ferment, the dark amber liquid has a pungent, salty flavor. The two most common types are Thai *nam pla* and Vietnamese *nuoc mam*, with the latter having a milder flavor.

FLOUR, WINTER-WHEAT Cooks in the American South depend on the flour finely milled from pure, soft winter wheat to give their biscuits extra flakiness. Extra grinding, sifting, and refinement create flour, such as the much-loved White Lily brand, with a finer texture particularly suited for baking. Self-rising soft-wheat flours incorporate salt and leavening for easier cooking.

FOIE GRAS Foie gras, the highest expression of French *charcuterie*, is whole fresh duck or goose liver from an animal that has been fattened by *gavage*, a process in which the animals are force-fed grain so their livers become enlarged and very fat. Because of its high fat content, the beige to tan liver hardens when chilled and is initially difficult to handle. It is first marinated, then placed over very low heat just long enough to cook it through and release some of its fat. A duck liver that is too large (over 1 lb/500 g) or too fat (indicated by a yellowish tinge) is liable to melt too quickly.

GALANGAL Similar in appearance to ginger, to which it is related, this gnarled rhizome has a mustardlike, slightly medicinal flavor. Known in Thailand as *kha*, in Indonesia and Malaysia as *laos*, and sometimes called Siamese ginger, galangal is available fresh and frozen whole, or as dried slices. If only the dried form can be found, use half the quantity you would for fresh. If it will be pounded or blended, reconstitute it first by soaking in warm water for 30 minutes until pliable; unsoaked pieces can be added directly to simmering liquids.

GARAM MASALA This keynote spice mixture of northern India also turns up in Southeast Asian kitchens. The blend—sold commercially or made at home—almost always features coriander seeds, cumin, cardamom, cloves, black pepper, cinnamon, nutmeg, and mace. It is used to season dishes at the beginning of cooking and is sprinkled over finished dishes.

GHEE Used throughout Indian cooking, ghee literally means "fat." There are two types: *usli ghee* (clarified butter) and *vanaspati ghee* (vegetable shortening). A recipe that calls simply for ghee is understood to mean *usli ghee*. Indian clarified butter differs from the European equivalent in having been simmered until all the moisture is removed from the milk solids and the fat is amber colored. This gives *usli ghee* its unique nutty taste. Clarification also increases the butter's storage life. *Vanaspati ghee* is a pale yellow, hydrogenated blend of various vegetable oils that is processed to look, smell, and taste very similar to *usli ghee*. Both are readily available; *usli ghee* can also be easily made at home.

To make usli ghee, heat ½ lb (250 g) butter in a pan over medium-low heat, uncovered, until it melts. Increase the heat to medium and simmer the butter, stirring often, until the clear fat separates from the milk solids, about 15 minutes. During this process a layer of foam will rise to the top of the butter and the butter will crackle as its milk solids lose moisture. When the milk solids lose all moisture, the fat as well as the milk residue will turn amber colored. When this occurs, remove the pan from the heat and let the residue settle on the bottom. When cool enough to handle, pour the clear fat, which is the *usli ghee*, into a jar, ensuring that no residue gets in. Alternatively, strain it through two layers of cheesecloth (muslin). Discard the residue. *Usli ghee* may be refrigerated, covered, for up to 6 months or frozen for up to 12 months. Allow to thaw before use. Makes ¾ cup/6 fl oz/180 ml *usli ghee*.

GINGER The edible root or rhizome of ginger is buff colored and smooth when young, and sometimes comes with slender, pink-tipped green shoots attached. When older, root ginger becomes a dull, deep buff color with slightly wrinkled skin; its flavor intensifies and the flesh becomes fibrous. It is peeled and grated, minced, sliced, or coarsely chopped for use as an edible flavoring of unique taste and appealing spiciness. Dried powdered ginger is not a suitable substitute; however, processed ginger products packed in brine or vinegar may be used, if rinsed first.

To make ginger juice, peel and finely grate fresh root ginger onto a piece of fine cloth, gather up into a ball and squeeze to extract the juice. The pulp can be discarded or saved for another use. 1 tablespoon of grated ginger will produce approximately 1½ teaspoons of ginger juice. Ginger wine is a seasoning and marinade made by combining 1 part ginger juice with 2–3 parts rice wine.

HERBS Choose fresh herbs that look bright, fragrant, and healthy. Avoid those that have wilted, yellowed, or blackened leaves or stems. To store fresh herbs, wrap them in damp paper towels then place them in a plastic bag and refrigerate for 3–5 days.

BASIL This sweet and spicy fresh herb is especially popular in the cooking of Italy and the south of France. It pairs perfectly with sun-ripened tomatoes.

BASIL, THAI Three types of basil are used in Thailand: *kraprow*, *maenglak*, and *horapa*. *Kraprow* has serrated green leaves with a tint of purple and a hint of anise flavor overlaying the familiar basil scent. *Maenglak*, also called lemon basil, has smaller leaves and a lemony scent. *Horapa* has purple stems, shiny leaves, and an anise aroma. All three can be used interchangeably and European sweet basil can be substituted.

CHIVES These thin green shoots, members of the onion family, are used fresh to add onion flavor to greens and mild-tasting ingredients such as eggs, cheeses, seafood, and poultry.

CILANTRO This lacy-leafed annual herb, also known as fresh coriander, has a fresh scent and bright, astringent flavor—an acquired taste for some. Cilantro leaves should be added at the end of cooking or used raw, as long cooking destroys their delicate flavor.

DILL This feathery, grassy-tasting herb is often used to season vinegars and pickling brines. It is frequently used to flavor cucumbers.

EPAZOTE This distinctly flavored, pungent herb is used in Mexican dishes, especially those with black beans. It can be hard to find, but is often available in Latin American markets.

KAFFIR LIME LEAVES The kaffir lime contributes its rich, citrusy flavor to curry pastes and other savory and sweet dishes through its dried, fresh, or frozen leaves and its gnarled rind. Its juice, however, is not used. Pesticide-free lemon or lime leaves may be substituted.

MINT More than 600 different types of mint exist, although peppermint and spearmint are the most common. Mint is typically used as an accompaniment to lamb and as a garnish.

OREGANO Related to mint and thyme, this strongly scented herb actually gains in flavor from drying, unlike most herbs. It is the signature seasoning of pizza and is added to many sauces and marinades.

OREGANO, MEXICAN Although similar in flavor to the more familiar Mediterranean oregano, Mexican oregano is more pungent and less sweet than its Mediterranean kin, making it a perfect match for the spicy, cumin-laden dishes of Mexico and the American Southwest. Add it at the beginning of cooking to allow time for its complex flavor to emerge and meld with others. Purchase small packets of the dried herb in Latin American markets.

PARSLEY Southern European in origin, this widely versatile herb adds its bright, fresh flavor to many different kinds of savory foods. The flat-leaf variety, also known as Italian parsley, has a more pronounced flavor than the curly type, which is used as a garnish.

POLYGONUM LEAVES Known also as Vietnamese mint and in Malaysia as *laksa* leaves or *daun kesom*, these slender green-and-purple leaves have an exotic, herbaceous flavor. They are added fresh to noodle dishes in Malaysia and to salads in Laos, Thailand, and Vietnam, where they are called *rau ram*.

ROSEMARY Taking its name from the Latin for "rose of the sea," this spiky evergreen shrub thrives in Mediterranean climates. Its highly aromatic, piney flavor goes well with lamb and poultry, as well as with vegetables.

SAGE Sharply fragrant, with traces of both bitterness and sweetness, this gray-green herb is often used in seasoning pork, veal, game, and sausages.

TARRAGON Native to Siberia, this heady, anise-flavored herb can perfume wine vinegar and Dijon mustards, flavor sauces and dressings, and season seafood, poultry, and eggs.

THYME This low-growing, aromatic herb grows wild throughout the Mediterranean. A key element of many slow-cooked savory dishes, it is considered a digestive aid.

HOOP CHEESE This moist, fresh curd cheese is pressed from skim cow's milk. Although sometimes dry enough to slice, its consistency is usually closer to that of farmer cheese or ricotta, which can be used as an adequate, though richer, substitute. Highly perishable, hoop cheese should be used within 3 days of purchase. Look for it in specialty-cheese shops or health-food stores.

JAMBON CRU *Jambon cru*, also known as *jambon sec*, is the raw, unsmoked ham of France. Prized raw hams such as *jambon de montagne* are dry-cured and air-aged in the mountains to create their finely textured and delicately flavored meat. Spanish *serrano* or Italian *prosciutto* are also good choices in recipes calling for *jambon cru*. For cooking, avoid packages of paper-thin slices, and instead ask the butcher to cut the ham into thicker pieces. Cooked ham, *jambon cuit* or *jambon blanc*, is also used throughout France.

JICAMA Sold year-round, this large, brown-skinned tuber, also called a yam bean, has a refreshingly crisp, mild white flesh that is most often eaten raw. Before serving, peel away the thick skin and the fibrous layer beneath it.

KARI LEAVES These small, shiny, highly aromatic leaves come from the kari tree, native to southern India and Sri Lanka. Although sometimes called curry leaves and used in curries, they bear no relation to curry powder and are not interchangeable with it. Rather, both their flavor and aroma are citrusy. Kari leaves are available in Indian grocery stores. Fresh leaves have the best flavor, but dried are usually more easily found and may be substituted; use double the quantity of dried leaves as for fresh. If kari leaves are unavailable, you can substitute 2 teaspoons minced parsley and 1 teaspoon grated lemon zest for every 20 kari leaves.

LEMONGRASS This stiff, reedlike grass has an intensely aromatic, citrusy flavor that is one of the signatures of Southeast Asian cooking. Use only fresh lemongrass, as it lacks good flavor when dried. Lemon zest, often mentioned as a substitute, can play its role but in no way equals its impact.

To prepare lemongrass, if a recipe calls for the tender midsection of a stalk, use only its bottom 4–6 inches (10–15 cm). Peel off any tough outer layers of the stalk to reveal the inner purple ring. To release the aromatic oils, smash or chop the stalk before use.

MANCHEGO CHEESE Spain's most famous cheese, this specialty of La Mancha, from which it gets its name, is traditionally made from sheep's milk, although cow's milk is now used as well. In its earliest days, it was made and eaten by the shepherds who tended large flocks in the area. Today it is available in Spain in fresh (*fresco*) and lightly aged (*semicurado*) forms, but the most common and widely exported type is labeled *curado*, and has been aged for at least 6 months. It has a rich, tangy flavor and a firm, somewhat brittle texture. Thinly sliced, it is served alone as a tapa or with fruit or quince preserves.

MANGO Mangoes belong to the same family as cashew and pistachio trees and are native to India, where they have been cultivated for thousands of years. Of the hundreds of varieties, the Alphonso is the most desired and therefore the most expensive. Mangoes are used green in curries and pickles, and ripe in puddings, chutneys, or by themselves.

To cube a mango, cut the flesh in a single piece from either side of the pit. Crosshatch the flesh of each piece, being careful not to puncture the skin. Push the skin side so that the piece inverts and the cubes separate from each other, then cut them away from the skin.

MANGO POWDER Made from unripe mangoes that have been peeled, dried, and ground to a pale gray-beige powder, mango powder has a strong aroma and sour tang. It is used as a souring agent and to tenderize meat. Lemon juice may be substituted.

MASA Kernels of dried field corn are treated with a solution of calcium hydroxide (powdered lime) and water to loosen and remove their tough outer skins and are then ground and mixed with water to make *masa*, literally "dough," used primarily for preparing tortillas and tamales. Fresh-ground *masa* comes in 5- or 10-lb (2.5- or 5-kg) plastic bags. Use as needed, divide the rest into small amounts, and freeze. Use fresh or frozen *masa* within 1 day of purchase or thawing.

MASA HARINA This flour is ground from dried corn and used to make tortillas and tamales. Two basic types are available, the fine-ground *masa harina* for tortillas and the coarser-ground *masa harina* for tamales.

MUSHROOMS Strict regulations govern commercial foraging practices throughout North America. More and more mushrooms once found only in the wild are now being cultivated, but despite advances in growing various types, the flavor of mushrooms harvested in the wild is superior to that of their cultivated counterparts, an opinion reflected in their higher prices. Only trained

foragers and knowledgeable mycologists should harvest mushrooms in the wild. A good selection of fresh mushrooms, both wild and domesticated, can be found in well-stocked grocery stores and farmers' markets.

CHANTERELLE Found only in the wild, delicately flared chanterelles have a distinctive nutty flavor. The best-known varieties include golden-hued yellow chanterelle, mild but chewy white chanterelle, and the flavorful black trumpet of death. They are all most plentiful from late summer to late autumn.

CREMINI Although closely related to common button mushrooms, these widely cultivated, small mushrooms have light brown, rather than white, caps. Also known as Italian brown and common brown mushrooms, cremini have a firmer texture and slightly fuller flavor than buttons, making them increasingly popular with cooks. Available year-round, they can be used interchangeably with their white-capped kin.

HEDGEHOG Also known as the sweet tooth and the *pied de mouton*, this flavorful mushroom was named for the small, teethlike projections on the underside of its cap. Hedgehogs grow on the forest floor, and most have caps that are creamy to buff in color. At their best when young, they have a flavor reminiscent of mild chanterelles, but they quickly become bitter as they grow larger. These wild mushrooms appear in January along the Pacific Coast and from July to November in the East.

OYSTER MUSHROOM Creamy to pale gray, this fan-shaped mushroom, available both wild and cultivated, has a delicate texture and a flavor that evokes seafood. Choose smaller ones, as oyster mushrooms become bitter and tough as they grow larger.

SHIITAKE Widely cultivated, this mushroom is now available beyond the Asian communities that first brought it to the United States. Light to dark brown, with a smooth texture, the shiitake appears in a broad variety dishes.

NUTS When purchasing nuts, seek out only those that are free of cracks, holes, and discoloration. To make sure the nutmeat is not dried out inside, shake the shells.

ALMONDS These oval nuts are the meat found inside the pit of a dried fruit related to the peach—which is why almonds pair so well with peaches and other stone fruit like cherries and plums. Almonds are delicate and

fragrant and have a smooth texture. They are sold unblanched, with their natural brown skins intact, and blanched, with the skins removed to reveal their light ivory color.

To blanch and peel almonds, put the shelled nuts in a heatproof bowl and pour boiling water over them. Let stand for about 1 minute, then drain the nuts in a colander and rinse with cold running water to cool. Pinch each almond to slip off its bitter skin.

CASHEWS Cashew trees measure up to 40 feet (12 m) in height and produce fruits called cashew apples (though actually pear shaped), inside of which the nut develops. When the fruits ripen, the nuts protrude from the end of them. The shells of the nuts contain an acidic, oily substance that can burn and blister the skin but which is neutralized by heating.

HAZELNUTS Cultivation of plump, sweet noisettes is small and limited. Rich and slightly sweet, hazelnuts appear as a garnish on greens, vegetables, and other savory dishes. Pressed into a fragrant oil, the nut adds depth of flavor to a variety of sauces and dressings. Avoid buying hazelnuts already chopped, as whole nuts have the best flavor and texture.

To toast and peel hazelnuts spread the nuts in a single layer on a baking sheet or shallow pan. Toast them at 325°F (165°C) for 15–20 minutes, or until they are fragrant, shaking the pan to ensure even coloration. Remove from the oven and, while still warm, rub the hazelnuts in a clean kitchen towel to remove their skins. As with all nuts, toasting hazelnuts deepens their flavor and improves their texture.

PEANUTS Not really a nut at all, but rather a type of legume that grows underground, peanuts are seeds nestled inside waffle-veined pods that become thin and brittle when dried.

PECANS Native to North America, the pecan has two deeply crinkled lobes of nutmeat, much like its relative the walnut. The nuts have smooth, brown, oval shells that break easily. Their flavor is sweeter and more delicate than that of walnuts.

PINE NUTS Umbrella-shaped stone pines grow throughout the Mediterranean, and their long, slender seeds (also called pignoli) are high in oil and delicately flavored. As with all nuts, a gentle toasting enhances their flavor.

PISTACHIOS Pistachios have thin, very hard, rounded outer shells that are naturally creamy tan in color but are sometimes dyed bright red. As the nuts ripen, their shells crack to reveal light green kernels.

WALNUTS The furrowed, double-lobed nutmeat of the walnut has an assertive, rich flavor. The most common variety is the English walnut, also known as the Persian walnut, which has a light brown shell that cracks easily. Black walnuts have a stronger flavor and tougher shells but can be hard find.

To toast nuts, spread them on a baking sheet and toast in a 325°F (165°C) oven until they are fragrant and golden , 10–20 minutes; the timing depends on the type of nut and the size of the pieces. Stir once or twice to ensure even cooking. Remove from the oven and immediately pour onto a plate, as they will continue to darken if left on the hot pan. Toast small amounts of nuts in a frying pan over medium-low heat, stirring frequently, until fragrant and golden.

PANCETTA A form of unsmoked Italian bacon, this long, flat cut of fatty pork belly is seasoned with black pepper, and sometimes garlic, cinnamon, and nutmeg, then rolled up tightly and salt-cured. Pancetta is used thinly sliced as a wrapper for savory dishes and chopped to flavor stuffings and sauces.

PARMESAN Parmesan is fashioned into wheels and then aged for 1–3 years to develop a complex, nutty flavor and dry, granular texture. "Parmigiano-Reggiano" stenciled on the rind ensures that the cheese is a true Parmesan made in Emilia-Romagna.

PILONCILLO This unrefined sugar commonly comes in hard cones that are grated or chopped before use. The most common ones weigh ¾ oz (20 g), while the larger ones weigh about 9 oz (280 g). In southern Mexico, the unrefined sugar is often made into thin, round cakes or into bricks. The darker the sugar, the more pronounced the molasses flavor. Well-wrapped *piloncillo* will keep indefinitely. Dark brown sugar may be substituted.

PLANTAIN Closely related to the banana, the large plantain, or *plátano*, is starchier and firmer. It is always cooked before eating. Fresh plantains have almost uniformly black skins when ripe and will yield to gentle finger pressure. Some recipes may call for the firmer texture of an underripe plantain that has only lightly spotted or yellow-green skin.

POLENTA Both cornmeal and the thick, porridgelike dish made from it, polenta is endlessly versatile. Soft polenta serves as a base for a hearty sauce, an accompaniment to roast meat or poultry, or a simple meal or snack on its own with a swirl of cheese.

PRAHOK A popular Cambodian seasoning sold in jars, this fish paste is more easily used as a seasoning if an extract is made from it.

To prepare prahok juice, put ¼ cup (2 fl oz/ 60 ml) of the fermented fish (including the meat) into a saucepan with 1 cup (8 fl oz/ 250 ml) water and bring to a boil over high heat. Reduce the heat to a simmer and cook, uncovered, stirring once or twice, for 10 minutes. Pour through a sieve placed over a bowl, pressing against the solids to extract as much liquid as possible. Discard the solids. Store the strained liquid, tightly covered, in the refrigerator for up to 2 weeks. Makes 1 cup (8 fl oz/250 ml).

PROSCIUTTO This high-quality air-cured Italian ham has a silken texture and a sweet, almost fruity flavor. The most exceptional hams come from Parma, in Emilia-Romagna, and from San Daniele, in Friuli, recognized by their flatter shape. The term *prosciutto crudo* refers specifically to this cured and aged raw ham, while *prosciutto cotto* is a mildly cured cooked ham.

PUMPKIN SEEDS Mexican cooks have long ground the hulled seeds of various pumpkins and other hard-shelled winter squashes for use as thickening agents. The whole hulled seeds may also be eaten as a snack or used as a garnish. Brief toasting helps develop their flavor and texture.

To toast pumpkin seeds, spread them in a dry frying pan over medium heat and cook, stirring continuously, until they just begin to darken. Transfer to a heat-resistant dish to cool; the seeds will continue to darken slightly from the residual heat.

QUESO Several types of *queso* (cheese) predominate in Mexican cooking. Melting cheeses include the pale, slightly tangy *asadero*; the flavorful, quite rare *queso Chihuahua*; and *quesillo de Oaxaca*, which resembles string cheese. Fresh cheeses, or *quesos frescos*, are soft, tangy, lightly salted cow's milk cheeses that are crumbled or sliced for adding to dishes. They are labeled

queso fresco or *queso ranchero*. When *queso fresco* is aged, it becomes *queso añejo*, a tangy, dry cheese, more authentically called *queso cotijo*, which is grated as a garnish for tacos, enchiladas, and other traditional dishes. Mexican Manchego resembles the Spanish cheese of the same name but is made from cow's rather than sheep's milk. Spanish Manchego may be substituted for the Mexican variety, which can often only be found in specialty shops.

RADICCHIO Pleasantly astringent, bitter, and crisp, this member of the chicory family may be found in various forms throughout Italy. The most familiar type is a compact, round head of white-ribbed burgundy leaves. In late autumn, markets offer the less bitter Treviso variety, which has spearlike purple leaves the shape of romaine (cos) lettuce leaves.

RADISH, PRESERVED A preserved form of the large white radish commonly known by its Japanese name, daikon, this Chinese ingredient is sold in plastic packages labeled "preserved white radish" or "preserved turnips." The brown-tinged strips add their pungent flavor to dishes that are cooked for a long time, such as braises and stews.

RICE WINE Rice wine is an indispensable addition to Chinese cooking, adding flavor and working as a tenderizer and seasoning in marinades. Rice wine can be purchased at most Asian food stores and well-stocked markets. Bottles labeled "cooking wine" may contain 5 percent added salt, so be sure to check the labels before seasoning a dish. Dry sherry or Japanese mirin can be substituted in most recipes.

ROCK SUGAR *Bingtang* or rock sugar—chunks of crystalline sugar—is used to make a clear, sweet syrup for soups and sauces. Crystal sugar can often be substituted.

SALT Some cooks contend that the iodine added to common table salt clouds stocks and clear sauces, and that the salt's fine grains lack the texture and depth of flavor of sea salt or kosher salt. Sea salt, gathered from evaporated seawater, retains small amounts of naturally occurring minerals, and it often carries a slight tint of gray or pink from these minerals. Available in both fine and coarse crystals, sea salt is excellent used in cooking.

Sprinkling it over dishes just before serving allows diners to appreciate its complex flavor. Kosher salt was originally developed for the preparation of kosher meats, but its flat, coarse grains dissolve quickly, an often-desirable quality for many cooks.

SALT COD, BONELESS This strong, briny-tasting, tender fish must be soaked in cold water to reduce its saltiness before use. Be sure to use filleted salt cod.

To rehydrate salt cod, immerse the fish in a bowl of cold water. Cover and refrigerate, changing the water 4–6 times, for 24–36 hours. The soaking time will depend upon how heavily salted and how thick the cod is. When ready, the fish will be puffy and lighter in color. Drain and proceed as directed in the recipe.

SESAME SEEDS Tiny sesame seeds, white or black, are used as garnishes and textural elements or to add a warm, nutty taste to many dishes. Because of their high oil content, they should be stored in the refrigerator.

To toast sesame seeds, cook them gently, stirring, for 3–5 minutes in a dry frying pan. Watch them closely to ensure that they do not burn.

SHALLOTS AND PICKLED SHALLOTS Covered in an amber-colored, papery skins, small, mild-flavored shallots are used as flavoring base for dishes in many different cuisines. Asian markets also carry jarred pickled shallots, which have been packed in a vinegar brine.

SHISO LEAVES Related to mint but with an aromatic flavor that faintly recalls ginger or cinnamon, these serrated, heart-shaped leaves tinder have purple undersides and are also known as perilla or beefsteak leaves.

SHRIMP PASTE, DRIED Intensely flavored, this Southeast Asian seasoning paste is made by salting, fermenting, and then drying shrimp (prawns). Depending on its source, the dried paste may range in color from pinkish tan to deep purple-black. Called *blacan* in Malaysia, *trasi* in Indonesia, *kapi* in Thailand, and *ngapi* in Myanmar, it is most often sold in hard blocks from which slices can be easily cut with a sharp knife. Do not confuse the dried paste with shrimp sauce, called *bagoong* in the Philippines and sometimes shrimp paste in English, a highly pungent, thick grayish sauce sold in jars. It can usually be found in Chinese grocery stores.

SOY SAUCE Typically made by fermenting and aging soybeans with wheat, salt, and water, soy sauce is an indispensable seasoning in kitchens in China and, to a far lesser degree, in Southeast Asia. Dark soy sauce gains its dark color, thicker consistency, and edge of sweetness from the addition of caramel. Light soy sauce has a thinner consistency and a lighter flavor. Japanese soy sauces tend to be milder tasting, slightly sweeter, and less salty than Chinese varieties.

SRIRACHA Named for the seaside Thai town in which it originated, this bottled, hot or mild, sweet-tart, all-purpose sauce is made from red chiles and resembles a light-colored ketchup. Keep in mind that even the so-called mild version is still quite hot.

SQUASH BLOSSOMS With their delicate flavor and vivid color, the yellow blossoms of summer squash taste wonderful and make a pleasant addition to soups and other cooked dishes. Harvest them from your own garden or buy them at farmers' markets. Blossoms should be freshly picked early in the morning, just before they open. Most gardeners take only the male flowers, leaving the rest to develop into future squash.

TAMARIND The sweet-sour pulp from the seedpods of this tree native to India a popular flavoring. Tamarinds are also known as Indian dates. The long, brown seedpods resemble fava (broad) bean pods. Tamarind paste and concentrate are also available. Tamarind pulp is sold in block form in most well-stocked Asian markets.

To make tamarind water, cut up ½ pound (250 g) of tamarind pulp into small pieces, place in a bowl, and add 2 cups (16 fl oz/500 ml) boiling water. Mash the pulp to spearate the fibers and seeds, then let stand for 15 minutes, stirring 2 or 3 times. Pour the liquid through a fine-mesh sieve placed over a bowl, pushing against the pulp with the back of a spoon to extract as much liquid as possible. Scrape the underside of the sieve to dislodge any clinging purée. Transfer to a jar and refrigerate for up to 4 days or freeze for up to 1 month. A tamarind concentrate, which dissolves instantly in hot water, is available in some Asian markets and can be used to save time. Makes 1½ cups (12 fl oz/375 g) tamarind water.

TOMATOES During summer, use vine-ripened fresh tomatoes for both uncooked dishes and for recipes such as tomato sauce. At other times of year, good-quality canned plum (Roma) tomatoes are best to use for cooking. The Italian San Marzano variety is generally considered to be the finest.

To peel a fresh tomato, use a small, sharp knife to score a shallow X in its flower end. Then, using a slotted spoon, dip the tomato into a saucepan of boiling water for no more than 20 seconds. Submerge the tomatoes in a bowl of ice water to cool. Starting at the X, peel off the loosened skin with your fingertips. To remove the seeds, cut the tomato in half crosswise and squeeze gently.

TORTILLAS These thin, flat rounds are the staple bread throughout much of Mexico. Many markets sell good corn and wheat flour tortillas, which are usually best to use in dishes where the tortillas are to be fried or cooked. To reheat tortillas, wrap stacks of 5 tortillas each in aluminum foil and warm in a 275°F (135°C) oven for 5–10 minutes. To reheat fewer, put the tortillas on a griddle and reheat for several seconds on each side. For making the crisp corn chips called totopos, use the thinnest corn tortillas you can find. If you prefer not to fry them, place them in a single layer on a baking sheet, top with a wire rack to prevent curling, and toast in a 300°F (150°C) oven for about 30 minutes.

VINEGAR, BALSAMIC While vinegar is most commonly made from red or white wine, Italy's most renowned vinegar, *aceto balsamico*, or "balsamic vinegar," is based on white grape juice that is reduced by boiling it down to a thick syrup, or must, then aged for many years in a succession of ever-smaller barrels made of different woods, each of which contributes its own taste to the final syrupy, sharp-and-sweet product. Rare and expensive, this true aceto balsamico is used sparely as a condiment, a few drops at a time, often over Parmesan cheese or ripe strawberries. More commonly available balsamic vinegar, appropriate for cooking or salad dressings, is made from a mixture of wine vinegar, must, and caramel coloring.

INDEX

ACKNOWLEDGMENTS

Weldon Owen wishes to thank the following people for their generous support in producing this book: Heather Belt, Carrie Bradley, Ken DellaPenta, Lucie Parker, and Kate Washington.

Recipe photography by Noel Barnhurst, except for the following by Andre Martin: Pages 58, 61, 63, 68, 69, 71, 72, 76, 78, 80, 82, 91, 92, 96, 100, 101, 102, 105, 106, 109.

Travel photography by Maren Caruso: Page ©13; Michael Freeman: Page ©54 (bottom), 56; Wolfgang Kaehler: Page ©57 (right); R. Ian Lloyd: Page ©57 (left); Jason Lowe: Pages 6 (top and bottom), 7, 8, 52–53, 54 (top), 55, 112 (top), 114, 115 (left), 166 (bottom), 168, 169 (right), 226; David Portnoy, Black Star: Page ©9 (left); Steven Rothfeld: Pages 4 (left), 5 (right), 9 (right), 14, 110–111, 112 (bottom), 113, 115 (right), 166 (top), 167, 169 (left), 230; Paul Solomon, Woodfin Camp & Associates: Pages ©164–165; Ignacio Urquiza: Pages 12 (top and bottom), 15 (left); Rachel Weill: Page ©15 (right); Ted Wood, Getty Images: Pages ©10–11.

Recipes and sidebars by Georgeanne Brennan: Pages 125, 126, 129, 130, 136, 140, 141, 144, 145, 146, 149, 150, 151, 155, 158, 161; Kerri Conan: Pages 22, 23; Lori de Mori: Pages 172, 174, 175, 181, 188, 189, 204, 208, 213, 216, 217; Abigail Johnson Dodge: Page 44; Janet Fletcher: Pages 27, 31, 32, 37; Joyce Goldstein: Pages 177, 178, 182, 187, 195, 198, 199, 200, 203, 211, 212; Diane Holuigue: Pages 117, 118, 119, 121, 122, 123, 133, 134, 135, 139, 142, 147, 152, 154, 156, 157, 160, 162, 163; Joyce Jue: Pages 65, 66, 75, 81, 84, 87, 88, 90, 94, 98, 99; Michael McLaughlin: Pages 47, 51; Cynthia Nims: Pages 21, 26, 36; Ray Overton: Page 18; Jacki Passmore: Pages 59, 60, 69, 70, 79, 83, 92, 93, 97, 103, 104; Julie Sahni: Pages 62, 63, 68, 72, 73, 77, 80, 91, 100, 101, 107, 108; Michele Scicolone: Pages 171, 176, 184, 185, 190, 191, 192, 196, 197, 201, 207, 209, 214; Marilyn Tausend: Pages 17, 19, 25, 29, 33, 34, 38, 39, 40, 41, 42, 45, 46, 48, 49.

Page 4 (left): The leaning tower of Pisa, which started to tilt even before its completion in 1274, has attracted visitors for centuries, among them Galileo, who conducted his experiments on the velocity of fallig objects from the top of the tipping *torre*. Page 5 (right): A baker and his assistant carry a tray laden with *panini* along a street in Abruzzo. In southern Italy, superb breads are made from *semolino di grano duro* (semolina flour milled from the center of the durum wheat berry). Page 218: Shoppers admire the breads at the famous Poilâne bakery in the rue du Cherche-Midi in Paris. Page 226: In the busy streets of Kunming, Muslim street vendors, in their traditional embroidered caps, do a thriving trade with their lamb skewers and other local delicacies. Page 230: Spigots release freshly pressed olive oil into bottles at Spains' Nuestra Señora de la Olivia.

Cover: Polenta Crisps with Anchovy Sauce, page 208.

OXMOOR HOUSE INC.

Oxmoor House books are distributed by Sunset Books
80 Willow Road, Menlo Park, CA 94025
Telephone: 650-321-3600 Fax: 650-324-1532
Vice President/General Manager Rich Smeby
National Accounts Manager/Special Sales Brad Moses
Oxmoor House and Sunset Books are divisions of
Southern Progress Corporation

WILLIAMS-SONOMA

Founder and Vice-Chairman Chuck Williams

THE SAVORING SERIES

Conceived and produced by Weldon Owen Inc.
814 Montgomery Street, San Francisco, CA 94133
Telephone: 415 291 0100 Fax: 415 291 8841

In collaboration with Williams-Sonoma, Inc.
3250 Van Ness Avenue, San Francisco, CA 94109

A WELDON OWEN PRODUCTION

Set in Minion and Myriad.
Color separations by Bright Arts in Singapore.
Printed and bound by Tien Wah Press in Singapore.

First printed in 2006.
10 9 8 7 6 5 4 3 2 1

Library of Congress Cataloging-in-Publication data is available.
ISBN: 0-8487-3140-9

First published in the USA by Time-Life Custom Publishing
Originally published as Williams-Sonoma Savoring:
Savoring France (© 1999 Weldon Owen Inc.)
Savoring Italy (© 1999 Weldon Owen Inc.)
Savoring Southeast Asia (© 2000 Weldon Owen Inc.)
Savoring Spain & Portugal (© 2000 Weldon Owen Inc.)
Savoring India (© 2001 Weldon Owen Inc.)
Savoring Mexico (© 2001 Weldon Owen Inc.)
Savoring Tuscany (© 2001 Weldon Owen Inc.)
Savoring America (© 2002 Weldon Owen Inc.)
Savoring Provence (© 2002 Weldon Owen Inc.)
Savoring China (© 2003 Weldon Owen Inc.)

WELDON OWEN INC.

Chief Executive Officer John Owen
President and Chief Operating Officer Terry Newell
Chief Financial Officer Christine E. Munson
Vice President International Sales Stuart Laurence
Creative Director Gaye Allen
Publisher Hannah Rahill

Senior Editor Kim Goodfriend
Assistant Editor Juli Vendzules

Designer Rachel Lopez

Production Director Chris Hemesath
Color Manager Teri Bell
Production and Reprint Coordinator Todd Rechner

Food Stylists George Dolese, Sally Parker
Illustrations Marlene McLoughlin
Text Stephanie Rosenbaum

A NOTE ON WEIGHTS AND MEASURES

All recipes include customary U.S. and metric measurements. Metric
conversions are based on a standard developed for these books and
have been rounded off. Actual weights may vary.